THE UNIVERSITY OF WINCHESTER

Martial Rose Library
Tel: 01962 827306

To be returned on or before the day marked above, subject to recall.

Dyke/Girl: Language and Identities in a Lesbian Group

Dyke/Girl: Language and Identities in a Lesbian Group

Lucy Jones
University of Hull, UK

First published 2012 by
PALGRAVE MACMILLAN

Palgrave Macmillan in the UK is an imprint of Macmillan Publishers Limited, registered in England, company number 785998, of Houndmills, Basingstoke, Hampshire RG21 6XS.

Palgrave Macmillan in the US is a division of St Martin's Press LLC, 175 Fifth Avenue, New York, NY 10010.

Palgrave Macmillan is the global academic imprint of the above companies and has companies and representatives throughout the world.

Palgrave® and Macmillan® are registered trademarks in the United States, the United Kingdom, Europe and other countries.

ISBN 978–0–230–29256–7

This book is printed on paper suitable for recycling and made from fully managed and sustained forest sources. Logging, pulping and manufacturing processes are expected to conform to the environmental regulations of the country of origin.

A catalogue record for this book is available from the British Library.

A catalog record for this book is available from the Library of Congress.

10 9 8 7 6 5 4 3 2 1
21 20 19 18 17 16 15 14 13 12

Printed and bound in Great Britain by
CPI Antony Rowe, Chippenham and Eastbourne

Contents

List of Transcriptions

Transcription Conventions

[	beginning of first overlap
]	end of first overlap
[[	beginning of second overlap
]]	end of second overlap
-	self-interruption or false start
/	latching (no pause between speaker turns)
(.)	pause of less than 1 second
(2)	timed pause
.	end of intonation unit; falling intonation
?	end of intonation unit; rising intonation
()	uncertain transcription
<>	transcriber comment
{}	stretch of talk over which comment applies
::	lengthening of sound
(XX)	emphatic breath out/sigh
@(10)	laughing, plus duration
<@ @>	laughing quality
<u>underline</u>	emphatic stress or increased amplitude
<* *>	rapid speech

Acknowledgements

This book details fieldwork which took place during my doctoral research at the University of Sheffield, and was written with the support of a sabbatical from my usual teaching duties whilst I was employed by Edge Hill University. I am indebted, of course, to the women in the Sapphic Stomper group for allowing me to spend time with them for the duration of my research. I am also enormously grateful to my friend and mentor, Emma Moore, who supervised my PhD and offered superb advice and guidance throughout the process. The analyses in this book have developed over a number of years and have been influenced, enhanced and inspired by feedback and comments from research groups at Edge Hill University, Lancaster University, Sheffield Hallam University and the University of California, Santa Barbara, as well as from audience members at conferences including Dialogic Language Use 2, IGALA 6, Lavender Languages and Linguistics 14 and 16, and the Sociolinguistics Symposia 17 and 18. I am very grateful to the colleagues – and sorry that I cannot name them all – who offered their own perceptive insights into my data at these events, each of which enhanced my analysis in some way.

I would like to thank Mary Bucholtz, not only for her inspirational work but for her time and generosity during the early stages of my analysis, and Bill Leap for his unfailing encouragement and interest since the beginning of my research. The book itself would not have come about were it not for the advice of Richard Steadman-Jones and Sara Mills, and I thank them both for their interest, encouragement and time spent talking through some of the key ideas within it. I am also thankful to Liz Morrish for reading through sections of this book and offering excellent, enormously useful advice with regard to both its content and structure.

I am so grateful for the love and support of my parents, Jan and Ian and Derek and Ruth, as the many years leading up to this book would have been insurmountable without them. Without my wonderful friends, they would have been less rewarding. Finally, I would like to express my thanks to my partner Kitty, whose photography features on the cover of this book. Her belief and encouragement in me have been unfailing and, without her practical and emotional support, I could never have completed this project.

LUCY JONES

1
Introduction

In the autumn of 2006, a conversation occurred between Sam, Marianne, Eve and Jill, some of the members of a lesbian hiking group that I had recently become acquainted with. We were in a family pub eating a meal, having just been for a walk nearby. We were discussing Jill's recent women-only walking holiday, and Jill told us about how long the hikes had been and what the accommodation had been like. The friendly atmosphere changed, however, when Marianne asked the question: 'Were most of the women dykes, then?' It was clear that Jill was irritated by this question – she told me that she had gone on the trip to appreciate the walks, not the women. When she claimed that she had not had those conversations and did not know the sexuality of her companions, Marianne asked: 'Well, did they look like dykes?' Again, Jill said that it was not something she had considered, and promptly changed the topic.

This was a typical interaction between the Sapphic Stompers,[1] a group of gay women that met regularly to walk together in the English countryside, and with whom I carried out the research for this book. Although the Sapphic Stompers did not spend all of their time talking about their sexuality, the varying attitudes that each woman in the group had about this sensitive topic often emerged in their conversations. Their interaction often included moments where they indirectly defined what a 'real' or 'proper' lesbian looked or behaved like, for example. Typically, this meant a style and practice they referred to as 'dykey'. This book considers the ways in which these women positioned themselves and others as 'authentic' lesbians through their discussions of what makes a woman a 'dyke'. It explores the meaning and identity of a Stomper lesbian, but also considers what it means to be a Stomper *woman*, looking beyond the women's sexuality alone

1

as a way of defining themselves. The Stompers' identity is considered in relation to broader social norms and values related to their shared experience, illustrating how individuals create their own meaning and shared sense of identity through their engagement. Central to this is Bucholtz and Hall's (2005: 586) proposition that identity is 'the social positioning of the self and other'. The approach taken here draws upon ideas from feminism, anthropology and queer theory, using concepts from linguistics to provide analyses of specific interactions. Through a sociocultural focus, it is shown to be possible to trace the relationships between local practice and social identity.

This is the first book of its kind to focus exclusively on lesbian discourse and identity. As will be shown in later chapters, recent research has considered the interaction of lesbian friends (e.g. Morrish and Sauntson 2007, Queen 2005), as well as the written discourses constructed by lesbian 'communities' for their members (e.g. Koller 2008, Turner 2008). The existing body of work on lesbian discourse does not, however, currently include a concentrated ethnographic study which investigates the links between broader ideological conceptions of lesbian culture and the local practices which might be shaped by them. Even in the twenty-first century, negative and offensive stereotypes about lesbians continue to exist, and (particularly older) gay women are often rendered invisible within a male-dominated gay culture. It is therefore important to attempt to capture snapshots of the experiences of gay women in order to represent – and try to explain – the realities of being a lesbian in a heterosexual, male-oriented world. It is my intention to provide one such snapshot in this book. This first chapter outlines the meaning of being a Sapphic Stomper, explaining the typical demographic of the group and outlining the relationships within it. It concludes with an introduction to the key concepts used throughout these pages in analysing Stomper interactions, before a plan of the book is presented.

1.1   The Sapphic Stompers

In 2006–7, when the research for this book took place, the Sapphic Stomper group was based in the north of England. Most of its members lived in Dayton (a city with a population over 400,000) where any events for lesbian, gay and bisexual (LGB) people were sporadic and typically occurred in late-night bars and clubs. Heavy consumption of alcohol and loud dance music were the norm, making up what was typically referred to as 'the gay scene'. In itself, as implied above, this excluded older LGB individuals given that there was little to reflect broader cultural tastes, and the 'scene' was dominated by people in their teens and twenties. The universities in the city had LGB societies, typically comprising undergraduate students between the ages of 18 and 21 and not open to the general public, and events aimed at a wider range of people (such as the first Dayton Pride[2]) were only just beginning to emerge.

As a result of this restricted scene, a small group of friends – lesbians who had lived in Dayton for some time and wanted to extend their social circle – decided to set up a social group intended to facilitate events and activities for lesbian women in the area. Using an existing facility on the internet, which enabled the creation of a free email-based mailing list, these women created the group 'Do You Know Everyone?' (DYKE) and advertised the group in the listings of national lesbian magazines and websites. This group was established in 2004 and, by 2006, had just over 100 people subscribing to the mailing list. The Sapphic Stompers advertised themselves through this mailing list with a link to a website that a few members of the group had created. The Stompers were established in 1991 and had previously been advertised through the gay media more generally, but their involvement with DYKE allowed new people to discover them. To join a Stomper walk, an interested woman would obtain information about it from either the website or the mailing list and then go along to the starting point of the walk at the specified time (typically on a Sunday morning). Any number of women might turn up for a walk, but on average there were between six and ten people per hike.

Upon encountering a newcomer, individuals within the group would typically ask only a few questions about their personal life, enough to show a polite interest but not so many that they might invade their privacy. As a result, they did not always know one another intimately and their interaction reflected this. They were typically middle-class white women, and they ranged in age from their mid-forties to their early sixties. There was an understanding that not everybody would be comfortable talking about their sexuality or their relationship status, and new members would never be asked outright about their family life. It was assumed that a woman was gay, single and childless unless they mentioned otherwise, but there was never a demand for this information to be provided. It was also assumed that the women were female-born rather than transgender, though – again – the discretion maintained by the Stomper members was such that this would not necessarily have been disclosed. In this sense, members were able to maintain some level of anonymity and, crucially, to present the version of themselves that they wished to and that they felt was appropriate in this context.

Often of primary importance in these introductory stages was the question of whether the new arrival was a keen hiker. The Stompers often went on walking vacations alone, with partners, friends, or through (typically women-only or lesbian-specific) holiday organisations, and spent much of their spare time outside in the countryside. In this sense, most of the women took hiking seriously, and expected potential members of the group also to be passionate about it. The most committed members of the group spent much of their time preparing and leading Stomper walks as well as meeting four times a year to plan a timetable. They often referred to themselves as the 'core' members and were identifiable as such by most of the other regulars.

For all of the core members, a primary reason for living in Dayton was to be close to a rural area. Typically, they originated from other areas in the UK – often the south – but had moved to the area in later life either for employment or retirement. All of the core members had lived in London at some point, and they talked enthusiastically about the fact that they now lived in or near to a city in such close proximity to the countryside. The hikes that the women engaged in were always a maximum of 45 minutes' drive from the centre of the city, as within just half an hour one could reach open land upon which hikers were free to roam. The women walked in these areas on routes which they planned themselves and which, typically, were between eight and ten miles in length. The walks were usually on undulating (yet not unstable) ground, and were suitable for relatively fit individuals but also not overly challenging for those new to the pastime. They typically took place on a Sunday morning twice a month and, in the summer months, twice on weekday evenings, and would usually take five or six hours to complete. Though the length of walks could have been covered in less time, the ethos of the group was to enjoy being in the outdoors, to spot wildlife, and to take in impressive views. In this sense, there was never a perceived need to move quickly whilst on a Stomper hike.

Passion for nature and wildlife was an important part of the overall Stomper identity; all of the core members and many of the regular members would try to name and identify species of butterfly, bird, plant or tree, and enjoyed demonstrating their knowledge of ecology and geography as we walked through the countryside. To present themselves as knowledgeable was a part of their practice generally, as the women were typically well educated, well read and articulate, and would often have discussions about current affairs. In itself, hiking was accessible to most of the women due to their income and free time, which, along with these displays of knowledge and intellectualism, reflected the typically middle-class status of the Stomper members. The activity of walking, as the Stompers considered it, was about the experience throughout the day as opposed to the achievements in terms of miles walked or heights climbed. This became particularly clear when new or infrequent attendees who were already members of other walking groups came along to a Stomper hike; they would often walk faster, protest at the regularity of stops, or wish to take a harder route than that planned by the leader.

On a typical walk, the Stompers would stop for two short rests and a lunch break, during which time they ate their own packed lunches and often drank from flasks of hot drinks or from bottles of water. It was not common practice to attempt to share food or treat the breaks as a picnic, but instead as a well-deserved rest from the walk. During these times, people would occasionally talk but, more often, would simply sit surveying the view. The moment and location at which a break occurred were decided upon by the walk leader, and it was expected that this leader would have carried out a trial walk before leading the Stompers on it. This was referred to as a 'reccy', a term which the core Stompers all used frequently to describe the practice run they would do before leading a walk for the group. The word was always used but never defined, though it is common in British hiking circles – its use originates from army slang, short for 'reconnaissance' or 'reconnoitre', meaning to become familiar with or inspect an area. Its use was an example of shared linguistic practice between the women, and symbolised not only their awareness of walking culture but also the importance of taking the role of walk leader seriously. The fact that a reccy was expected from a leader illustrates the time commitment that the women would make to the group, not only planning and leading a walk, but spending an additional day rehearsing it, too. Stompers always went along with the leader's decisions and navigation, and it was not appropriate to question choices made or directions taken by that leader (though the women would often criticise aspects of the walk between themselves, without the leader's knowledge). Typically, the leader of the walk was also a member of the core group.

Another shared practice of the core Stompers related to the money that they spent purchasing the best equipment for their hikes (such as walking poles, rucksacks, boots and clothing). For a newcomer to achieve membership, they needed to demonstrate similar enthusiasm.

Often, newcomers would return after one hike with the group with new equipment, presumably having decided that they enjoyed the hobby enough to spend the money, realising what was required to do it in comfort, and noting what the other Stomper women wore, used and carried. Whilst the wearing of clothes with the brands of certain well-respected outdoor clothing companies was practical, it was also a part of the women's style. Indeed, the few times that we encountered newcomers wearing training shoes as opposed to walking boots, the women would mock them for being ill-prepared novices, with one Stomper once despairing of what she referred to as 'the trainer brigade'. To clearly mark oneself out as a group member, therefore, it was important to wear the 'right' clothing, and this was of clear importance to the core members.

Six women made up this core group, and they reflected the typical demographics of the Stompers as a whole. The core women were mostly in their fifties or sixties, in (or retired from) professional occupations, home owners, had all been educated up to at least graduate level, and were all white British citizens. Typically, the Stomper women identified as feminists, having experienced a period in the 1960s or 1970s where consciousness-raising and discourse about 'women's liberation' were widespread, particularly amongst the middle classes and lesbians. Although the interaction of less frequent members will be considered in the chapters that follow, the core group members were those with whom I spent the most time. As a result, the majority of the analysis in this book is focused on their engagement. The six core Stomper women are introduced below. They are **Claire, Eve, Hannah, Jill, Marianne** and **Sam**.

1.1.1 The Stomper members

Claire was in her early forties, and the youngest member of the Stompers by almost a decade. This was a source of banter between her and the other women, as she frequently (playfully) mocked them for being 'prehistoric' or 'dinosaurs' in order to illustrate her relative youth. She had lived in Dayton for 11 years, coming originally from a city 40 miles north and then living in London for some years whilst studying for a doctorate. Claire became involved with the Stompers as soon as she arrived in the city. Working in a skilled, technical role for a large company, she considered her colleagues to be her main social network in Dayton, and she gave this as the main reason for joining the Stompers. She knew nobody in the area upon gaining employment there, wanted to make other lesbian friends, and thought that taking up a hobby would be a good way of enhancing her social life.

Claire was never a keen walker before joining the Stompers, though her attitude towards the activity changed as she spent more and more of her spare time hiking, both with and without the group. Whilst Claire also enjoyed socialising in pubs and bars, the women in the group were not typically interested in such activities. She found this difficult, sometimes feeling bored or apathetic towards the group, yet it was the only contact that she had with other lesbians. For her, this was extremely important. In an interview with me, when I asked her whether she attended the group because of the walking or because of its lesbian status, she said: 'the most important part is that it's lesbian just so you can be yourself and you don't have to be worrying any of the time about what you might say'. For Claire, then, the group represented safety and comfort due to the people within it not questioning her sexuality or judging her for it.

Eve had been a central member of the group for four years, responsible for leading the Stomper planning meetings and organising the calendar of walks. Eve was a self-employed professional in her mid-sixties, managing and chairing local government meetings and committees. She was educated to Master's level, identified as a feminist, and frequently engaged in discussions regarding the connections between gender and sexuality, considering her own experience of being 'other' as due to her discomfort in wearing 'feminine' styles. Her relationship with the Stompers was formed primarily through her love of walking and, whilst she felt secure in the group because (as she said in an interview) 'it's nice not to have to explain yourself, it's nice to be in a situation where you assume you've got certain things in common', she did view it primarily as 'a walking group that happens to be lesbian'.

Hannah was in her early sixties, having retired in her late fifties from work as a civil servant, and the Stomper group played an important part in her social life as well. She was instrumental in the creation of the Stomper group in the 1990s and had formed some strong relationships through it, though not with any of the core Stompers involved in this study. The walking was the primary reason for her joining the group as she was passionate about it as a hobby, though she also enjoyed the company of other women in a big group. She felt that it was a refreshing change to many of the 'individualistic' elements of current society and reflected the experiences she had as a younger woman and a feminist. She regularly led walks for the group and typically attended the planning meetings, though was also in the process of trying to broaden her social circle as she was becoming tired of spending all of her spare time with gay women.

Jill was the newest member of the group, having recently retired from a professional, self-employed role and moving to Dayton in her mid-sixties. Jill took the group very seriously and came to the area primarily due to the Stompers' existence; she met some women on a walking holiday who were involved in the group and invited her to visit the area, which she promptly 'fell in love with'. As a result, the Stompers were the only people that Jill knew upon first moving to the area and they were a crucial part of her social life. Though Jill enjoyed walking with the Stompers, having long been independently interested in the hobby, she often grew frustrated with the Stompers as she felt that the group was 'too lesbian' in its focus. She argued that she had 'very little time for gay women's groups', partly because she disliked the label 'lesbian', viewing herself primarily as a feminist, but also because they were so often not political; if lesbian groups had to exist, she felt that they should be activist in nature. For her, though, the Stomper group was an opportunity to spend time engaged in her favourite hobby while also meeting new women who were her 'kind of people: middle aged and middle class'.

Marianne also joined the Stompers immediately upon moving to Dayton, and had been involved with the group for nine years. In her early fifties, she was employed in a highly skilled profession yet was committed to the Stompers in her spare time. She led walks and organised Stomper holidays, and attended every planning meeting that she could. She described herself as middle class and had engaged with feminist groups as a student. Her identification as a lesbian came in part, she felt, from her views about patriarchal society. Marianne strongly identified as a lesbian and, other than her work colleagues, her friends were exclusively gay because she felt more comfortable in such groups. Though she enjoyed walking, she engaged with the Stompers primarily to be in the company of other lesbians, explaining that she felt at ease because 'you don't have to go through all the other stuff of "are you married, have you got children" … you don't have to even think about answering those questions'.

Finally, **Sam** had recently retired from a professional job, for which she had obtained a number of postgraduate qualifications, and was in her mid-sixties. Unlike the other core Stompers, Sam had only 'come out' relatively recently and lived in an area 30 miles away from the other members. The first time she ever hiked was with the Stompers, having heard about the group at a DYKE event. Before this, she had not been a regular walker and had not been a part of any other walking group but, since joining the Stompers, described it as 'an adrenaline rush to be in the open space'. Though she joined the group primarily to meet people, she felt 'hooked on walking'. Though Sam's dedication to the group was clearly formed from a new-found love of hiking, illustrated by her regular leadership of Stomper walks, the lesbian side of the group was also crucial to her. Before becoming a part of the Stompers, she identified as a feminist, but had little experience of any specifically lesbian groups and knew little of gay culture. The group was intrinsic to her discovery of this.

Each woman in the group interpreted their relationship with it slightly differently, then; all went because they enjoyed the activity but not all of them felt that its lesbian status was important. For some, such as Jill, the lesbian focus was completely incidental and even, at times, irritating, whereas for Sam, for example, it was vital. All of the women considered the Stompers to be an important part of their social life, however, and had been engaged with the group for long enough and with enough frequency to consider themselves a central part of it. The women's commitment to the group was clear, as they routinely reserved up to two Sundays and two evenings per month to attend Stomper events.

Whilst the group's ethos was based around their passion for nature and the countryside, the activity of walking also clearly facilitated their engagement as lesbians. It gave this otherwise unconnected group of women a reason to be together and, despite their individual orientations or opinions about their sexuality, their part in the group was maintained through the shared assumption that they all identified as lesbian. Unsurprisingly, individual relationships developed between the women yet, despite the core members' regular engagement, it was not inevitable that *close* friendships would emerge. When they did, the women involved would often still only engage within Stomper contexts. The main friendships in the group were between **Claire** and **Marianne**, platonic and friendly ex-lovers; **Claire** and **Sam**, who got on well within the group and occasionally went together to DYKE events; **Jill** and **Hannah**, who regularly shared lifts to the Stomper walks; and **Marianne** and **Eve**, who were good friends within the group and often accompanied one another on a reccy of their walks. There were two poor relationships in the group, however, both of which involved Sam. **Sam** had failed to form neutral or positive ties with either **Marianne** or **Eve** after she experienced failed romances with both. The latter women's bad feeling towards her was compounded by their friendship with one another, and when moments occurred in which Sam and one of these women were present, they tended to avoid direct interaction. Despite the conflict between them, however, all three continued to attend the Stomper walks and meetings. This illustrates the importance of the group to them as, although their attendance at the walks was optional and therefore their interaction theoretically avoidable, they considered their membership to the Stompers to be more important than the relative unease that they felt when together.

The other relationships in the group were relatively neutral. This reflects the fact that these women had little (other than their sexuality and the hiking) in common to create a more intimate friendship, yet no reason to actively dislike one another. It also reveals the typically non-intimate nature of the group's dynamics. The ties between the women were uniplex (see Milroy 1980: 179) in that they usually only knew one another through the group and typically had no interaction together outside of it, and this had a clear impact on the ways that the Stomper women made sense of their time together. The women were committed to maintaining their engagement, despite awkwardness between certain members and disagreement in what the group was 'for', making the Sapphic Stompers a fascinating site within which to view the construction of mutual identity.

1.2   Focus of the book

The following chapters will reveal how the Stompers negotiated their differing perspectives in order to construct a shared sense of self, by focusing in minute detail on a range of interactions that occurred between them. Central to their engagement together was a jointly created sense of what it meant to be a woman and a lesbian – this defined who they were and their membership to the group, and they negotiated these ideas together in order to create a Stomper identity. The chapters which follow, as a result, deal with gender and sexuality as concepts which can be reworked within interaction. That is to say, they are viewed as *ideological* concepts.

To posit that gender and sexuality are ideological is to invoke a concept core to Marxist theory: *ideology*. Ideology can be defined, for the purposes of this book, as ideas which create structure and order in society. Central to Marxist thought is the view that the ideas of the ruling classes are, essentially, the ruling ideas. In other words, those with the most influence in society are able to create a world which reflects their own needs and desires. Ideologies, within this structure, are the versions of truth and reality put forward by those with power. The critical position on gender which is taken here, then, views the assumptions typically made about what is 'naturally' male or female as ideologies and part of the 'gender order'. Gender ideologies include, for example, the presumed 'fact' that women are 'naturally' caring and nurturing and, therefore, that they are most suited to a primary role of rearing children. One might argue that this allows men to maintain a patriarchal system whereby they are more likely to enter the workforce and women are less likely to achieve powerful positions in society. Similarly, men are typically viewed as 'naturally' strong and tough, an ideal reinforced by the representation of masculinity in war stories or action films. In comparison, women tend to be viewed as the 'weaker' sex, a position which again allows men to take on more positions of power and responsibility. Many differences which are defined as specific to *either* men *or* women, which connect each sex to particular 'modes of dress and social roles and even ways of expressing emotion and experiencing sexual desire' (Bem 1993: 2) may therefore be seen as ideological in nature. They are culturally constructed expectations and notions of what is 'normal' or, to use a term which stresses the culturally accepted *assumption* of what is typical, 'normative'.

A focus on the ways in which these ideologies are invoked through language use, and the ways in which language may be used to construct ideological meaning, is fundamental to a *sociocultural linguistics* view of gender – the approach taken in this book. As will be illustrated in later chapters, however, notions of normative gender may also be contested. The Gramscian notion of hegemony is particularly relevant here, in that the powerful messages which exist within our culture – everything from the newspapers that we read to the television shows that we watch – *influence* rather than *determine* the way that we view the world and, in this sense, may also be challenged. This is evident when the ideologies associated with sexuality (where heterosexuality is typically seen as the norm and homosexuality is viewed as anomalous or a perversion) are considered, in that what is normative is continually challenged through the actions of gay, lesbian and bisexual groups. Alternative identities and positions can develop in societies which transgress that which is ideological, for example, as the presence of 'camp' men or 'butch' women illustrates. The chapters which follow demonstrate that such transgressive identity construction can occur through interaction; speakers may create positions which subvert popular ideas about what is 'normal' through their talk together. Prevalent ideologies of gender and sexuality are therefore both repeated and reworked by individuals through their engagement in their social world, as is shown in the interaction of the Stompers in this book. As will be revealed, group-based and individually realised identities are produced as a result of interaction, meaning that such phenomena as 'lesbian identity' are always mediated by ideologies of gender and sexuality.

1.2.2   Plan of the book

In Chapter 2, the theoretical approaches which have led to the sociocultural linguistics framework used in this book are outlined. Specifically, concepts which have been central to recent developments in variationist sociolinguistics, such as the community of practice approach and notions of stance and style, are redefined for an interactionist study of language and identity. Through the introduction of interactive moments occurring in the Stomper group, the theoretical framework for an understanding of identity construction in relation to both interactive contexts and the broader ideological structures underpinning those contexts is introduced. In Chapter 3, this framework is considered in terms of its significance to the concept of sexuality, which is introduced here in relation to broader cultural concepts and research within sociocultural linguistics.

Crucial to the sociocultural linguistics framework is an approach which implements an ethnographic methodology; the information on the Stomper women presented in the current chapter has begun to illustrate this, and Chapter 4 provides further detail of the methodology involved in collecting this information. Through an account of the ethnographic methodology used in this study, this chapter outlines the emotional, ethical and practical obstacles which may be involved in such a study. This chapter offers a guide to those new to ethnographic research, before the following chapters present in-depth analyses of interactions between the Stompers.

In Chapter 5, the two principal identities constructed by the Stomper group are discussed – 'dyke' and 'girl'. The women position themselves as legitimate Stompers in accordance with their own constructed authenticity, and a relationship to their sexuality is highlighted through this. They are shown to use widely available cultural resources associated with lesbianism – specifically those which position lesbians as differently gendered from heterosexual women – but to do so varyingly and flexibly in accordance with their identity goal at a given moment. Chapter 6 continues by showing how the women rework the heteronormative category of 'woman' as something which is meaningful to their shared experiences as a group and their assumed *mutual* experiences as white, middle-class, British lesbian women in their middle age. Rather than showing their construction of lesbian authenticity as *constrained* by wider hegemonic ideologies surrounding their sexuality, the analysis of one in-depth conversation between the women shows that, whilst they achieve their joint sense of self via such stereotypes, they are agents in their mutual implementation of them for their own gain. Nonetheless, the gender binary is again shown to dominate all aspects of their construction of individual and group-specific selves.

In Chapter 7, the importance of political awareness and intellectualism to the group is revealed. Through the analysis of interactions in which the women discuss the role of politics in their lives and position themselves as well informed, the Stomper identity is shown to be multifaceted and not always specific to their sexuality. Chapter 8 leads on from this to present the last of the data and analysis, showing that the sociocultural context in which the women's engagement takes place defines their notion of authenticity. Specifically, this chapter demonstrates how the apparent homogeneity within the group may be disturbed and displaced, yet authenticity may still be achieved. Chapter 9 sums up by providing an overview of the theoretical frameworks used throughout the book, before Chapter 10 concludes by arguing that, due to the clear influence of the gender binary on Western societies, heteronormative ideology is likely to impact upon even fundamentally queer identities.

As this book progresses, it aims to develop a new way of approaching discursive data in the study of language and sexuality. By establishing the sociocultural linguistics approach as a key framework in the investigation of identity construction, it engages with current debates surrounding the community of practice, ethnography, sexual identity and desire. Through the micro-level study of the Stompers, it offers a new way of understanding membership in such a group, and demonstrates how a sociocultural focus makes it possible to trace the relationship between local practice and social identity. The following chapter begins with a discussion of how Stomper members could subtly, yet coherently, position themselves as queer through their interaction, before the many analytical theories and approaches used to account for this are introduced and examined.

2
Sociocultural Approaches to Linguistics

In early December 2006, I found myself in conversation with Marianne (a core member of the Sapphic Stompers, introduced in Section 1.1.1). We were talking about Christmas events at our respective workplaces, telling one another about the parties that had been planned. As she told me about what was scheduled at her workplace, she stated that she was often uncomfortable at such events because she never knew what to wear. She described the other women in her firm as wearing party dresses and high heels, whereas she would never be comfortable in such attire. She presented the dress and heels combination as an expected uniform for such events, and herself as standing out as different in her trousers and shirts. It was apparent that Marianne did not expect this to be much of a revelation to me; indeed, I shared her experience and offered examples of similar situations that I had found myself in.

In this moment, neither Marianne nor I made any mention of the fact that we were both lesbians, yet it was implicit in our conversation that our sexuality had some relevance to our clothing choices. As two gay women, we were drawing on certain stereotypes and ideologies about lesbian style and quite clearly aligning ourselves with them; this allowed us to go some way towards creating a mutual lesbian identity. This book contains many descriptions of times such as this: fleeting, interactional moments whereby two or more speakers contribute to a conversation, draw on broader ideologies and, in doing so, project a certain *persona* – a type of 'identity image' which is specific to that context and that moment (Coupland 2007: 237). In this book, ethnographic moments and recorded interactions will reveal the construction and negotiation of personae which were meaningful to the Sapphic Stompers' overall shared identity, and this analysis will explore, through the use of a sociocultural framework, the many linguistic routes taken to achieving this identity. This theoretical approach, as introduced and outlined in the current chapter, may be defined as *interactionist* in nature. This is explained below.

2.1 Interactionist sociolinguistics

Interactionist approaches – those which interpret language as meaningful only within an interactive context and which view it primarily as a communicative tool – are fundamental to the sociocultural linguistics approach. As mentioned in Chapter 1, a central aspect of sociocultural linguistics is what Bucholtz and Hall (2005: 586) refer to as social positioning: the ways that speakers frame themselves and others as particular types of people through a variety of linguistic techniques. This approach enables a view of language as a resource for the creation of shared meaning between social actors. Rather than being individually produced, Bucholtz and Hall view identity as an intersubjective product of interaction with others on a local level and in relation to broader social structures (Bucholtz and Hall 2005: 598). For example, a moment such as that detailed between Marianne and me, above, can be understood from this perspective by considering the sociocultural context surrounding it; our shared membership of a lesbian group and declaration of ourselves as gay prior to this particular conversation clearly led to our invoking lesbian stereotypes surrounding non-feminine clothing style. Had one or both of us been straight, for instance, it might not have been so inevitable that we would position ourselves in the way that we did in this moment – as women who do not conform to the feminine styles expected of us. A focus on the context in which interactions take place is therefore intrinsic to the sociocultural linguistics approach and reflects an interactionist approach to language.

An interactionist approach to sociocultural linguistics differs in significant ways from what is often thought of as sociolinguistics 'proper', though it is frequently placed within the broad umbrella term. For instance, in the above example, the specifics of which words, syntax, phonological or prosodic patterns Marianne and I used in speaking to one another are interesting to interactionist sociocultural linguists inasmuch as they reveal how we communicated and what meaning that communication had. Whereas a traditional *variationist* approach may be primarily interested in the frequencies of such linguistic items and their statistical correlation with clearly defined social identities (such as male, female, young, old), the approach taken here is instead concerned with how such social categories are created and made meaningful *within a local group context.* In this way, it avoids taking identities such as 'working-class female', for instance, as a static marker – as Woolard (1985: 738) argues, this can result in broad theories that do not necessarily represent actual language use in all communities. Eckert's (2000) work illustrates a move towards this perspective within variationist sociolinguistics, whereby analysis which correlates statistical linguistic usage with local groupings of speakers is advocated. This reflects a significant shift within sociolinguistics, one which moves on from broad 'speech communities', defined by Labov (1972: 120) as a group of speakers who share and participate in the same linguistic and social norms, towards an in-depth consideration of the speaker set-up in which particular linguistic items are used. In this way, variationist research – the traditional approach to sociolinguistics – may take language as a tool in the construction of locally meaningful identity, not simply as the phenomenon which reflects it.

Although research such as this may investigate variation in language by analysing the statistical significance of specific, meaningful linguistic markers, and despite the fact that such an approach tends to be seen as the primary form of sociolinguistics (Cameron 1990: 82), the research presented in this book differs in its aims. Instead, it focuses in on the moment of interaction to a much greater degree than is possible through quantitative analysis alone, due to the overall patterns which must be found amongst large groups of speakers. Concentrating on qualitative, discursive data from a small group of speakers, the approach taken here is influenced by anthropologically inspired work such as that of Gumperz and Hymes (1964), approaches which may be defined as the 'other strand' of early research into the relationship between language and society. To differentiate between traditional variationist approaches and those more concerned with context, this 'other strand' may be relabelled 'sociocultural linguistics'.

Sociocultural linguistics research is concerned with individual moves made, interpreting all aspects of language (rather than specified variables) as of potential significance to its analysis. This is not to reject all that variationist sociolinguistics has achieved in developing its focus on local groups and identity construction, of course. Indeed, the analysis in this book takes as fundamental to its approach one of the key developments in recent variationist sociolinguistics: the *community of practice* (CoP). It endeavours to provide clarity in how this significant development in recent variationist research may be used within qualitative analysis. The CoP is therefore introduced and outlined in the following section.

2.2   The community of practice

The community of practice approach, developed for sociolinguistics by Eckert and McConnell-Ginet (1992), is fundamentally concerned with the engagement and interaction of speakers as part of a collective. A CoP can be defined as:

> … an aggregate of people who come together on a regular basis to engage in some enterprise (…). In the course of their engagement, the community of practice develops ways of doing things – practices. And these practices involve the construction of a shared orientation to the world around them – a tacit definition of themselves in relation to each other, and in relation to other communities of practice. (Eckert 2005: 16)

As Bucholtz (1999: 210) states, the CoP approach positions the shared *engagement* of speakers as definitive of their community membership. The Sapphic Stompers' regular walks together are illustrative of this – had they not frequently engaged together, they would have been unable to form any shared sense of self. Shared *enterprise*, referred to in the above quote, is a prerequisite of CoP membership because it fuels the engagement of individuals and defines what it means to be a member of that group. In the Stomper CoP, for example, the women's desire to walk together emerged from their mutual love of hiking and their need to be around people who, they could assume, had a similar outlook on life to them. Another example of this would be work colleagues who 'engage in daily gripe sessions' (Eckert and McConnell-Ginet 2003: 562). Such a regular activity defines the work context in which members are placed and allows them to jointly create a shared orientation to that context. Furthermore, the meanings specific to this activity become connected to the usage of particular context-specific *practices*; newcomers to the work environment will gradually learn the meaning of those practices – such as nicknames for colleagues – only by becoming part of the griping. Through their engagement, speakers develop a sense of their own place in a given environment in relation to the others within it. The product of their interaction is thus a coherent and recognisable *social identity*, such as being 'a Sapphic Stomper'.

Initially developed as a pedagogical theory (Lave and Wenger 1991), the CoP posits that speakers learn how to interact within communities by learning the meaning of the practices of those communities. In this sense, 'lived participation' is key to the acquisition of social identity.

This is, in essence, the result of an understanding of (and engagement in) 'shared ways of doing things' (Wenger 1998: 3), and it positions speakers as learning how to 'do' their identity through group membership. During my time hiking with the Stompers, for example, I learnt about the group's practices, appropriated them via my participation with the group, and began to use them within Stomper contexts in order to perform a Stomper identity. By being part of the group for a prolonged period of time, I began to learn about what was acceptable and appropriate in terms of humour, for instance. As mentioned in the previous chapter, the women were typically very polite, and their avoidance of vulgar or crude language or jokes was an aspect of this. By witnessing moments where newcomers made remarks which were intended to be humorous but were met by silence, criticism or simply a raised eyebrow (such as the occasion when a newcomer took a joke about the 'nipple cap' of her water bottle too far), I learnt what was typical in the group. In learning about the regular practices of a group such as the Stompers, we learn what it means to be a member of that group and, in time, acquire a group-specific social identity. As researchers, it is desirable to view such practices as meaningful to a group if we ourselves take part in it through ethnographic fieldwork (discussed in more detail in Chapter 4).

The CoP provides a new way of thinking about the concept of community; in variationist sociolinguistics, the 'speech community' under study is typically defined by the researcher and, as Bucholtz (1999: 207) argues, moulds speakers into an ideologically consensual group. A speech community is not tangible and is based on presumptions of what it means to inhabit a certain space; in this way it is comparable to Anderson's (1983) notion of an 'imagined community', in which people do not necessarily know one another and will probably never meet, but share something in common (such as the identity of 'a Londoner'). This sociolinguistic model of 'community' cannot allow for a view of how *individuals* might use language to create their own meaningful social groups (Bucholtz 1999: 209), since this perspective sees speakers as agentive and requires a knowledge of actual people engaging with one another. In contrast to the speech community model, then, the CoP allows researchers to deal with issues of both heterogeneity and mutual engagement, enabling a view of speakers as constructing their own meaning through their language. Though this educationalist model was first adopted for the quantitative study of sociolinguistics, its fundamental aim – to understand how language creates shared social identities – requires in-depth understanding of the sociocultural context in which interaction occurs and, as such, also has a role to play within sociocultural linguistics. In this sense, it is logical that this variationist model should be employed for use in a qualitative theoretical framework, as it is in this study, in order to best explore the construction of identity. The focus on identity that the CoP can enable is discussed below.

2.2.1 The community of practice and identity

It has been argued, so far, that a theoretical outlook in which speakers are seen to construct their own meaning in an agentive way is central to an interactionist, sociocultural linguistics approach. The concept of the community of practice, though typically used in variationist sociolinguistics, enables an exploration of this through its focus on individuals within specific interactional settings. In this sense, the CoP approach reflects the original propositions of the ethnography of speaking (Hymes 1962) – that we should aim to understand the context in which language and social practice occur as well as the broader structures within society. Research using CoPs has shown that the model does enable this perspective, as shown by Eckert's (2000) focus on two extreme social groups – the Jocks and the Burnouts – present in one American high school. 'Jock' and 'Burnout' were labels used by the students who inhabited each group and were known throughout the institution. Eckert found that students who engaged in a given CoP simultaneously learnt and contributed to the meaning attached to its practices. In this sense, she argued that membership of a CoP is based on a feeling of shared social experience, and is achieved through engagement in established CoP norms and practices. Yet CoPs must also be considered in relation to the wider world (Eckert and McConnell-Ginet 2007: 31), and the identities constructed within them as existing in relation to other social experiences. A vital element of Eckert's research, therefore, was the finding that the practices of the Jocks or Burnouts were related not only to their local experience, but to broader socio-economic class orientations. The Burnouts, for example, represented a working-class ideal of detachment from the institution, which was manifested on a local level through (amongst other things) the shirking of school rules and the use of drugs on the school premises. Conversely, an individual's move towards being part of the Jock CoP would be achieved through practices associated with collegiality and academic success, themselves part of a middle-class ideal. The Jocks and Burnouts were not random categories, therefore, but ways for the students to collectively make sense of their own social experience or place in the world. In this sense, the two categories were 'the very means by which adult social class [was] embedded in the adolescent order, hence reproduced' in that context (Eckert 2000: 48).

Broader structures of gender were also found to be of great significance in Eckert's study. She found that the role of gender in linguistic variation was dependent on the CoP to which the speakers belonged; there was clear gender difference in the language use within both groups, but the degree of this difference depended on the CoP and varied significantly between them. In this sense, Eckert found that gender was crucially intertwined with a speaker's membership of a particular CoP. Qualitative research focused on CoPs has also provided insights into the role of gender, such as Bucholtz's (1999) study into 'nerds' in an American high school. She found that the manner in which girls achieved their (desired and consciously constructed) nerd identity was by subverting the norms of femininity through various 'identity practices'. For example, Bucholtz (1999: 217) shows one of the nerd girls choosing a 'mildly scatological – or at least "gross" theme' for a poem in order to subvert the expectations of 'normal' topics for girls. In choosing to interact in non-normative, ideologically unfeminine ways such as this, the girls were able to construct a non-normative gender identity and, in turn, show a rejection of their 'cool' (normatively feminised) contemporaries (Bucholtz 1999: 211). In this example, as with Eckert's, the girls' gender identity was defined in direct response to their cultural experiences within the school context.

Such research reveals that gender – as with other broader social structures – exists both on an ideological level and a context-specific one. This is also the case for the Stomper CoP, whose members' identification as women will be shown, in later chapters, to reflect the typical political perspective of those involved in the group as well as their interaction as a CoP. Work such as that of Mendoza-Denton (2008) demonstrates the importance of understanding a CoP's relationship with broader structures; her research into Latina girl gangs in a high school in California reveals a complex construction of femaleness alongside the construction of Mexican ethnicity. In the site of her study, affiliation to one of two gangs was based on the rejection or acceptance of hegemonic American culture, styles and ideals, with Spanish or English language usage signalling one of these contextually specific Latina identities. As with the findings of Bucholtz (1999) and Eckert (2000), Mendoza-Denton also noted that gender performances were intertwined with CoP membership, as styles of dress and appearance resonant with American or Latina culture were employed by the girls dependent on the CoP to which they belonged. For example, members of the Spanish-speaking CoP often wore make-up which darkened their skin colour, dyed their hair black and even wore colour-changing contact lenses in order to emphasise their ethnic roots (Mendoza-Denton 2008: 157). In this sense, again, their femaleness was meaningful only within the context of their gang affiliation and their subsequent relationship to their ethnicity.

CoP studies have, therefore, illustrated the need to consider gender as it is constrained by the context in which it is produced. Yet work using the CoP did not set research concerned with language and gender into motion; approaches to gender within sociolinguistics emerged as a field of inquiry in its own right in the 1970s. Within this area, as detailed below, constructionist approaches have become central to analyses of language use.

2.3   Gender and language

'Gender' is a concept which exists on a broad, ideological level as well as on a local, context-specific level, as the studies outlined above illustrate. Work using communities of practice have shown that gender – typically femininity – can be interpreted and realised in very different ways depending on various intersections such as age, class and ethnicity (and, as the current study will show, sexuality), and this understanding reflects the most current gender-focused work in linguistics. Earlier investigations emerged from feminist linguists in the 1970s and 1980s, however, such as Lakoff (1975) and Spender (1980). During this time of second wave feminism (the 'first wave' having been primarily concerned with equal rights and the emancipation of women), issues surrounding women's sexuality, their roles within the family, at work and in society more broadly were of primary significance (see Freedman 2001: 4). The concerns of feminist linguists at the time were therefore mostly concerned with women's subordinate 'place' in a patriarchal society. Lakoff (1975), in particular, argued that this position was both created and perpetuated by the language that women were socialised into believing was appropriate for them to use. Although this notion was subsequently critiqued by scholars who interpreted her work as labelling feminine styles as deficient, she did – as Bucholtz (2004: 126) argues – highlight male power and the *ideological* pejoration of women's language.

From concerns about 'women's language', work centred on 'difference' (such as Maltz and Borker's (1982) reinterpretation of Gumperz's

(1982) work on miscommunication) and dominance (such as O'Barr and Atkins's (1980) claim that stereotypical 'women's language' was actually *powerless* language reflecting women's inferior position in society) emerged in the 1980s. Research from this period argued that men and women use language differently, explaining this as a product of their socialisation into masculine and feminine roles. In this way, such work began to suggest that gendered behaviour was culturally constructed. Yet gender *categories* typically went unquestioned in this early research, as feminist scholars aimed to find linguistic support for the subordination of women. In using predefined categories such as 'female' and 'male' and presuming what the identities attached to those categories meant, such research may be perceived as inadvertently perpetuating the notion of dichotomous gender *difference*. The generalisations made in an attempt to prove widespread gender inequality arguably led to the 'hall of mirrors' effect (Wareing 1996), whereby initially quite specific claims about particular speakers became seen as widespread, generalisable facts. Isolated research into mixed-sex groups (for instance, West and Zimmerman 1987) and single-sex groups (such as Coates 1996) thus began to be misinterpreted as representations of how *all* men or women (again, as opposite and fundamentally different categories) used language.

   More recently, the field of gender and language has considered approaches from elsewhere in gender studies which view 'gender' as 'the cultural interpretation of sexual attributes' (Salih 2004: 23). This reflects the influence of postmodernism upon feminist theory, whereby objectivity, truth and reality are seen as illusions (Spiro 1996: 759). It also represents an extension of theories of ideology and cultural hegemony (see discussion in Section 1.2), as research in recent years has endeavoured to question essentialist notions of gender in accordance with the post-structuralist feminist aim of deconstructing fixed analytical categories. This view problematises the naturalised concepts of 'femininity' and 'masculinity' within Western culture; when differences between men and women are observed, they are typically explained as *natural* differences (Connell 2005: 10), such as men being more capable of leadership than women due to a historic system of patriarchy. Via Judith Butler's postmodernist account of gender as a culturally produced and 'inscribed' phenomenon, whereby repeated behaviours become viewed as natural and in some way internal, an understanding of gender as a performance has instead emerged within linguistics.

   Butler's (1990) concept of *performativity* deals with the construction of an 'unnatural' gender identity through stylised *acts* or performances.

For example, the act of wearing make-up may be interpreted as a 'performance' of a particular woman's femininity, since she styles herself in a way which reflects broader cultural concepts of what a woman looks like. The very fact that she applies cosmetics in order to alter her appearance demonstrates that this 'femininity' is not 'natural', of course. Research within linguistics has used the concept of performativity in order to explore both gender and sexual identities in relation to language use. In this sense, language has begun to be seen as a performative act (one clearly connected to Austin's (1976) speech act theory), with gender viewed as a cultural construction (see Barrett 1997 and Cameron 1998 for examples of this). Such a focus clearly moves on from a traditional sociolinguistic concern with how speech reflects who people *already* are, to a postmodernist account of how the way that they use language *creates* who they are (Cameron 1998: 272) and, as a result, sits well within the focus of sociocultural linguistics. The following section explores the relevance of constructionist theories in relation to sociocultural linguistics in more detail.

2.3.1 Constructionist approaches in sociocultural linguistics

Gender identity in sociocultural linguistics may be interpreted as both a reproduction and a context-specific reworking of naturalised notions, or ideologies, of masculinity and femininity. As shown above, recent sociocultural linguistics work concerned with gender has been particularly focused on the means by which these ideologies are performed and projected through language use. This clearly contrasts with – yet emerges from developments in – earlier approaches in the field of gender and language, with a more explicit focus on the context in which language is produced being prevalent in recent research. When considering the broader sociocultural context underpinning a given conversation alongside minute, fleeting moments of interaction, as in the current study, it is beneficial to use clear analytical frameworks. Within sociocultural linguistics, two important concepts have emerged which enable an understanding of the process by which ideologies are communicated, and by which local-level identity positions are established: *indexicality* and *stance*. These are considered in turn, below.

2.3.1.1 Indexicality

Indexicality is the process by which ideologies are projected through language, and which ties language use to its social context. It shows how local, micro-social contexts relate to broader, macro-social frames of sociolinguistic analysis (Silverstein 2003: 193) by exploring the connection between language use and meaning. Central to this notion is that speakers connect given linguistic moves and features with iconic representations of the social groups that are stereotyped as using them (Irvine and Gal 2000: 37). In this way, for example, swearing can be indexical of masculinity due to its associations with aggression; the ideological link between men and aggression enables a linguistic move such as swearing to be associated with masculinity. In Silverstein's model, this may be referred to as 'second-order' indexicality; the 'first order' concerns simply the association made between language and a social identity (such as 'masculine language'), whilst the 'second order' involves cultural meaning that is attached to this association (such as aggression being a male trait). For other theorists, such as Ochs (1990, 1991), these two orders occur in well-defined stages: directly and indirectly. 'Indirect' indexicality again concerns a mediating ideological link, and is termed in this way to highlight the fact that the ideological link between a linguistic feature and a macro-level, demographic category (such as 'female') is not direct and inevitable.[1] This highlights the importance of considering the local sociocultural context in which language is used and acquires meaning – the perceived function or role of language will depend on the social group with whom it is associated, and the interpretation of this will differ between cultures and contexts (see Ochs's 1991 research in Samoa for more on this).

Fundamentally, then, indexicality is concerned with how interlocutors make sense of their own and others' use of language to invoke meaning. Despite the variations between Silverstein and Ochs, it is clear from both approaches to indexicality that language and its associated meaning must be interpreted as dependent on *culturally specific* connotations. In order to understand those connotations, it is necessary to understand the context in which they are built. It is possible to view indexical relations as emerging from more than just individual linguistic items (such as swear words), however; they may also emerge from entire turns in an interaction.

An example of this can be seen from early on in my fieldwork, when I would engage with Stompers and non-Stompers through DYKE events. One evening, this involved a drink in a local gay bar, at which Claire, Marianne and I found ourselves chatting. Specifically, we were discussing the trend (at the time) for heterosexual men to wear pink teeshirts, shirts and sweaters. This led to Claire's comment: 'I'd never wear pink – I'm too butch to wear pink!'. By suggesting that she was 'too butch' to wear pink, Claire clearly invoked the cultural stereotype of pink as a feminine colour. She also invoked the stereotypical lesbian category of 'butch' which, by positioning it as a social identity for which the wearing of pink clothing would be incongruent, she aligned with non-femininity. By overtly claiming this butch identity category for herself, Claire indexed a lesbian identity at this moment. Given the context of our interaction, this is very clear. Had a gay man, a straight man or a straight woman made the same statement, the social identity being indexed would have differed significantly (as a hyper-masculine, heterosexual male, for instance). As it stands, the ideology put forward, which mediates the link between not wearing pink and being a lesbian, is of lesbians being somehow more masculine; this gives credence and renewed salience to the 'butch' category (the significance of which will be clearly illustrated in Chapter 5) and is significant to lesbian culture. As Rose and Sharma (2002: 1) suggest, by observing interaction within local communities and understanding its meaning to a given group, it is possible to view the reproduction and maintenance of ideologies such as this one. Importantly, as this moment shows, it is possible to view entire participant roles or interactive moves as indexical of broader social identities, not just individual linguistic variants or specific turns.

   A sociocultural approach which uses indexicality to understand and interpret practices as part of a system of meaning relevant to the people who use and act upon them (see Irvine 2001: 21) may be defined as 'bottom-up' in its focus. As Bucholtz (1999: 207) argues, such work is concerned with the participant's viewpoint rather than the ('top-down') interpretations of the analyst alone being privileged. Approaching CoP research from this perspective allows for a clear understanding of the indexical relationships between language practices and local social groups or categories, through its focus on the meaningful links between the identity being constructed in a given moment and broader social roles. In the case of Claire's 'too butch to wear pink' comment, for example, my awareness that the women valued the notion of butchness and embraced certain masculinised stereotypes of lesbianism (as will be illustrated later in this book) helped me to understand that this comment was not self-deprecating or ironic in nature. Though it may have been framed as a humorous remark, it was relevant to the group's overall identity construction in its reassertion of what was valued in the Stomper CoP. In this sense, Claire used the opportunity to project and perform a particularly butch persona, knowing that it had salience for the overall group identity.

   The performance of a given persona can, in itself, index a wider ideological category – in Claire's case, 'butch' indexes 'lesbian', just as

Eckert's 'Burnout' indexes middle-class ideals on a broader level. For Bucholtz and Hall (2008: 406), the 'moment-by-moment dynamics of interaction and language use' of group members can be understood in relation to the sociocultural context in which it occurs, allowing an understanding of how these identities are constructed. The role of indexicality is central to their framework as, in Bucholtz and Hall (2005), three indexical levels involved in identity construction are put forward. The *ideological level* is considered to consist of the broader structures which constrain and define identity categories such as 'lesbian'. Through an understanding of these broader categories, it is possible to engage with the meaning of the personae produced on the *ethnographic level*, or the context in which speakers interact (as part of a lesbian hiking group, for example). In addition, the *interactional level* is the point where meaning is made and styles are negotiated, such as in conversation at a gay bar amongst Stomper members. These three indexical levels enable a view beyond generalised patterns of language use and towards a focus on the actual point at which that language is produced. A concern with the production of discourse between inter-actants involves a consideration of how speakers orient themselves to ongoing talk, of course, and a sociocultural linguistics approach can show how even temporary and fleeting interactional moments – such as the impulsive claiming of a butch persona – tie into broader levels of identity (Bucholtz and Hall 2005: 595). One such approach to this is to consider *stance-taking* in interaction.

2.3.1.2   *Stance*

Stance-taking, whereby one takes up 'a position with respect to the form or content of one's utterance' (Jaffe 2009: 3), reveals the ways in which speakers position themselves in relation to something articulated within an interaction. The definition of a stance is far from universal, though may be broadly characterised as the use of conversational strategies or discourse features in order to position oneself in line with or against another speaker (Coupland and Coupland 2009: 228) and also by taking up positions in relation to other speakers' utterances and the objects that they evaluate through those utterances (Du Bois 2007: 168). The responses that might have been given to Claire's direct claim 'I'm too butch to wear pink' help to explain this; had one of her interlocutors responded to her statement with an evaluative, dialogical statement of agreement such as 'yes, you're too butch to wear pink', this would be an example of stance-taking, as would a more combative stance such as 'you're not butch, so you could wear pink'. Irrespective of the alignment intended, stance typically occurs in response to another speaker's position, role or action, and is therefore intrinsically co-constitutive.

Stance-taking can also show how speakers position themselves in certain roles which are meaningful to others within a particular context, thus constructing personae. For example, as Weeks (1987: 31) shows, stances can include the alignment of oneself with a particular ideological identity category, such as through 'outing' oneself as a gay man or a lesbian, as well as with specific personae such as Claire's 'butch'. Stances may also be taken to align oneself with or against a (tangible or ideological) group that one may be a part of. In Pichler's (2009) research, for instance, upper-class, white British private-school girls are shown to position themselves in opposition to the stereotypical personae linked to their social class. In avoiding a 'posh' identity, they instead construct a 'cool' persona (2009: 4), for example. All stances which are taken, both by individuals and collectively as a group, relate in some way to broader notions of identity, either by indexing an ideological category or positioning oneself as a particular 'type' of person which is salient on an ethnographic level. Their role in the indexical levels of identity construction presented by Bucholtz and Hall, above, is therefore very clear.

This focus on stance as a positioning tool is fundamental to the sociocultural linguistics approach and to the analysis in this book. In the chapters which follow, speakers will be shown to position themselves on an *interactional level* through stance-taking and other interactionally specific moves. At times, particular word choices or discourse patterns will be remarked upon, should they bear relevance to what is being indexed. This interactional level will be considered in line with local identity positions which are meaningful on an *ethnographic level*. The personae which mean something to the Stomper CoP, in other words, will be shown to be constructed through these stances. In turn, these personae will be shown to be indexical of broader, macro-level categories on an *ideological level*. This analytical framework utilises the three indexical levels of identity construction defined in Bucholtz and Hall's (2005) sociocultural linguistics approach, and enables an understanding of identity in relation to both the interactive context and the broader ideological structures underpinning it. The following section will introduce the sociocultural linguistics approach in more depth, demonstrating its relevance to the current study.

2.4   Principles of sociocultural linguistics

As shown in the previous section, the sociocultural linguistics approach provides a useful analytical framework; speakers' engagement in a given interaction – through such dialogical moves as stance-taking – may be understood in relation to the ethnographic context of that interaction and the personae under construction, which in turn have an indexical relationship with the broader cultural context. In the case of the Stompers, the relationship that the core members have with one another must be understood both in terms of what it meant to be a member of this particular walking group – their ethos and expected practices – but also in terms of the wider cultural context of being a lesbian (and what that meant to them, as middle-aged, middle-class, white British women). Without this clear understanding of the sociocultural context on both an ethnographic and broader cultural level, it would not be possible to accurately understand the means by which the women constructed contextually specific identities.

In addition to this theory, which Bucholtz and Hall term the *indexicality principle* (2005: 593), the sociocultural linguistics approach that they advocate entails four further principles. As with their focus on indexicality, which ties together linguistic moments with broader social meanings, the remaining principles all provide a more nuanced way of approaching language and identity. They are influenced by cultural anthropology and subsequent interactionist approaches to sociolinguistics, as well as by postmodernist interpretations of gender and sexuality. Firstly, the *emergence principle* states that identity is socially created and grounded and emergent through discourse of some kind. That is to say, it is 'fundamentally a social and cultural phenomenon' (Bucholtz and Hall 2005: 588). When Claire positioned herself as 'too butch' to wear pink, for example, she actively created the 'butch' persona and aligned herself with it. She had to announce it in order to position it as a relevant category before she could claim it for herself. In this sense, her apparent 'butch' identity was something which emerged from her talk, and it was made meaningful by her alignment of it with masculinity.

Secondly, the *positionality principle* demonstrates that identities are produced through stance- and role-taking and can, therefore, be temporary and dependent on the context of an interactive moment. It also reveals that the typical roles speakers ascribe to themselves construct their social identity within a group. In the case of the core Stompers, it was commonplace for the women to position themselves as knowledgeable about map-reading and the areas in which we hiked; by taking stances which showed this knowledge, they took on roles such as 'expert hiker' or 'navigator'. The meaning of these roles is specific to the context – they would not necessarily garner respect in a non-walking situation but, in the Stomper group, indexed an authentic identity. To describe something as being 'authentic', such as a given practice, style or attitude, then, refers to its *legitimacy* within a given context – whether it is a valued and recognised position to take.

Thirdly, the *partialness principle* points out that any construction of identity can only ever be partial, since identity exceeds the individual self. Bucholtz and Hall see identity as a social achievement, yet one constrained by social structures – no speaker can ever produce an identity in complete independence from existing identity categories, and this will shift across discourse contexts (2005: 606). Again, the importance of the interactive moment, and its relationship to imposing ideological structures on identity construction, is highlighted through this principle. For example, to position oneself as uncomfortable wearing dresses and heels, as Marianne was shown to do earlier in this chapter, is meaningful in the Stomper context only because of the broader stereotypes and ideals surrounding lesbian style (as typically 'butch'). Without this broader cultural context, and Marianne's and my shared assumption that it meant something to us both, we could arguably not have relied on a discomfort with feminine styles to be indexical of the same sort of (lesbian-based) social identity.

Fourthly, Bucholtz and Hall (2005: 598) argue in the *relationality principle* that identities acquire social meaning in relation to other available identities and other people. They propose a framework of three pairs of *tactics of intersubjectivity* for analysing the relational ways in which speakers position both the self and others. These are: *adequation* and *distinction; authentication* and *denaturalisation; authorisation* and *illegitimation.* The first of these concerns the ways in which differences between individuals within a community are played down in order for them to appear as a homogeneous unit (adequation), and the process by which similarities that might undermine the group's identity as 'different' from others are suppressed (distinction). In Stomper interactions, this was commonplace; members would frequently align themselves with one another by discussing topics that they assumed would be relevant, based on what they had in common – walking and sexual orientation. In doing so, they avoided topics of conversation which would highlight differences between them, such as their careers or personal lives. The women would also regularly invoke stereotypes – as has been shown in Marianne's and Claire's turns in this chapter – significant to the ideological identity category which they could relate to, such as by indexing a butch persona. In doing so, the women positioned themselves as a group of people who were similar to one another but yet different from mainstream (heterosexual) society, thus reinforcing their notion of a shared group identity.

The second set of tactics aims to explain how identities are reified, or made real. Authentication concerns speakers' use of a variety of resources to create contextually legitimate identities (such as the learning of social practices key to meaning-making within a CoP). In contrast, denaturalisation shows how identities can appear to be false. This might, for example, be the deliberate claim-staking of an identity incongruent with that typically constructed by an individual in order to draw attention to the ideological nature of what is expected of them. The Stomper women would often index exaggerated, overtly feminine personae, or claim to be a 'girly girl', for example. This enabled them to highlight, through an ironic performance, the identity that they did *not* hold. In creating a sense of legitimacy and erecting symbolic boundaries around what the group represented (and what they did *not*), it was possible for the Stompers to make their own shared identity appear more tangible.

Finally, authorisation and illegitimation are tactics utilising power or ideology to affirm or dismiss an identity. The tactic of authorisation might occur when speakers wish to demonstrate their own legitimacy as a member of their community or a participant in the discourse moment and, therefore, might align themselves with some institutional or hege-monic structure in order to do so. In contrast, illegitimation is a tactic employed to make certain identities appear non-normative or illegiti-mate. For the Stompers, as will be outlined in Chapters 7 and 8, political awareness – specifically feminism – played a large part in defining their identity. The women used the shared assumption that – as women of a certain age, sexual orientation and socio-economic background – all members of the group were feminists. If something which conflicted with a perceived feminist ethos was stated, then, individual women could justify their displeasure or surprise at the statement by invoking that which the group recognised as being 'right': feminist discourse. The act of aligning oneself with an authoritative stance or ideology, of course, enables individuals to position themselves as entitled to do so; in turn, this allows them to present themselves as a legitimate member of a CoP. This notion of legitimacy and, specifically, what is authentic style and practice in the Stomper group, will be explored in much greater depth in the chapters which follow.

These three sets of tactics highlight the central argument of a sociocul-tural linguistics approach: that identity is an interactional phenomenon which is intersubjectively constructed through discourse. Within any interaction, some or all of these tactics may be employed in order to construct a stance and, in doing so, a local group persona. By considering the tactics of intersubjectivity in an analysis of interactive data, it is possible to view language as occurring in the moment, as significant to the aim of that moment, and as relevant to the context-specific identity positioning taking place. Though the tactics may be considered useful parameters for the analysis of varied aspects of identity construction, however, from 'nerd' identity positioning (Bucholtz 1999) to the construction of Asian selves (Young 2008), to the performance of authority and authenticity by flight attendants (B. Clark 2010), they were (as outlined in the following chapter) initially advocated for the study of sexuality (Bucholtz and Hall 2004). As such, they are rigorously tested in the analysis of lesbian interaction in the chapters which follow.

2.5 Concluding remarks

This chapter has introduced a range of research which may be brought together under the umbrella term 'sociocultural linguistics'. It has shown that sociocultural linguistic approaches to gender must view masculinity and femininity as ideological constructs, notions which are performatively reproduced within interaction and which can be understood on a local level by scrutinising that interaction. The principles and tactics put forward by Bucholtz and Hall (2004, 2005) have also been shown to enhance our understanding of indexicality, a concept fundamental to interactionist sociolinguistics, by exploring the relationship between momentary moves and stances, ethnographically salient identity positions and personae, and broader ideological categories. It has been argued that this approach provides a coherent way to analyse the linguistic construction of social identities such as gender and sexuality.

To date, studies engaged in exploring the relationship between language and sexuality, specifically, remain relatively few in number. Even fewer have engaged explicitly with the principles laid out in this chapter. The following chapter therefore examines the approaches that *have* been taken in this area and discusses current debates in the field. It culminates by arguing that an ethnographic, bottom-up approach such as sociocultural linguistics can enhance our understanding of language and sexuality, before the later chapters in this book illustrate this through the analysis of interactions between the Stomper women.

3
Approaches to Language and Sexuality

In the previous chapter, it was shown that a sociocultural approach to language use may enable an understanding of identity as an interactional phenomenon. Through stance-taking in conversation, we are able to perform particular personae, which are given meaning due to their indexical relationships with broader ideological categories. This chapter explores Bucholtz and Hall's claim that sexuality is 'a relational and contextual socio-political phenomenon' (2004: 506), a position which allows them to advocate theoretical approaches which use their proposed tactics of intersubjectivity and principles of sociocultural linguistics to investigate the relationship between language and sexuality. This chapter begins by introducing post-structuralist approaches to sexuality and examining its relationship with gender, before moving on to briefly review recent studies taking place within 'queer linguistics', particularly those concerning lesbian discourse and identity. In outlining some key aspects of lesbian culture, the chapter explains the ideological context of the Stomper group's interaction before it moves on to provide a detailed critique of current debates within the area of language and sexuality.

The view of sexuality posited by Bucholtz and Hall (2004) reflects the post-structuralist approach which, as shown in Section 2.3.1, influenced work within language and gender research by moving beyond an assumption of inherent gender (reflected by language) towards a view of language as a tool used in the construction of (gendered) identity. In much the same way that gendered roles can be viewed as a product of social practice, the categorisation of individuals by their sexual orientation can similarly be viewed as a cultural construction. As gender is often assumed to have predefined meaning, different sexualities have social meanings ideologically imposed upon them, too. Foucault

(1978) explores the concept of sexuality with relation to the privileged role of heterosexuality in society; he argues that the perception of heterosexuality as 'normal' is a historical construct, an ideal which maintains the moralistic view of sex as primarily an act of reproduction and classifies homosexuality as deviant or abnormal (1978: 43). This is known as *heteronormativity*, a term mentioned briefly in Chapter 1 and coined by Warner (1991) to mean an ideological notion of what is 'natural' with regards sexuality. Sexuality is also viewed as intrinsically linked to gender, in the sense that masculinity and femininity are ideologically binary and viewed as a logical romantic pairing (hence heterosexuality maintaining a normative status). Any conceptualisation of homosexuality has to therefore take heteronormativity into account, as work within the discipline of *queer theory* – outlined below – illustrates.

3.1   Queer theory

The term 'queer' is a reclaimed epithet; it has been used in a homophobic way against gay men and women for decades, but has now been redefined and implemented in an academic context to refer to all non-heteronormative behaviours and desires. Queer theory emerged through postmodernist approaches to culture and society, directly influenced by a Foucauldian understanding of sexuality, and has provided a new way of viewing homosexuality. This new approach to sexuality moves beyond the historical theorisation of homosexuality as a psychological illness or deviant practice; until the latter half of the twentieth century, homosexual behaviour was routinely explained through the concept of gender 'inversion', whereby a psychological disorder led to the misalignment of a person's sex and their gender identity (see, for example, Henry 1948). Such a view assumed that it was natural for a man to be 'male', for example, a definitive element of which was his sexual attraction to the female. In this sense, homosexuality was seen as a curable affliction, but it also led to prevalent cultural ideologies about the gendered identity of gay men and women, who were assumed to be effeminate and masculinised respectively. Rather than assuming that there is a definitive ideological dichotomy between the sexes, with gender options allowing men (who are masculine) *or* women (who are feminine), one of queer theory's aims is to view homosexuality as a social phenomenon and discursively produced identity, not as an inherently inverted self.

   Butler's (1990) work on performativity (see Section 2.3) is often cited as the beginning of queer theory, combining a feminist understanding of constructionism and female oppression with a detailed critique of the performative nature of both gender and sexuality. The main objective of queer studies and queer theory, then, is to challenge essentialist categories and assumptions, particularly (but not restricted to) those surrounding sexuality. In challenging these categories and assumptions, queer theory contests heteronormativity in a way which reflects feminism's challenge of patriarchy and misogyny in society and academia; by deconstructing, critiquing and attacking homophobia and 'the hegemonic centrism of heterosexism'[1] (Whittle 1996: 202). Whilst studies of gay and lesbian experience are clearly placed within the theoretical lines of postmodernist feminist critiques of gender (in that they respond to ideological preconceptions about gender as innate and binary), however, it is clear that there is a particular need to move beyond the recognised boundaries of gender in order to understand non-normative sexual behaviour. This can include, as will be illustrated throughout this book, specifically in Chapter 5, queer orientations to ideological positions such as 'masculine' and 'feminine', reworking and subverting them for a homosexual context, yet maintaining them at the same time as pervasive categories. Research combining queer theory with linguistics – often referred to, perhaps unsurprisingly, as queer linguistics – has endeavoured to explore the manifestations of such non-heteronormative identities through a focus on language use. Central to this, as it is with queer theory more generally, is an understanding of gender and sexuality as culturally defined and performatively produced concepts. For this reason, Bucholtz and Hall's (2004, 2005) sociocultural approach has particular relevance to queer linguistics.

3.2 Queer linguistics

As indicated above, queer theory concerns all non-normative experiences and behaviours, typically viewing identities as culturally constructed and fluid. Queer linguistics shares this concern. As well as homosexuality, studies within queer linguistics include bisexuality (such as Rust 1996, Madison 2012 and Thorne 2012) and transsexuality (Namaste 2000 and Valentine 2003, for instance), as well as, for example, sadomasochism (such as Nichols 2006). Studies within queer linguistics are typically characterised by an approach which utilises queer theory and post-structuralist feminism and, in this sense, have directly influenced the emerging field of sociocultural linguistics. An example of this is Rusty Barrett's work (1995, 1998). Barrett details the linguistic performativity of a number of African American drag queens – gay men performing cabaret acts at (in this case) gay bars. The speakers in Barrett's study used language which was indexical of white, heterosexual women in combination with forms indexing black, homosexual male identity. By framing drag as a performance of gender, Barrett challenges heteronormative, essentialist assumptions about the relationship between biological sex and gender behaviour (1995: 209). He also questions the assumption that using a linguistic feature that is indexical of a social identity necessarily reflects a desire to identify with that group. Rather than sharing some white, heterosexual female social identity, for example, the drag queens in his research are found to utilise linguistic forms indexical of this to subvert the ideological mainstream, and to creatively construct an ironic persona (Barrett 1998: 140).

Barrett's approach combines performativity theory with an understanding of language as a multifaceted, context-specific resource, and in this sense reflects the aims of sociocultural linguistics. Studies contributing to the growing field of queer linguistics share these aims, with research which explores the relationship between language and the performance of sexual identity (such as Hall 1995 and Podesva 2007), which focuses on the representation of gay people's language (for instance Queen 1997 and Livia 1995) and which investigates the discourses of queer culture (such as Chirrey's (2011) analysis of advice on the 'coming out' process). Little work currently exists, however, which directly employs an interactionist approach to the study of language and sexuality, despite the prevalence of such research within language and gender.

A notable exception to this is Queen (1998), who considers the interaction of a group of gay male and female speakers. Queen demonstrates how these speakers used co-constructive techniques to build a queer network around the shared notion of their membership of an imagined queer community. The individuals in this study used a range of techniques to construct a joint identity based upon their mutually queer sense of self, including the raising of topics which reflected a shared cultural knowledge about what it meant to be gay (Queen 1998: 206–10). Queen also looked at the discourse patterns of the speakers, focusing on their turn-taking and interruptions, finding that they frequently co-narrated in order to build their sense of community and camaraderie. That this occurred despite their previous lack of acquaintance with one another reflects the fact 'that they consider themselves to be part of a broader, queer community' (Queen 1998: 210).

Queen's early research in this area has been, along with Barrett's (1998), central to the developing field of queer linguistics. It demonstrates the necessity for research to recognise the complex relationship between queer identities and the sense of collective belonging felt by many gay people as a result of their difference. In its focus on the interactive construction of momentary queerness, it also clearly reflects Bucholtz and Hall's (2005) concern with identity as a connection between context-specific personae and broader ideologies. Though research into language and sexuality which takes this approach has *begun* to emerge, however, this work has so far overwhelmingly been concerned with discourse related to gay male (such as Gaudio 1994, Jacobs 2002 and Podesva 2007) and trans-related (Behan 1995, Edelman 2008 and Leap 2008, for instance) experiences and identities. A very limited body of work considering language and lesbian identity has emerged in comparison. This reflects, perhaps, the nature of lesbian culture compared to that of gay men, in particular; the political context of lesbian identity and experience differs considerably, and lesbian life has often been less prevalent in gay culture more broadly. This context is considered below, before work exploring lesbian language is outlined.

3.3   Lesbian language and culture

As the previous section has shown, research into the connection between language and sexuality is certainly emerging and developing, and has clearly been influenced by postmodernist thought and work within sociocultural linguistics. Yet linguistic investigations which consider lesbian culture and identity remain few in number. The chapters which follow (which more closely examine the Sapphic Stomper group) will demonstrate that the sociocultural context of lesbian identity is complex, multifaceted, and deserving of greater consideration. In many ways, the Stomper identity will be shown to reflect many of the ideologies that are prevalent in lesbian culture; in particular, the women associated with the labels 'butch' and 'femme' in striking ways. These are terms which are highly prevalent within lesbian culture[2] (and queer culture more broadly), as illustrated below.

Due to ideological notions of sex and gender as innate and intrinsically connected, along with the influence of scientific explanations for gender 'inversion' (detailed above), there is arguably an expectation for lesbian women to be more 'masculine', a common definition or explanation for being *butch*. A butch identity is often also explained as a politically motivated stylistic performance, one which rejects normative femininity and what Roof (1998: 29) refers to as 'the highly impractical feminized appearance demanded by patriarchy'. Yet, given the performative nature of gender and the constant reification of binary opposites, as well as the prevalence of naturalised gender ideology, it is unsurprising that the notion of *femme* lesbians (seen to reflect the 'natural' styles of womanhood, unlike the 'unfeminine' butch) also exists and is placed in ideological opposition to a butch identity; this 'makes sense' within normative culture (see Vicinus 1992: 480). As Richardson (1996: 280) argues, the idea of two women being involved in a sexual relationship is problematic within a mainstream, heteronormative frame of reference, since women are ideologically considered to be sexually passive. For two women to be sexually engaged, therefore, at least one must be more 'masculine' (i.e. butch), and the other typically less active (i.e. femme). In this sense, they 'reproduce' a male/female structure. Despite the fact that these traits may be perceived as emerging from mainstream, heteronormative culture in order to define and explain a queer phenomenon within its own prescribed parameters, however, it is evident that 'butch' and 'femme' remain intrinsic to lesbian culture. As will be outlined in Chapter 5, for example, the Stomper women negotiated their way around one another's differences and found a sense of shared self by employing these two stereotypes; they performed specifically butch or femme personae, claimed alignment to the labels through their stances, and defined them as clear categories through their interaction.

This is, perhaps, unsurprising; as Sauntson argues, sexuality 'tends to be discursively constructed using culturally recognisable sex and gender categories as its key terms of reference' (2008: 274). In other words, broad ideologies and cultural norms surrounding the category of 'lesbian' are essential for the construction of a salient lesbian identity. The use of such culturally recognisable categories can be problematic, however; the categories of 'butch' and 'femme', for example, are semantically loaded and politically charged. There can be confusion surrounding the meaning of butch and femme; these terms can be interpreted as simply role-playing or adoption of heteronormative masculinity and femininity. Many feminist scholars have positioned the categories as dangerous – as reproducing patriarchal ideology (Rich 1980) and unequal distributions of power within relationships (Wilson and Weir 1986: 137). It may also be argued, however, that – far from perpetuating harmful gender ideologies – the categories of butch and femme actually *challenge* heteronormativity (Butler 1990: 31), since their very existence reveals 'the constructed nature of the heterosexual matrix' (Hemmings 2002: 9). Whether the categories are embraced and adopted as coherent identities or not, it is clear that – to many women – they are meaningful. This is not to argue, of course, that *all* lesbians identify with these two labels, but that they are likely to be *familiar* to women who engage in some level of queer or lesbian culture. For this reason, linguistic research into lesbian culture and identity has often focused on the two identities and endeavoured to understand their manifestation in specific, unrelated contexts. Below, an outline of some relevant research in this area is presented.

3.3.1 'Lesbian language'

Research into the relationship between language and lesbianism has been plagued, somewhat, by the generalised phrase 'lesbian language'. This terminology conjures up ideas of homogeneous language use or secret codes between all women (who, presumably, identify with their sexuality in exactly the same way), and reflects early attempts to identify a coherent 'gay language' (such as the glossaries of Legman (1941) and Rodgers (1972), both concerned with the language of homosexual men). Perhaps in avoidance of this, linguistic work which has explored a specifically lesbian context has typically focused not on identifying ways that gay women (and only gay women) use language, but instead on two key areas. Firstly, research has investigated the ways that lesbians tend to be represented through discourse and, secondly, how language can be used to index broader lesbian culture-specific stereotypes in order to construct some aspect of lesbian identity or community. This section will briefly introduce work in these two main areas in order to highlight commonalities between a range of studies. These commonalities will be seen repeatedly in the chapters which follow, illustrating the relevance of broader lesbian culture on local lesbian interaction.

3.3.1.1 Lesbian representation

Research into how lesbian women are represented is popular within cultural studies and queer theory more broadly, with scholars arguing that lesbians are typically positioned in the media either as menacing (Inness 1997) or titillating (Maher and Pusch 1995), as well as exploring the historical association of masculinity with gay women (such as Doan 2001). In this sense, much of the research has focused on homophobic or misogynistic trends within mainstream culture. Within linguistics, in contrast, work considering how lesbian women are represented has typically focused on lesbian culture itself by looking, specifically, at texts written by lesbians for lesbians. For example, Livia (1995) explores the use of the butch/femme dynamic in lesbian popular fiction. She finds that couples within lesbian stories are frequently constructed within this frame of reference, with each woman typically occupying one side of the dichotomy, and are scripted as using language which mostly reflects existing stereotypes of 'men's language' and 'women's language' respectively. This illustrates, of course, both the prevalence of the butch/femme stereotype and the cultural transmission of it. Irrespective of whether 'real' women actually relate to the categories in coherent ways, it is clear that their engagement with lesbian culture might well lead them to believe that they ought to.

A further example of such research is Queen's (1997) investigation into the characterisation of lesbians in fiction. Queen identified linguistic features commonly used by butch characters in popular lesbian comic strips, including language features (such as swearing and flat intonation patterns) stereotypical of working-class urban males (1997: 244). In addition, the characters were found to utilise forms of 'women's language' and stereotypical gay men's styles. Queen argues that the use of these styles in a new (specifically lesbian) context allows lesbian women to rework them and thus give them new meaning, creating a 'uniquely lesbian language' (1997: 242). Though this does seem to imply a certain homogeneity between all women identifying as lesbian, and appears to seek out a definitive 'lesbian language' which cannot, realistically, be used by *all* lesbian women, Queen's work is an example of early investigations into the role of language in lesbian identity and culture and, importantly, investigates the representation of lesbian speech rather than its use in conversation. It highlights the expectation that exists within lesbian culture that there is a lesbian-specific way of communicating or behaving which, again, indicates that broader ideologies and stereotypes (such as lesbians being more 'mannish') are likely to play some role in lesbian identity construction.

Research has also developed, in recent years, to investigate the relationship between lesbian women and broader society. Turner (2008), for example, explores the language used in a British lesbian magazine to construct a sense of community and sameness with its readers; typically, she finds that the authors position themselves and their readers (all, presumably, lesbian) as 'us' and those who engage in mainstream or specifically heterosexual practices as 'them'. Koller's (2008) account of the representation of lesbians in a variety of discourse contexts, such as in pamphlets, magazines and TV shows created by lesbians, for lesbians, since the 1970s, also identifies a coherent 'us/them' theme. Yet Koller shows that this polarising technique occurs not only between 'us' as lesbians and 'them' as heterosexuals or men, but between 'us' as (for example) butch lesbians versus 'them' as 'womanly women'

(Koller 2008: 94). As with Turner's work, this foregrounds the perceived need for definition and clarity in terms of what it means to be a lesbian; for those women who view their sexuality as part of their identity, it is clear that cultural ideologies and stereotypes have been prevalent within lesbian media for generations. In this sense, again, it is important to consider how the global context of lesbian culture might impact on local instantiations of lesbian identity. It is through consideration of interaction between lesbians, such as in the small body of research outlined below, that it is possible to begin to explore this relationship in detail.

3.3.1.2   Lesbian discourse and interaction

Studies into the role of language in lesbian communication, as suggested above, have not been great in number, yet research in this area is beginning to increase. Early examples include Morgan and Wood's (1995) recordings of lesbian friends in conversation which, they argued, revealed the collaborative co-construction of lesbian identity as the women worked together to create a lesbian space (1995: 235). Whilst some of the conversational topics were about lesbians, however, little in the interaction actually demonstrated what being a lesbian meant to the group as a whole or to each individual member. Although the data reveals the importance, for this particular group of women, of constructing a shared sense of self, it does not enhance our understanding of what is important to them *as lesbians*. This reflects a danger, perhaps, of assuming that what speakers do necessarily reflects who the researchers have defined them as being.

In contrast to this, Queen's (2005) later work reveals the use of joke-telling in an interaction to define what is humorous for lesbian women, specifically. Taking two groups of gay women, one of feminist activists and the other a softball team, Queen looks at jokes as examples of in-group markers which assume a shared knowledge between the speakers and signify their relationship. The jokes in her study reflect certain lesbian stereotypes, such as those surrounding hair length (that lesbians have short hair), clothing style (such as lesbians wearing comfortable shoes), and so on. Queen demonstrates that the women actively construct their own identity as lesbians by employing global lesbian ideologies. In doing so, she reveals the importance of recognising the impact of broader structures.

Similarly, Morrish and Sauntson (2007) advocate a study of lesbian identity which considers how 'linguistic resources are deployed and manipulated within a given context' (2007: 40). They are the first to directly apply Bucholtz and Hall's (2005) framework to a qualitative account of lesbian interaction, and demonstrate that the women in their study construct identity positions for themselves as either 'lesbian' or 'woman' dependent on whether heterosexual women are present or not. This reveals the complex ties between gender and sexual identity and the different constructions the two can have. Recent work by Wagner (2010) continues in this vein, focusing on same-sex female couples and their interaction as parents. In considering their construction of power dynamics when dealing with their children, Wagner shows the lesbian couples in her study to be flexible by sharing the disciplinarian roles. Wagner's research shows that, rather than merely reproducing heteronormative familial structures, it is possible to take up numerous (gendered and neutral) positions at any one time.

Research such as this clearly demonstrates that the invoking of wider cultural resources, such as stereotypes, may enable a joint understanding of what it means to be a lesbian. In this sense, a shared notion of self might well be achieved within specific contexts, based around mutual identification with this social, globally resonant category. Wood (1999) contributes to this evidence by considering a range of coming-out stories, through which the women in her study discursively construct their sexual identity. She demonstrates that the ideologies that her participants used to situate themselves in their narrative frame overlap, despite the fact that the women are unconnected and demographi- cally disparate. Typically, these reflect an awareness of heteronormative scripts and the participants' own deviation from them (1999: 52) – the feeling that one was 'always different', for example. Such research indi- cates that, on a broad level, being a lesbian within mainstream society may result in certain shared experiences of homophobia or discrimina- tion, for example. This again demonstrates the prevalence of ideological structures on the way that individuals construct their identity, and explains the desire of many gay people to associate with those sharing not only their orientation to a given sexual identity category, but their experiences as a minority group.

Research in the area of lesbian language and interaction, as evident by the relatively small number of studies here, is still emerging. What is typically missing from this research, to date, is a focus on the ethno- graphic context from which any data emerges. This is problematic, since without an understanding of the way that stylistic moves are used to construct group identities, it is difficult to view the *meaning* of broader stereotypes in relation to the co-construction of a shared sense of self. Instead, we simply discover that the stereotypes are salient and make assumptions about what they must mean to our participants. By taking a bottom-up, ethnographic approach, however, it is possible to assess this from the perspective of the women involved rather than attempting to account for the moves they make in line with the researchers' preconceptions. As outlined in Section 2.3, this approach has enabled new insights into the study of language and gender, yet such a focus in an investigation of lesbian interaction remains comparatively overdue. For this reason, in the analysis of Stomper interactions provided later in this book, the meaning behind individual stances will be explained through an ethnographically defined understanding of the meaning of those stances, using the indexical framework outlined in the previous chapter. Yet before the Stompers may be reintroduced via a discussion of this ethnographic process, it is important to consider *all* aspects of language and sexuality. So far, identity has been the focus of this chapter, yet an additional focus has emerged in recent years: that of *desire*. Below, the identity and desire arguments are outlined, and a critical perspective on the debate is presented.

3.4   Sexual identity and desire

This chapter has so far outlined developments in the evolving field of language and sexuality, showing how queer theory has begun to play a central role in research considering the representation and interaction of gay and lesbian people. It has shown that work within lesbian discourse has considered the relationship between broader ideologies and local interactive contexts, and has argued that the ethnographic contexts which mediate the ways in which identities are constructed must be fully explored. Of course, the assertion that such research is needed in order for the field of language and sexuality to develop cannot go unchallenged. Indeed, it may be argued that, by concentrating on sexual identity and its relationship to language, we are in danger of neglecting other valuable areas of research, such as the relevance of desire. This is considered, below.

The desire approach, introduced by Cameron and Kulick (2003), has led, over the past decade, to a debate about the progression of the field of language and sexuality. On the one hand, Cameron and Kulick (2003, 2005) argue that studies of desire would be fruitful for research into language and sexuality, whilst Bucholtz and Hall (2004) explicitly argue against this approach due to its implication that identity ought to be put aside 'for a while' (Cameron and Kulick 2003: 105). In defending their stance, Cameron and Kulick (2005) make it clear that they are 'not calling for questions of identity to be *replaced* by other questions', but instead for 'them to be *supplemented* with other questions' (2005: 110, italics in original). In explaining their approach to language and sexuality, Cameron and Kulick argue that such study should encompass more than that which might be considered queer (2003: 7). Furthermore, they suggest that language and sexuality research should focus not only on identity but on 'other dimensions of sexual experience' including 'fantasy, repression, pleasure, fear and the unconscious' (2003: 106). In doing so, they argue that we should consider how desire for a subject is articulated and reified, using linguistic data to 'map out the workings of desire' (2003: 131). Central to Cameron and Kulick's (2003) argument is that the current approaches to sexuality typical within linguistics are preoccupied with the notion of identity. In order to advocate a focus on desire, therefore, they critique studies of identity as reliant on oblique labels and categories, overly concerned with predictable and problematic notions such as 'the gay community' or 'authentic gayness', and missing the erotic element of sexuality. Below, these issues are considered in light of what the sociocultural linguistics and community of practice approaches can offer.

3.4.1   The critique of identity work in queer linguistics

Cameron and Kulick argue that analysing queer identity is problematic due to the complex and multifaceted identification individuals have with labels such as 'lesbian' or 'gay'; individuals may struggle to articulate their sexualities through the imposed identity categories available to them (2005: 114). An alternative view of this, however, can be achieved by considering the community of practice approach. As illustrated already (see Section 2.2), the CoP allows the researcher to assess how global categories are reproduced in myriad ways by individuals on a local level, and how new categories are created to both represent and challenge existing labels. As will be explored in the following chapters, the Sapphic Stompers' interaction provides evidence of this. Rather than simply embracing a version of 'lesbian' which was pre-existing and already defined, the women in this CoP actively negotiated what it *meant* to be a lesbian *to them*. Though they appropriated lesbian-specific stereotypes, such as butch and femme, these were also not accepted wholesale – they were *re*appropriated for their own purposes, turned into CoP-specific personae, and then indexed through stance-taking. Whilst Cameron and Kulick quite rightly argue against work which views sexuality as predefined by rigid categories, sociocultural linguistics also challenges these approaches by viewing the categories as both constraining *and* facilitating. The framework enables an interpretation of identity as fluid social positioning in line with culturally relevant roles (Bucholtz and Hall 2005: 586), not of language use correlating in a straightforward way with ideological, globally prevalent categories and labels.

Whilst ideological categories may constrain, then, speakers still tend to find ways to deconstruct and rework them for their own social gain and sense of place in the world. As the data analysed in this book will illustrate, social categories – though seemingly limiting – also form a basis for constructing social groups and local personae (Eckert and McConnell-Ginet 1995: 472). The Stomper group would not have existed if it were not for the coherent category of 'lesbian', for example, that concept which – in some way – defined them all and brought them together as a group. For Cameron and Kulick, though, such a concept of shared identification with a broader category brings potential issues. In particular, they argue against research which positions the language of given speakers as representative of the sexual category with which those speakers identify – what Kulick (2000: 258) refers to as a 'linguistic code'. If researchers assume that all gay people share some fundamental quality or identity, they are perhaps likely to believe that there is some shared language between them. However, as Morrish and Leap (2007) point out, there is in fact very little contemporary research which has discovered such a code or made an assumption about the homogeneity of all queer speakers. Indeed, 'no researcher who studies [queer]-centred language has ever claimed to be searching for unique linguistic features – or has ever claimed to have found them' (Morrish and Leap 2007: 20). Whilst this suggests that Cameron and Kulick may, in fact, concern themselves with an issue which is not particularly prevalent within queer linguistic research, their concern about *how* language can be correlated with queer identities nonetheless deserves further consideration. Recent research exploring identity as occurring within interaction, and categories as concepts which are reworked through local practice, deals directly with this concern.

Through the use of an analytical framework which encompasses indexicality, for example, it is possible to view language as indexical of certain ideological, stereotypical categorisations of gay people, such as falsetto with gay men. Such language may indeed be used to index 'gay-ness' at the global level, but this enables the positioning of oneself in line with *local* personae which reflect *ideological* gay categories. If we are primarily concerned with this local-level identity construction and we consider the local sociocultural context behind the construction of such personae, we need not, therefore, make broad stereotypical claims about how 'all' gay people speak. Cameron and Kulick have been concerned by the potential for this kind of naïve theorising, and the sociocultural linguistics approach is one which enables an alternative, clearer perspective. Whereas Cameron and Kulick suggest that we move on from considering such ideological identity categories and move to new intellectual ground, therefore, a sociocultural approach actually allows us to investigate these categories in a more nuanced way by studying how they are reified within local contexts. In this way, rather than attempting to find features which are specific to queer speakers and in some way relating that to a queer identity, research may investigate the referential links of particular styles of language, in a given context, to varied sexual identities.

Cameron and Kulick also suggest that sexual identity itself is a problematic concept to investigate, however. They argue, for example, that language and sexuality research has, so far, tended to focus on 'predictable debates' about issues of community and authenticity. In expressing their concern for the development of language and sexuality, they suggest that such debates may be misleading and may result in an incomplete account (2003: 105). Yet, one could argue, the debates that they characterise as 'predictable' are so prominent due to their importance. The concept of the 'gay community' is clearly ideological, as illustrated by Queen (1998) above, and also Barrett (1997), and alternative theories of community have been put forward which recognise that it is not a tangible or homogeneous concept. As will be argued in the chapters which follow, indeed, the CoP is a viable means of exploring the role of an ideological 'gay community' on the construction of identities in interaction by examining a community on a smaller scale.

In terms of the critique of 'authenticity', this is a concept most extensively researched by Leap (1996). His research explores how speakers employ a variety of linguistic means to identify themselves and others as gay, and to create a shared sense of gay (male) experience. Though Kulick (2000: 264) critiques Leap's early work for reinforcing a notion of homogeneity and exclusivity by attempting to establish what an authentic gay language is, this work is of considerable importance due to its illustration of the role that language plays in the *construction* of what it means to be gay. As Bucholtz and Hall's (2005: 601) tactic of intersubjectivity 'authentication' shows, authenticity need not only mean a rigid and predefined notion of what is real. Instead, we can focus on what is *constructed* as 'genuine' or 'legitimate' through social interaction. This may include, for example, members of a lesbian CoP negotiating what 'real' lesbianism is, as is found repeatedly through the

data that follows in this book. In contrast to the stance of Cameron and
Kulick that the notions of 'community' and 'authenticity' are predictable and in themselves problematic, therefore, the research detailed in
the chapters which follow focuses explicitly upon them.

3.4.2 Desire and identity as complementary concepts

As outlined above, a focus on desire is presented by Cameron and Kulick
as a new way of exploring language and sexuality, with a key aim of
the approach being to view those aspects of sexuality which are subconscious, such as the erotic, rather than performed or a result of social
positioning. In doing so, one would be sure to understand all aspects
of what manifests itself culturally as 'sexuality', and one could focus
on how desire is communicated. For Cameron and Kulick, this would
concern 'not only whom one desires but also what one desires to do
(whether or not with another person)' (2003: 8). This focus on desire,
in terms of the ways in which speakers articulate or communicate what
they want, has already been considered – albeit, so far, to a limited
extent – within the field of language and sexuality, however. Harvey
and Shalom's (1997) edited volume, for example, brings together a
collection of scholars exploring 'the linguistic encodings of desire'
(1997: 3). In this sense, it has not been disputed that 'desire' may be
a fascinating area to research. However, the apparent suggestion that
desire might supplant research into sexual identity has led to some
consternation within the field, resulting in research attempting to bring
together approaches to identity and desire rather than further polarising
them. Though research into the subconscious may not fit within this
endeavour, a consideration of sexuality as something which is erotic
and intimate, as well as simply social, has now developed.

An example of this is Sauntson and Kyratzis's (2007) edited volume,
which focuses on sexuality as a social identity *as well as* an activity
shaped by desire (2007: 4). Included within this volume is a consideration of talk about desire, with Pichler's account of adolescent girls
engaged in 'sex talk' featured. Pichler (2007: 91) demonstrates that,
whilst the girls in her study are ostensibly discussing the adult world
of sex and desire, in doing so they also construct other key aspects of
their social identity, including their ethnicity, age, gender and class.
Similarly, whilst the communication of what one desires via dating
advertisements may seem ostensibly to be about sexual longing and
preference, research such as that of Thorne and Coupland (1998) has
found that such a context is also a site for the construction of a specifically sexualised self; dating adverts allow 'idealistic identity formations'

as well as 'playful, fantastic relationship projections' (1998: 254). In this sense, as Morrish and Leap (2007: 17) argue, desire itself may be best examined and explained within research which focuses on identity.

Whilst the consideration of desire within the field of language and sexuality has led somewhat to a focus on the erotic, however, it may also be useful to consider 'desire' in a broader, non-sexualised way. When 'desire' is interpreted not only as a longing for something which is explicitly sexual, for instance, it is possible to view much of the research into constructions of identity presented in the previous chapter as, instead, the communication of desire. For example: if wishing to fit socially into a particular context, such as an illegal party, one of Eckert's (2000) participants might use forms symbolic of Burnout identity. In this hypothetical instance, it could be said that the speaker is expressing a desire to belong. Similarly, when a Stomper such as Marianne expresses her discomfort with wearing skirts and dresses to such events as work parties, as presented in the previous chapter, she may be viewed as expressing her desire to be recognised as different from her heterosexual colleagues. This is not to dismiss a focus on the communication of sexual desire, but rather to suggest that desire in broader terms might be integral to many of the ways in which speakers position themselves as certain types of people. Again, focusing on CoPs may be a way to mediate this. If the practices of speakers, who engage together in CoP activity, reflect their shared aims as a group, we may also interpret this as their desire to be a certain type of person – to perform an authentic persona and play a part in constructing what it means to be a CoP member. Identities emerge through interaction, but only as a result of mutual negotiation and meaning-making; if CoP members do not understand what is desirable within their group, they cannot – and will not – play a part in the construction of a group identity. Rather than rejecting Cameron and Kulick's recommendation that we consider the communication of desire in relation to sexuality, then, the analysis in this book endeavours to highlight and explore moments whereby, through their social positioning, the Stomper women seem to express their desire to be interpreted in a certain way.

3.5   Concluding remarks

This chapter has outlined current approaches to language and sexuality, arguing that the sociocultural linguistics approach provides a way of understanding how social identities which emerge from sexual orientation may be communicated and reified through interaction. Crucially, it has been shown that this requires researchers to relate such interaction to both its ethnographic context and the broader sociocultural influences which surround it. Without a bottom-up approach such as this, it is impossible to understand how broader ideological categories such as 'gay' and 'lesbian' are both reworked and responded to as a result of a shared desire to orient oneself to such labels. To truly understand the interaction of a CoP such as the Stompers, indeed, who define themselves as a group because of their shared claiming of the ideological category 'lesbian', one must interpret their local practices and stances in light of what matters to them as a unit. To do this, one must understand the meaning of the local personae which are created through those stances and, in turn, must understand how and why those personae index the broader categories that they do. As outlined in Chapter 2, this knowledge and understanding is fundamental to a bottom-up perspective. As indicated above, research into language and lesbian identity has not, until now, fully explored the indexical relationships between local interaction and broad, ideological categories, because such research has not employed an ethnographic methodology. The following chapter argues for the implementation of such a methodology and outlines the processes which may be involved in it. Through personal reflection and accounts of the ethnography which facilitated the analyses in this book, the chapter reveals just how this revealing, yet often tumultuous and emotionally draining methodology enables a view of identity construction in progress.

4
Doing Ethnography with the Stompers

So far in this book, the Sapphic Stomper women have been introduced as a group who regularly got together for hikes in the countryside, and who identified as lesbians. It has been mentioned that the data which features in later chapters was acquired through an ethnographic methodology, and that I myself became a member of the group in order to best interpret that data. Yet the process of ethnography itself – the 'integration of both first-hand empirical investigation and the theoretical and comparative interpretation of social organisation and culture' (Hammersley and Atkinson 1995: 1) – has not been explicated, despite the central role it played in both the collection and analysis of this data. This chapter is dedicated to outlining this process, and does so with three aims. Firstly, by providing an account of the ethnographic process, I hope to enhance the reader's understanding of the context in which the Stompers interacted. In doing so, the significance of their unique relationships with one another and with the broader sociocultural context will be foregrounded, enabling a more nuanced interpretation of the analyses which follow. The second aim of this chapter is to demonstrate why ethnography is so crucial to work such as this, both by providing the context which will enhance readings of the later chapters, but also by outlining the theoretical development of the methodology in order to advocate its use for sociocultural linguistic studies. Thirdly, and perhaps most importantly, I hope that this chapter is of practical use to those embarking on this type of research for the first time. My experiences of fieldwork are laid bare here, and I hope that the honest portrayal of my encounters during this process – including accounts of hurdles that had to be overcome – will be of use to those critically assessing or planning their own ethnographic methodology.

4.1   Ethnography and communities of practice

Ethnography, as will be shown in this chapter, is beginning to be used with some frequency within linguistics, perhaps because it draws parallels with the participant observation method often used within variationist sociolinguistics (see e.g. Milroy 1980) and, in this sense, is familiar. Ethnographic research typically requires a researcher to be actively involved in the practices that they observe (Tusting and Maybin 2007: 578), enabling a valuable insider's perspective on the meaning of those practices to the group using them. Indeed, for this research, I spent 15 months hiking with the Stomper group whenever they met. As Tusting and Maybin point out, however, 'the involvement of the researcher in social action inevitably changes the language practices under study' (2007: 579). As with the observer's paradox (Labov 1972: 113) – the difficulty of observing 'natural' or vernacular language use, given that such language use is more likely to be produced when a speaker is *not* being observed – engaging in ethnography runs the risk of somehow falsifying the interactive setting under observation. Yet if language use is viewed as having indexical meaning within a community at particular interactive moments, we can never obtain truly 'natural' data, only that which is suited to the context in which a recording takes place. As Wolfson (1976) argues, a speaker will have different speech styles for different situations. If we take Bucholtz and Hall's (2005) view of identity – as emergent in interaction as opposed to pre-existing – we may aim to understand language production as it is meaningful *in a given context*. In order to view language in this way, we must fully understand that context and how language is stylistically or symbolically meaningful within it. Ethnography, as this chapter will argue, can provide this understanding. Due to its clear focus on local practice and social identity, the CoP approach enables, and takes ethnography as central to, its theory.

The need to understand language use within a given context informs the use of ethnography in studies of CoPs such as the Stompers. Ethnographic research within CoPs has led, for example, to analyses of gender (detailed briefly in Section 2.2.1), specifically femininities (Bucholtz 1999, Moore 2003) and masculinities (such as Kiesling 2001 and Lawson 2006), and has also revealed much about ethnicity (Mendoza-Denton 2008), age (Rose 2006) and socio-economic class (Eckert 2000). Studies into CoPs have typically emerged in response to an institution because, as illustrated in Section 2.2, a focus on CoPs demands a view of both wider social configurations and a local context.

In fact, Eckert and McConnell-Ginet go so far as to argue that CoPs 'cannot be understood without viewing their relation to the institution' (2007: 33) and to other CoPs within that institution (2007: 29). Without these boundaries, it is argued, it is not possible to understand what individuals are creating a shared sense of self *in response to* (such as the Burnout identity, which clearly exists as a way of rejecting the institutionally imposed norms and rules surrounding curricular and extracurricular activities in a given high school). Of course, the CoP was initially developed to enable a view of active learning through participation within institutional contexts such as the school and, in this sense, it is logical that such institutions have been the site of CoP study.

In comparison, however, not only was the research for this book not situated within a school or other institution, the Stomper CoP existed as a solely self-composed social group. There were no formally imposed physical sites or tangible institutional structures in relation to which the CoP members constructed their sense of themselves. Within the parameters of the CoP approach, as set out by Eckert and McConnell-Ginet, research within such a context should be untenable. As Davies (2005) argues, for example, the impact of jointly participatory meaning-making on speaker roles and CoP structures can only be seen when within an institutional context. Without the context of a school or workplace, for instance, she argues that 'there may not be such a perceptible locus for a potential community of practice' (Davies 2005: 563). In the analyses that follow this chapter, however, it will be shown that – for the Stompers – prevalent ideologies of patriarchy and heteronormativity acted as imposed institutional structures in their own right. Given their constraining nature, it will be argued, they are equal to physical boundaries in terms of their influence on how social beings interpret their own identity. It is largely in response to this ideological structure, after all, that the Sapphic Stompers will be shown to construct their identity: rejecting, embracing, reworking and indexing various norms, ideals and stereotypes associated with homosexuality, heterosexuality, womanhood and lesbianism. This directly challenges the firm notions of the CoP and tests its use outside of the contexts in which it has typically been implemented.

This is not to suggest that ethnographic fieldwork outside of the typical, institutional CoP context, as in this study, is necessarily a straightforward process. It can be fraught with complications and obstacles, and it was clear from my own experiences with the Stomper group just why, on a practical level, research into CoPs within institutional settings can appear to be more feasible than those which exist outside of such a context. The setting and structure of the Stomper CoP, as outlined below, had a significant impact on the data and analysis featured later in this book; in no small part, this was due to the very self-constituted nature of the group.

4.2   Ethnography with the Sapphic Stompers

As explained in Chapter 1, the Stompers ran a mailing list and advertised themselves online. However, it was through DYKE ('Do You Know Everyone') that I first heard about the women. At an advertised event in July 2006, I met several women who were also involved with the hiking group. After hearing about my research, these women invited me to attend a walk the following weekend. My immediate concerns in response to this were twofold: to alert the women present to my status as researcher and to attempt to make myself welcome in the group. All research involving participants who will potentially be recorded and whose data will be used must be executed with ethical considerations in mind – it is essential that those who take part in research are able to make informed choices about their participation and that those researching them make efforts to protect their rights and their safety. The ethical ramifications of linguistic research of this type are not often discussed in academic forums, yet – in order to protect one's participants and oneself during the fieldwork process – they are integral to any modern decision-making and planning for investigative research. For this reason, I outline the techniques that I employed in order to proceed ethically in this research (as well as the implications of proceeding ethically on the data that I collected) below.

4.2.1   Proceeding ethically

Each time that I met a new woman during my early walks with the group, I made a concerted effort to introduce myself and to explain my intellectual interest in the Stompers. When asked if they had any objections to my being present during walks, few expressed any reservations, though it remained important that the women were able to choose not to be involved with the project at any time. Verbal agreements were made with all of the women that I met on any of the walks that I attended, with written consent collected at a later date if I involved them in any audio recordings. After only a few hikes with the Stomper women, my continued and regular presence came to be interpreted as indicative of my enjoyment of the walk activities. For instance, I once heard myself being referred to by a regular member as 'a keen walker', and the women often assumed that I regularly hiked outside of the group. In a relatively short space of time (approximately four months), the questions about my research became less common and I felt that I was beginning to be viewed as a group member rather than, primarily, a participant observer.

I came to feel that my ethnography was going well, since the women seemed to feel relaxed around me from this point on. Along with this sense of self-assurance, however, came many feelings of guilt. Specifically, I began to worry that I was abusing the women's hospitality for the benefit of my own agenda. My concern that I was somehow using the women unfairly was quelled by their enthusiasm in taking part and their consent to the use of their data, though the nature of our engagement was such that some bonds were formed between us. Some of the women began to invite me to their homes for meals, or to social events such as theatre trips or drinks in the evenings. I felt that these invitations were based not on their keenness to be involved in my fieldwork but rather to spend time socially with me as a person who was developing a relationship with them. Indeed, the fact that I was so familiar with them and with the other members meant that they could talk about their fellow Stompers with me in both favourable and critical terms, though it was never clear whether they interpreted these conversations as private or as a resource that I could exploit for the furthering of my own ethnography.

Goodwin et al. articulate similar experiences within long-term ethnography whereby participants spoke over lunches, or in other non-field-specific contexts, in ways which suggested that they did not expect their contributions to be used as data (2003: 571). They dealt with any topics mentioned in these moments by attempting to revisit them during conversations that *did* occur in recognisable, field-specific contexts. As the topics of conversation that *I* encountered in such situations appeared to be given in confidence, it was not always possible to revisit them when in the company of others. At the same time, I found it impossible to view any engagement that I had with the women as anything other than an ethnographic moment that I would make extensive notes on after the fact. As my discomfort grew, I began to start rejecting invitations to non-Stomper events, especially those where I would be alone with just one or two of the group's members. In doing so, I hoped to make my role in the group clear, without damaging my relationship with the women that had come to trust me. It also ensured that I viewed the women in moments when they were 'being' Stompers, rather than individuals in another context (with the different identities that may have been part of that). Whilst my observations during non-research moments have inevitably influenced my view of the individuals in relation to the group, in order to behave ethically and responsibly towards the women I have chosen to exclude interactions from these moments in the analysis which follows. This decision is an effort to respect the private lives of some of the women who clearly came to view me more as a friend than a researcher when in non-field contexts, and may not have considered themselves under observation at this time.

The difficulty in distinguishing between field and non-field contexts illustrates my growing awareness of my own legitimacy during the research process. I was constantly aware of how the other women behaved towards me, and this in itself was emotionally exhausting. Nonetheless, with time, I came to feel that I was becoming a 'real' member of the Stomper CoP. This process, as I interpreted it, is outlined below.

4.2.2   Gaining legitimacy

Despite the complex and emotionally intensive role that this fieldwork demanded, my engagement with the women both within and outside of the Stomper setting enabled me to gain a considerable level of legitimacy as a member of the group. Whilst I was never able to be a neutral or typical member due to my motives as a researcher, the levels of legitimacy that I achieved certainly informed my knowledge of the group's practices. For example, my own identification as a lesbian assisted me in becoming accepted by the Stompers. Were I heterosexual, it is quite feasible that the women might have felt as though they were being studied as some kind of 'exotic' phenomenon. Furthermore, my knowledge and experience of certain aspects of lesbian lifestyle and culture awarded me a certain 'insider' status. Whilst ethnographers such as De Andrade (2000: 277) sometimes find that their shared identification with or prior knowledge of participants may complicate research, the assumed shared cultural experience between me and my participants was crucial to my involvement in the CoP. It broke down barriers that may have existed otherwise and gave my research credence; they assumed that I shared their views and experiences of homophobia, for example, or gay marriage.

Whilst certain cultural experiences were shared between us, however, the Stomper women were typically middle-aged whereas I was in my mid-twenties during the time that this research took place. This did have an impact on our relationship; it tended to be assumed, for example, that I knew nothing of lesbian culture prior to the twenty-first century, with the women often (light-heartedly) mocking me for this. Though I was initially concerned that my age would prevent me from being seen as 'one of the group', I quickly became viewed as an 'apprentice' to this established CoP, and my youthfulness seemed to help me to fit this role. The notion of apprenticeship, first established for the CoP by Lave and Wenger (1991), emerges from the concept that one's identity as a group member is achieved through the development of engagement in shared social practices, and the gradual learning of the meanings of those practices. Upon first engaging with CoP practices, an individual may have peripheral knowledge sufficient to allow their continued engagement. At this stage, when practices are being acquired, that individual may be interpreted as a 'legitimate peripheral participant' (Lave and Wenger 1991: 37). With full membership, when the practices are acquired and understood, those meanings may be negotiated by that individual. In order to learn the practices of the Stompers, then, I needed to be considered a legitimate peripheral participant and to engage with them to some extent. Davies (2005: 566) presents this requirement of participation and engagement as a flaw in the internal structure of a CoP; newcomers to a group need to learn the practices of the CoP before gaining the legitimacy required to become a member of it, yet cannot engage with those practices before gaining some membership. My experience suggests, however, that the 'legitimacy' required of me by the group was not to understand the meaning behind or typical nature of their practices, but rather to reflect an important demographic of the group and to demonstrate some reason for belonging. In my case, expressing an interest in their primary activity (hiking) and sharing a broad sexual orientation provided me with this initial legitimacy.

Though there were aspects of my own experience that differed considerably from the women's (namely my age), my ability to engage with them intellectually and my enthusiasm in learning more about lesbian culture outside of my own experience resulted in them 'educating' me on topics such as lesbian icons or television shows from before I was born. In this sense, I was not only an apprentice in terms of my gradual learning of their social practice as a walking group, but in terms of their coaching me in (what they viewed to be) our shared cultural history. In return, the women often treated me as a useful resource because I knew about the developments on the local scene that might be of interest to them. Evidently, the learning of information worked both ways; we fed into one another's cultural knowledge of queer issues by virtue of our differing ages, experiences and social activities outside of the group. Together with my continued involvement in group activities, this facilitated the women's perception of me as a legitimate Stomper and, presumably as a result of this, I was welcomed into the group.

I was also treated as an apprentice hiker, with the women suggesting areas I might like to visit and advising me on the best equipment for the walks that we went on together. In turn, as with Lave and Wenger's (1991: 21) concept of an apprentice acquiring a shared social identity through learned participation, I began to gain some authenticity as a Stomper member. I learnt and acquired the appropriate styles of language, such as high-register lexis demonstrating intellectualism and education (reflecting the experiences of most members), and the use of euphemism in place of taboo language (reflecting the typically polite interactional style of the women). Over time, as I engaged more and more with the Stomper group, I began to notice when an occasional walker or newcomer would interact in an inappropriate way, learning through the women's responses to it exactly what norms (and subsequent values) had been contested. As a result, I was able to adapt my own behaviour in line with those norms. To this effect, my prolonged and involved participation with the group enabled me to gain an insider's perspective but also, again, some legitimacy amongst its members.

In contrast to other CoP studies, this occurred relatively swiftly. Moore (2003), for example, details the 'distrust' and 'suspicion' that she felt from her potential participants in the high school she was studying (2003: 38). In a school context, of course, an adult automatically assumes some authoritative status when interacting with children. Unlike studies such as Moore's, in my research the distribution of power was, to some extent, reversed. I was 15 years junior to the youngest Stomper member (Claire) and, for that reason, not necessarily taken particularly seriously. Furthermore, I was an outsider entering an established group with no culturally imposed right to be there (unlike an adult within a school context). I was therefore dependent on the women's acceptance of me into the group and on them allowing me to attend their walks regularly. As illustrated above, they did. With time, a number of regular Stompers began to hint to me that I should think about leading a walk (taking charge of the location, navigation, and decision-making surrounding speed and rest breaks). This was something that only the more regular members would typically do, however, as the women most actively involved in the group (the core Stompers, introduced in Section 1.1) were also central to its organisation and composition. By providing me with a turn in which to lead a walk, therefore, the group effectively made space for me and acknowledged me, to some extent, as a core member.

Evidently, then, the women's trust in me grew over a period of time. I took my cues from them, in terms of how welcoming they were, as to when it was appropriate to engage in certain phases of my data collection. By not rushing into the process, but instead waiting for the women to be comfortable with me, it was possible to get extremely open, valuable data. Involved in the overall process were three stages and three separate methodological techniques: the taking of fieldnotes, the use of interviews and the recording of the women's interaction. This method of triangulation allowed me to gradually gain an understanding of the group, to collect a range of different types of data and to understand the perspectives of my participants as CoP members and as individuals. The three aspects of data collection involved in the study are outlined below.

4.2.3 Collecting data

An ethnographic approach relies, fundamentally, both on the immersion of a researcher within a sociocultural context and the taking of extensive fieldwork notes. In particular fieldwork settings, it is not practical or possible to make recordings, such as in Gaudio's (2001) research into homosexuality and race in West Africa. Due to the sensitive nature of his research and interviews, he relied not on audio recordings but on reconstructed quotes from his fieldwork notes, presenting his data in a narrative style to provide the reader with a clear insight into the ethnographic context of his study. Due to the physical, outdoor nature of the activity in which I was involved, it was not always possible even to write fieldnotes in a notebook, however. For this reason, I made only brief notes to remind me of particular interactive moments or events that occurred whilst on the walks, using a notebook where possible. More commonly, I used the text messaging facility on my mobile phone. It was usual for the women to have mobile phones with them on walks and, as such, when I used mine for note-taking, their awareness of it was reduced. I was also able to quickly and easily store information in a range of weather conditions. I made brief notes when possible whilst walking and then wrote them up in more detail as soon as possible after the event, a method based upon what Sanjek (1990: 144) refers to as 'headnotes': those fieldnotes which rely on memory rather than systematic note-taking whilst in the field.

In order to ensure that I shared the Stompers' interpretation of their group and its typical practices, I also asked women that I met on the walks if they would be willing to be recorded talking to me one-on-one about their experiences in the group. I waited until I had been engaged in the field for six months before beginning to conduct informal interviews, allowing me to gain the women's trust and affording me the time to identify the core Stomper members. These interviews – held in the women's homes to reduce the inconvenience to them and to put them at their ease – supplemented my understanding of who they each were. They inform much of the information provided about the Stompers in Chapter 1, as well as in the analyses which follow.

The third aspect of the data collection was obtaining recordings of the women's engagement together. Twelve months into my fieldwork, once I had interviewed Claire, Marianne, Jill, Hannah, Eve and Sam, I began to record these same women in conversation together. It was not possible to record the women during the regular, advertised Stomper walks, as they feared that newcomers would be deterred from coming again if, upon making the already difficult step of joining a lesbian group, they were to have their conversations recorded. For this reason, it was decided at one of the women's quarterly planning meetings that I would use the Stomper's website and mailing list to advertise walks and events with the specific intention of them being recorded. Although invited, no members other than the core Stompers came along to these events, but all six women were recorded in a variety of contexts. The recordings took place during hikes, during lunch breaks, over dinners which followed the walks and at a social event at Jill's house.

Though it would have been useful to consider the role of less frequent Stompers in terms of their manipulation of group practices in comparison to the core members, the nature of the CoP's practice meant that I was unable to focus on occasional walkers as they were simply not present regularly enough for me to do so. This demonstrates a key issue regarding CoP research: only the most prominent members of a group come into focus when that group is not placed within an institution. Researchers have gained valuable data from peripheral CoP members (such as Moore's 2003 'wannabes') due to those individuals existing within a structured system and thus being accessible to that researcher. In a non-institutional context, such access is more difficult to ensure. The focus on the six core Stompers, however, enabled a close consideration of individual practices and identity work, such as unusual or changing stance-taking, and my understanding of their styles and identities throughout the 15 months of ethnographic fieldwork afforded me a unique insight into their interaction and meaning-making. In this way, I could best analyse their language and could use a sociocultural linguistic framework to do so.

4.3   Ethnography and reflexivity

In order to account for the Stompers' practices fairly whilst simultaneously understanding their meaning from a subjective standpoint, it was important to remain reflexive throughout the fieldwork. As Bucholtz and Hall argue, ethnography 'demands that we put ourselves into the picture and examine our own role in the research process' since, as researchers, we are 'inextricable from the research we do' (2008: 160). As a result, it is crucial that ethnographers understand how their own experiences within the research process might impact upon their interpretation of language practices. For example, my role within the Stompers as an ethnographer was not, and could not be, purely objective. I was involved on a personal and social level with the women in my study and, as such, formed opinions and thoughts which were biased towards my own experiences. Both in terms of my understanding of the women's interaction from the perspective of a relative insider, and the fact that I approach my analysis as a feminist, my interpretation was subjective. For post-structuralist feminist scholars in particular, the concept of objectivity is questionable and problematic; any interpretation must be situated within a given research context, despite the political orientation of the researcher (Haraway 1991: 156). For example, my understanding of what was typical, acceptable or permissible in the Stompers was achieved through my developing awareness of my own changing attitudes and behaviour as I moved from being a legitimate peripheral participant towards increasingly full membership of the CoP. However, this understanding was also undoubtedly influenced by my own predefined notions of patriarchy, lesbian culture, misogyny and heteronormative ideology. Eckert (1989) argues that it is practically impossible to ignore one's own prior or separate experiences whilst engaged in ethnography, and that they will have an inevitable impact on a researcher's understanding of the field:

> There is no special way to deal with the potential interference of personal experience. My responsibility as an ethnographer was not to forget my own story, but to know it well and to refer to it constantly to make sure that it was not blinding me to what I saw or focusing my attention on only some of what I saw. (Eckert 1989: 27)

My prior experiences as a feminist and a lesbian led to my empathising with the Stomper women and feeling that I understood their perspective on matters associated with their sexuality and their gender from the very beginning of my fieldwork. It was important, as a result, to remind myself throughout my fieldwork that my perspective was not wholly objective. This relates to the notion of 'ethnosensitivity' (see Alim 2004), whereby a researcher's awareness of their own role and their subjectivity within their field must be taken as paramount to their analysis. An example of this in relation to sexuality comes from Bolton (1995), who argues in his ethnography of Brussels' gay communities that what he saw, felt, heard and thought during his research was crucial to his interpretation of the world he was experiencing (1995: 148). His identification as a gay man had inevitable influence on his understanding of the culture he witnessed and, rather than record his thoughts separately to his fieldnotes, he considered them an intrinsic part of his data analysis. This practice differs from the earliest anthropological research of the likes of Malinowski (1935), who engaged with his participants yet wrote ethnographies from an objective perspective, not including his own thoughts, reactions or experiences. More recently, Geertz (1973) was arguably the first anthropologist to engage in thoroughly reflexive practice by considering his own interpretation as key to his understanding of the context around him (see Rampton 1992: 69). In following such reflexive practice, I used my fieldwork notes to record not only specific occurrences during my fieldwork but to also write a diary of my experiences, including my fears, confusion, emotions and thoughts. This allowed me to explain the ongoing process of my understanding and interpretation. It also allowed me to look retrospectively at my fieldnotes, reflect on my early interpretations and assess how my developing understanding of the Stompers' practices had emerged in line with my own developing membership in the group. In doing so, I have been able to more effectively account for what it meant to be a Stomper as a result of my learned participation.

It could be argued, of course, that I was *not* best suited to interpret or analyse the interaction of the Stomper group, given that I was originally an outsider. Whereas previous researchers, such as De Andrade (2000), Kaminski (2004), Bani-Shoraka (2008) and Chen (2008), have belonged to the communities they studied and utilised their existing relationships to facilitate their ethnographies, I had no prior links with the Stomper group before beginning this fieldwork. Yet whilst the role of 'native' is clearly valuable and helpful to an ethnographic understanding of a community, the process of learning how to be a member as an initially peripheral participant has its own important role to play in a reflexive ethnography. For example, the process that I went through in learning to be a Stomper was crucial to my developing ability to see the way that indexical links between linguistic practice and cultural meaning worked for this CoP. Part of moving from the periphery towards full membership involved my understanding of certain styles and subsequent adoption of this same language at appropriate moments, for example. Had I been immersed in the group and part of that practice already, I might not have been so acutely conscious of it and so keen to interpret it. Not knowing the women and not understanding their practices was precisely what enabled me to interpret them as a researcher and as an apprentice Stomper. In this sense, I was also intensely aware of my own practice.

As Alim (2004: 52) argues, linguistic anthropologists need to be able to be reflexive in this way – to consider their own language use as well as that of their participants. He details his own style-shifting towards a hip-hop community that he was studying, and describes his developing accommodation towards an African American style. His argument that 'the language of the speaker collecting the data is as much a part of the study as the one providing the data' (2004: 53) reflects the significance and importance of learning meaning through one's own engagement, and demonstrates why reflexive ethnography is so crucial to a socioculturally informed analysis. What was clear to me, as my fieldwork progressed, was that my own practice underwent change to fit in with that of the Stompers. My ability to reflect upon this, due to my heightened awareness of my own language use, allowed me to gradually understand what was significant and meaningful to the group. For this reason, I involved myself in the interactions that I recorded, and I analyse my own speech as well as that of my participants in the chapters which follow. The analytical method used in doing so is outlincd below.

4.4   Analysing interaction

Analysis is an ongoing process when using an ethnographic method, as the immersion of oneself within the interactive site from which language practices emerge requires constant scrutiny of all that occurs. However, the formal analysis of transcribed data may also often signal the end of the fieldwork process. Whilst the interactive context in which a conversation is produced is captured in time by virtue of its being recorded at that moment, the broader ethnographic context will continue to evolve and change. This has an inevitable impact on the way that the researcher interprets a particular recording. My own fieldwork came to a natural conclusion 15 months in, for example, once I became aware that relationships within the CoP were shifting as new members joined and some of the core Stompers began to attend with less frequency for various reasons. This inevitably altered the dynamics of the group and meant that I began to interpret the actions of individual Stompers in slightly different ways than I had when the recordings had been made. It is of the utmost importance that an ethnographically informed analysis represents a specific moment in time – it can do no more than this, as social groups (and their practices) will always transform in due course. An analysis should therefore relate to the understanding that an ethnographer had *at that moment* as well as in relation to broader structures and the wider ethnographic context. Discourse analysis allows such a contextualised interpretation, as explained below.

4.4.1   Discourse analysis

The term 'discourse' refers to everything from magazine articles (such as in Turner 2008 and Talbot 1995) to transcribed conversations between friends (as in Tannen 2007 and Coates 1996). It is used here in the sense of communication and discussion rather than in the ideological, Foucauldian sense, whereby discourses are frameworks which represent the world (Foucault 1972: 49). Discourse analysis itself encompasses a wide range of approaches to discourse, being 'neither a single theory nor a single method' (Bucholtz 2003: 45), but those engaged with it agree that discourse – or interaction – is the site at which meaning is created. Gee and Green (1998: 125), for instance, argue that discourse analysis enables the researcher to view interactive moments as indicative of the broader practices of a community, and to explain how people create identities, categories and meanings by talking to one another. Similarly to Coates and Jordan's (1997) analysis of a group of gay and lesbian friends, who jointly 'other' heteronormative practices in constructing their own queer identity, a range of discursive practices emerge from the data detailed in the following chapters. These practices reveal the patterns of participation that the Stomper members employed in meaningful ways, yet the data also shows that a range of linguistic techniques can be employed to achieve identity aims. This reflects the approach of Morrish and Sauntson (2007), who aimed to 'examine the way linguistic resources are deployed and manipulated within a given context, as a means of enabling speakers to collectively produce temporary meanings and identities' (2007: 40). The analysis, therefore, focuses not on the prevalence of particular linguistic features, or the quantitative occurrence of them, but on the effect that the women's use of them to negotiate meaning at one specific moment in time had on their value system as a group. Whilst individual discourse markers are considered and analysed in detail, such as the lengthening of a vowel, the use of expletives, or an instance of non-standard syntactic construction, the analysis of these markers occurs only inasmuch as it reveals something of the broader patterns of co-constructed identity within the CoP. Linguistic features are considered, then, if they appear to contribute to the stance-taking of interactants and the indexing of broader categories, not in terms of how they are used varyingly across the group. Through the focus on language use as it is relevant within a given interactive moment rather than across a number of interactive contexts, it is possible to gain a nuanced understanding of how temporary, transient identities are constructed through talk.

4.5   Concluding remarks

This chapter has shown that the experience of ethnography is intrinsic to the analytical outcomes of a piece of sociocultural linguistic research. At times, ethnography can be emotionally challenging and ethically difficult, with the researcher required to become a version of themselves who absorbs the context in which they have become situated. Yet the understanding that is achieved from a sustained period of ethnographic observation also enables an insightful analysis of interaction between members of a group context which is incomparable to other approaches. In this way, ethnography is immensely rewarding and indisputably essential, albeit with its own particular practical obstacles to overcome. The analysis which follows will demonstrate, through a selection of key moments from the women's interactions, that an in-depth understanding of the ethnographic context (such as that outlined in Chapter 1) affords the analyst a unique opportunity to interpret and identify the construction of identity in action.

5
Dyke and *Girl*

The sociocultural context of the Sapphic Stomper women's interaction has been presented so far in this book. The Stompers were typically middle-aged, middle-class, white British lesbians who shared certain assumptions about lesbian culture (see Section 3.3 for a discussion of this) and about one another's engagement in it. In particular, it has been alluded to that the core Stomper women utilised the broader stereotypes of 'butch' and 'femme' in their social positioning and identity work (Section 3.3.1). This chapter provides in-depth analysis of their interaction to reveal how their stance-taking towards these ideological categories allowed them to construct a CoP-specific version of authentic lesbianism.[1] Specifically, the women are shown in this chapter to construct their own context-specific personae *Dyke* and *Girl*. The chapter begins with a discussion of the relevance of butch and femme to the group, by presenting an ethnographic account of the Stomper CoP's response to these ideological notions.

5.1 Lesbian normativity

As argued in Section 3.3, 'butch' can be loosely defined within lesbian culture as a non-feminised style of womanhood. The term is used within lesbian communities, therefore, to refer to women that adhere to more ideologically 'masculine' styles and practices. The Sapphic Stompers also used this term, locally defining it for their own purposes as an 'authentic' style of lesbianism. Throughout their interaction, they favourably oriented their stances towards it in order to project a legitimate Stomper identity. Indeed, it was evident from the earliest stages of my fieldwork with the group that the women typically viewed butch styles as signalling lesbian identity, such as on occasions where unknown women were assessed as being lesbians or not. This happened regularly as a result of the way that the walks were set up. Each of the Stomper hikes was structured in such a way that anybody attending that walk would join at a predefined start point. Because the individuals attending may be unknown to the leader and other regular members, the women tended to wait at the meeting point until ten minutes past the specified start time in case others joined them. At these moments, guesses would be made about any other women in the vicinity – often a car park starting a popular route – as to whether they were a potential member or not. I myself went through this experience when I entered the group for the first time: upon arriving independently at the advertised start point, I identified a group of women that I thought were most likely (out of the other people in the area) to be Sapphic Stomper members. I judged this based on locating the women most likely to be lesbian, and found myself using stereotypical symbols of lesbianism to do so. The three women that I approached, for example, all had short or cropped hair and a dog with them with a rainbow-striped collar.[2] As a result of these cultural cues, I approached them to ask if they were members of the Sapphic Stompers walking group (which they were). Thereafter, I always knew at least one person on each walk and did not go through this process again, but did observe numerous situations where it was assumed that a woman matching the stereotypical butch identity would be likely to be a lesbian. Such moments are outlined below.

5.1.1   Looking like a lesbian

On a walk towards the end of my fieldwork, I arrived at the starting point to find Hannah, Jill and another regular walker waiting by Jill's car. We waited a few minutes for any other Stompers (or potential Stompers) to arrive. We noticed a woman in her fifties with a closely cropped haircut sitting in her car in the corner of the car park, looking in our direction. Hannah said 'I wonder if she's one of us?' and Jill replied 'well, she's got the regimental haircut!' The idea of having a hairstyle which matches some predefined uniform clearly connects lesbianism to a specifically stylised category or 'regiment', a notion connoting membership and homogeneity. The fact that the hairstyle in question was one which would more normatively be associated with men also indicated that, to be a part of this particular 'regiment' (i.e. a lesbian), one would engage in more masculinised styles. Furthermore, the use of 'us' by Hannah indicated a certain inclusivity in terms of both being a Stomper *walker* and a Stomper *lesbian*, indicating that being a lesbian and being a part of the group could be seen to go hand in hand.

The fact that butch stereotypes were used by the Stompers in order to identify an unknown person as a lesbian demonstrates how important global as well as local ideologies are in the articulation of identity. Indeed, it demonstrates that there is a typical style of presentation which may be appropriated in order to present oneself as an authentic lesbian when meeting other gay women.[3] Hair length, in particular, was a particularly salient symbol of lesbian identity for the group; on one occasion during my fieldwork, a non-core Stomper member (Deb) had been discussing a woman that she had met at a recent DYKE event. Another Stomper, Kay, asked Deb 'so what did she look like?' to which Deb replied 'erm … about five foot six, brownish [laughing] short hair'. Overhearing this conversation, Claire joked 'oh that's really helpful – like every other lesbian, then!' The stereotype that lesbians have short hair was clearly articulated in this moment. The fact that Deb laughed before saying 'short hair' also placed this as humorous because she was, quite simply, stating the obvious. On a different walk, Jill had been talking about a woman who had come along to a previous hike but that the other women had not yet met. She said to Sam, 'I can't remember her name – I don't know if you'd have met her'. Sam then asked, 'what does she look like?', to which Jill replied 'she's got blonde hair, she's short and she wears glasses'. In this moment, Jill did not think it relevant to mention the hair length or style of the woman that she was describing, and the question was not asked. This suggests that it was implicit that a lesbian would have short hair; had she had long hair, perhaps, this would have been remarked upon (certainly, I was the only woman throughout my fieldwork who had hair which was long enough to necessitate it being tied back, and this was pointed out on occasion). By omitting the detail of hair length, despite remarking on the hair *colour*, the presupposition here was that it could be assumed that a lesbian has short hair unless mentioned otherwise. The ethnicity of the women was similarly never articulated – the norm in the group was whiteness and, as such, it would only be remarked upon if a woman was non-white.

The women's assumption that short hair is normative for a lesbian reflects the broader stereotype of butch styles in gay women, in the sense that short hair is ideologically associated with men and masculinity. In addition to the ideology of butch as being the most *typical* way of being a lesbian, the women constructed a clear opposition against women who represented heteronormative femininity, positioning them as 'inauthentic' lesbians. For example, at a DYKE event early on in my fieldwork, Marianne, Claire and I were in a gay pub during the early evening. We noticed two women in a corner kissing one another passionately. The women were both wearing tight-fit jeans and T-shirts, make-up and had long hair; in terms of their appearance, they reproduced stereotypically 'feminine' styles. In response to seeing them, Marianne said: 'I know I'm being stereotypical, but they just don't look like lesbians!' Claire responded, 'I know!' to which Marianne added, 'they're probably just bi-curious'.[4] This not only clearly equated wearing make-up, fitted clothes and having long hair with a non-lesbian look, it also linked authenticity to appearance: non-butch equals non-lesbian. The use of the term 'bi-curious' also suggests that a 'real' lesbian defines herself as singularly interested in women (rather than being 'bi') and as actively experienced (rather than 'curious').

In this moment, Claire and Marianne categorised two women who were clearly in some form of sexual relationship as bi-curious due simply to their observation that the women's appearance did not conform to lesbian stereotypes. In this sense, their *appearance* was enough to outweigh their apparently homosexual *behaviour*. This not only demonstrates the significance of physical style to the women's identity, but shows that being non-butch was conflated with heteronormative femaleness and, of course, that this equated to being inauthentically lesbian. That Marianne acknowledged that she was conforming to stereotypes suggests that she was aware that her statement did not necessarily reflect reality, though the fact that she preceded her statement 'they just don't look like lesbians' with 'but' excused the fact that it was stereotypical of her to say so. This, combined with 'just', positioned her claim as truthful and as an inescapable fact. This also shows that her awareness of the stereotype did not impinge upon her belief that there is a certain way of looking 'authentic' as a lesbian. This notion was clearly shared by the other Stompers, at least within the context of the CoP, as the remainder of this chapter aims to demonstrate. The women's positioning of butch or masculine styles will be shown, typically, to have been articulated as being 'dykey', whereas those practices or styles viewed as more feminine were presented as 'girly'. Importantly, the former was seen as 'real' lesbian identity and the latter as inauthentic. By introducing the constructed persona of Dyke[5] and then, in direct contrast, revealing the women's complex stance-taking away from a Girly self, this chapter explains the relationship between authenticity and butchness in the group.

5.1.2   Constructing meaningful personae: Dyke and Girl

Given the prevalence of an ideological gendered binary (of butch and femme) within lesbian culture, it is not surprising that the Stompers would use these notions to position themselves and others. Indeed, this facilitated their identity construction. An example of this came one autumn day during a Stomper hike. Whilst walking uphill, I found myself getting very warm very quickly despite the cold weather. When those of us present paused at the top of the hill to take a rest, I removed my padded jacket and then my thin sweatshirt. Upon removing the second layer of clothing, two of the women joked that I was 'showing off my dykeyness' and 'being hard'. It was clear that they were suggesting that the act of removing a sweatshirt in cold weather was somehow 'butch' in nature, though to appreciate quite why this link was made, it is useful to break down the ideologies being invoked in this moment. This is possible through a consideration of indirect indexicality (Ochs 1991, see Section 2.3.1.1). Taking one's clothes off in cold weather, for example, clearly carries a direct connotation of toughness or hardiness. These are qualities which would typically be associated with men – they point to ideological images associated with survival experts or soldiers, masculine characters who engage in 'manly' acts. In itself, then, an act which directly indexes toughness and hardiness also indexes non-femininity, since the ideological binary structure that governs social constructions of gender routinely places the sexes in a dichotomous frame. By defining a 'tough' act as being 'dykey', then, both the action and the label itself are categorised as non-feminine. In this way, an indirect index is constructed between a non-feminised act and being a Dyke. This shows that, whilst taking a layer of clothing off in cold weather might always directly index hardiness in the first order, the cultural meaning of this to the Stompers (or the indirect index) is that Dykes engage in these sorts of acts due to them being somehow intrinsically non-feminine.

This link between Dykey behaviour and non-femininity was also clear during the final stages of a walk with the group on a hot summer's day. Several women including Marianne, Claire and myself stopped outside a pub for a cold drink. Whilst sat outside, the majority of the women had non-alcoholic drinks or half-pints of beer. When a newcomer, Lisa, sat down with a full pint, it was commented on how she was the 'dykiest' of us all. In the UK, drinking a pint of beer has historically been seen as 'unladylike', with a half-measure or glass of wine seen as more appropriate for a woman.[6] To associate the 'unladylike' practice of drinking pints with embodying the qualities of a Dyke, therefore, again demonstrates a clear link with non-femininity.

It is evident, then, that an ideological link between lesbian identity and non-femininity was played out in the interaction of the Stompers, revealing an indexical connection between gender and sexuality which is evident on a broader scale than just that of this local CoP. For instance, Cameron's (1998) analysis of fraternity men shows them asserting their masculinity by presenting themselves as *heterosexual* in contrast to a less 'masculine' man in their peer group. Similarly, Kiesling's (2001) study illustrates how the accusation of homosexuality can be a discursive tool used to delegitimise a young man's masculine identity (2001: 260). In addition to this, Pascoe (2007: 337) has found that the epithet 'fag' is routinely applied to young American males if they do anything to demonstrate 'incompetence' as a male. Such research reveals that the ideological connection between homosexuality and inverted gender is salient in the present day. As the researchers cited here demonstrate, a person's *actual* sexual orientation or gender is often inconsequential to the choice of sexuality and gender labels used to define them. To position 'masculine' acts as being Dykey, therefore, is not to claim that a Dyke is a man, or performing a male identity. Instead, it is reasonable to argue that the Stompers' interpretation of a Dyke is to some extent synonymous with the broader category of butch; butchness is typically viewed as a lesbian-specific, non-feminised version of womanhood, *not* as a performance of a male identity.

The indexical links between butchness, the Dyke persona and masculinity must be carefully unpicked before embarking upon an analysis of the women's construction of a Dykey persona. As the above discussion indicates, the meaning that the women attached to the position of Dyke was specific to their own experiences and expectations. Although a 'butch lesbian' or a 'dyke' may already be meaningful on a mainstream, ideological level, it is clear that these categories also have a more nuanced meaning within a local context. This is supported by research such as Mendoza-Denton's (2008) study with Mexican girl gangs. These girls used the term 'macha' to describe some of their practices, and Mendoza-Denton initially assumed that this term was connected to machismo or, at least, masculinity (2008: 169). When defined by one of her participants, however, it became clear that the term's group-specific meaning of 'macha' was of taking responsibility and looking after one's own, and that they themselves did not view the term as connected to maleness or masculinity. Similarly, Kiesling's (2004) study of the term 'dude' shows that, though synonymous with 'man' or 'guy' in broader culture, in particular CoPs 'dude' indexes solidarity and coolness (2004: 282). This illustrates the importance of understanding group-specific terms and practices from the perspective of those within that local context and of looking beyond its hegemonic connotation.

In much the same way, the Stompers' use of Dyke operates as more than merely a synonym for 'butch'. Though the term 'dyke' often carries a pejorative meaning in broader culture, used as an offensive or homophobic term towards lesbians, the Stomper women use it in a positive way (as will be illustrated below). Zwicky (1997: 22) argues that the word is often used as 'a reclaimed epithet, a term of derision that has been to some extent rescued as an expression of pride'. The women's use of it, therefore, may reflect a politicised identity as well as their membership of a minority social group. The following chapter will argue that the term relates to their specific orientation to wider ideologies of masculinity and femininity, specifically to an intellectual endeavour to 'other' heteronormative practices. It was also meaningful to the group as a reworking of butch stereotypes and held a nuanced, context-specific relationship to the butch identity category. The current chapter will reveal that, as opposed to simply reproducing a butch category through the indexing of masculinity, the Dyke persona was actually achieved through the rejection of more feminised (therefore traditionally and heteronormatively *female*) roles and stances. In this sense, it was fundamentally relational, existing only because of that which it was not – a Girl.

The salience of the Girl persona was first apparent on a particularly long hike in the spring, as several women and I found ourselves ahead of the remainder of the group. We paused by a gate to allow them to catch up, drinking from our water bottles and adjusting our equipment. One of the women on the walk, Deb, removed her coat and, as she did so, had it pointed out to her that her fleece jacket was the same colour as her T-shirt. Deb responded to this by saying 'oh no, I didn't realise!' in mock dismay, to which another woman remarked that Deb must be 'one of the girlies'. With us all laughing at this, Deb pretended to hang her head in shame as she said 'oh no, I'm one of the girly girls'. The fact that it was seen as marked and inappropriate for Deb to be wearing coordinated colours was signalled by her announcement of dismay ('oh no'), and her subsequent attempt to reduce the extent of her 'error' by excusing herself and claiming not to have been conscious of it. This suggests her immediate awareness that she had done something inappropriate or, at least, not in line with the group's norms. It is also an example of a stereotype about lesbian culture being used to position a particular ideal as authentically lesbian; in this case, that lesbians do not colour-coordinate their clothes. The fact that doing this is presented as being 'girly' shows some of the connotations of this persona as being vain and image-conscious. Using the diminutive of 'girl' further expresses the silliness and non-necessity that come with being concerned with one's attire. Deb's response, her repeated 'oh no' and sarcastic alignment of herself with 'girly girls', makes it clear that to be girly was to not fit into the group.

The relevance of the Girl persona is best understood in contrast to the Dyke persona, given the binary nature of the women's construction of these two identity resources. For this reason, the following section begins with an analysis of an interaction in which a Dyke is constructed. It then returns to this notion of girliness by exploring the Stompers' complex association of non-lesbianism or non-Dykeyness with the coherent persona of Girl.

5.2   Lesbian authenticity

It has been suggested, above, that the Stomper women constructed a binary opposition between the way in which they would typically position themselves – in line with the butch-identified label of Dyke – and that which was feminised, girly or 'femme'. As will be argued below and in the following chapter, the Stompers' interaction repeatedly aligned girliness with inauthenticity as a lesbian. In order to project an authentic lesbian identity (in line with Stomper values), as a result, the women typically exercised an avoidance of stances which indexed a feminised persona due to its ability to undermine their own lesbian authenticity. Furthermore, they embraced that which was more butch, or Dykey. In the interviews carried out during my fieldwork, I asked the women what various categories meant to them, including the term 'dyke'. Overwhelmingly, this was viewed positively by the women; Hannah defined the term as referring to an 'in-your-face butch lesbian', someone who was strong and proud of who they were, and both Sam and Marianne described the term as synonymous with 'lesbian' but also as connoting butchness 'in a good way'. This is significant, of course, because the interchangeable nature of the term with 'lesbian' in this group demonstrates the extent to which the women aligned butchness and authentic lesbianism. The following section explores this further, revealing the ways in which this indexical alignment manifested itself through the women's interaction.

5.2.1   Androgyny as 'vague' authenticity

Towards the end of a walk between myself, Marianne, Sam and Claire (see Section 1.1.1 for a profile of each woman), we engaged in a conversation which I audio-recorded. The conversation led from a discussion of *Cagney and Lacey*, a 1980s television drama about two female police officers. Though the characters in the show were portrayed as heterosexuals, the three women enjoyed telling me about how this series used to be popular with lesbians due to the independent nature and feminist traits of the protagonists. Due to my age and experience, I knew little of the show, and the women regaled me with information about it. After commenting that it sounded as though this was a 'genius' show, I went on to suggest that the women watch *The L Word*, a drama series about lesbian women in Los Angeles, first broadcast in the UK in 2004. The resulting conversation, which begins with Marianne's rejection of the show, is transcribed below.

Interaction 5.1   *The L Word*

Claire (C), Marianne (M), Sam (S), Author (L)

```
 1  M:    I wasn't impressed with it
    C:                                        /It's not exactly- Cagney and
    L:                              What the L Word?/
```

```
 2  S:          [I still haven't got] I still haven't got past the pilot I've got the
    C:    Lacey [wasn't exactly the L Word]
```

```
 3  S:    first series but I just (.)  They just so do not look like lesbians/
    M:                              (XX)                                    /I
```

```
 4  M:    <inaudible>
    C:              But the L Word is genius as well
    L:                                      That's that is the problem (.)
```

```
 5  M:                                          [They all- they all
    C:                            [They're a::ll unrea [listic (.) Cagney and
    L:    ridiculously like (.) feminine [and
```

```
 6  M:    they're all talking how] I've never heard any lesbian talk      [about
    C:    La::cey were unrealistic.]                              They said [that
```

```
 7  M:    other women]
    C:    there would] never be two female police officers who were partners that (.)
```

```
 8  L:    there is one who (.) looks like she is (.) and she's the one that everyone
```

```
 9  M:    [That is] bisexual? No? Oh
    L:    [fancies]                 No she's the one that everyone fancies though
```

```
10  S:                                      [Which one is she?]
    C:                              She's [not rea::lly] androgynous::s
    L:    because she's like androgynous looking
```

```
11  S:                                                      Oh that
    C:            /Sha::ne
    L:    She's er/        she's also the one that sleeps around a lot
```

```
12  S:    one [Shane.]                                Shane
    C:                                                      Yeah the one who
    L:         [Yeah]  (.)  ridiculously thin though.    Shane yeah
```
```
13  S:             [Well yeah she's the only one who looks] vaguely like a dyke
    C:    really is [bisexual is <inaudible>]
```
```
14  S:    actually
    M:          True.
    C:                                          [I thought Guinevere-]
    L:             But you see and everyone fancies [her which suggests-] (.) that
```
```
15  S:                   [that she's the only dykey one @]
    C:    Guinevere Turner's [in it as well and she's a lesbian]
    L:                                           Which one's Guinevere?
```

This extract of conversation begins at the point where Marianne constructs a negative stance towards *The L Word*, stating that she 'wasn't impressed with it' (line 1). The other women involved in the interaction then begin to respond to Marianne's stance, critically evaluating it and positioning it as unrepresentative of authentic lesbians and lesbian culture. In line 3, Sam argues that the actors playing the characters 'just so do not look like lesbians', allowing her to put forward the notion that there *is* a specific way of looking like a lesbian. Using the adverb 'just' allows Sam to problematise the appearance of the characters and validate her argument as, in conjunction with 'so', she positions their inauthenticity as inevitable. This argument is thus presented as being factual, allowing Sam to position herself as understanding what *is* appropriate for a lesbian to look like and, therefore, to articulate an authentic lesbian self in the process. Marianne then continues with her original negative stance, dialogically supporting Sam's claim in doing so. In line 6, she mirrors Sam's syntactic construction by using 'lesbian' as a concrete noun and suggesting that the women in the show ('they all') speak in a way which does not reflect how she has 'heard any lesbian talk'. In doing so, Marianne puts forward the notion that there is a specifically lesbian style of speaking (which the women in the show do not use). This reinforces Sam's earlier claim and, in doing so, completes the women's co-construction of the ideal that there is a coherent way of 'doing' a lesbian identity. Importantly, Marianne also uses her turn to position herself as authentic in comparison to the *L Word* characters by referring to her own experience ('how I've never heard') and awareness of what real lesbians do ('any lesbian').

From line 6, as Marianne takes the floor from Claire, it is clear that the characters are considered as inauthentic due to their apparent femininity, a stance initially constructed by me (line 5) in an effort to present my own legitimacy based on my ethnographic understanding of the values of the group. Though this may have impacted on the direction of the women's conversation, it is also a claim which is frequently made about the show. Indeed, Heller (2006: 56) suggests that the characters in the show are presented in ways which are conventionally feminine and, therefore, non-threatening to a mainstream audience. In other words, there was a lack of butch representation in the show, at least in the earlier series that the Stomper women had seen. Sam and Marianne's positioning of the characters as not looking or talking 'like lesbians' is, therefore, tied into this more general critique of the show for representing only ideologically femme women. In itself, this invokes the idea that there can be an authentic style of lesbianism (and, conversely, an inauthentic style of lesbianism), implying that only two 'options' exist. This reflects the broader heteronormative system of gender (see Section 1.2 for a discussion of this), in that these two 'options' are presented as binary – one must be butch *or* femme. Marianne's turn, specifically, also posits that lesbians embody a distinct category of their own as, in lines 6–7, she uses two categories in opposition to one another; 'lesbians' and the 'women' that they talk about. Though Marianne clearly aligns lesbians as women, too – shown through her construction of the *other* women that they discuss – she does position the two as being intrinsically different. In doing so, she constructs the notion that being a lesbian and being a woman are not one and the same. This desire to position lesbians as distinct from the heteronormative woman is mirrored later in the conversation, as we begin to discuss the character of Shane.

The character of Shane is played by the actress Katherine Moennig, whose hair is styled in a short, 'messed-up' cut and who stands out from the other characters – typically found in dresses, skirts and feminine tops – by being dressed in jeans, unisex vests and shirts for the majority of the show. From line 8, as I introduce Shane, a clearer link between authentic lesbianism and non-femininity emerges. My introduction of this character was, initially, an attempt to defend *The L Word* from the criticism of the Stomper women, and I begin by suggesting that she resembles an authentic lesbian because she is 'like androgynous looking'. The construction of this turn is significant as my reluctance to explicitly position the actress as looking authentically lesbian is revealed; I use 'like' to mitigate my claim and suggest some *quality* of androgyny, and 'looking' in order to suggest that she *appears* to be androgynous (rather than that she embodies this style). It is clear from

Claire's claim in line 10 – that Shane is not 'really androgynous' – that my hedging was necessary, as she takes a stance which directly opposes my own. Claire minimises the aggression in her stance by using the truth marker 'really' (though this may also be interpreted as an intensifier to indicate that Shane was not *very* androgynous), yet her turn leads to those present being required to define androgyny (in order to establish whether Shane qualifies to be defined as such).

Claire's stance against Shane being androgynous is not accompanied by a claim that she is too butch to be gender neutral. Instead, it seems that her implied meaning is that the actress playing Shane is too *feminine*. This seems particularly likely given that the producers of the show have previously been accused of using this actress to introduce a 'boyish' rather than 'butch' character – she is frequently found to wear make-up, for example. Moore and Schilt (2006: 161), for example, argue that Shane's promiscuity and fewer feminine styles and gestures than the other characters allowed the show to include a supposedly butch character without 'alienating squeamish viewers'. In this sense, Claire's claim may be contextualised by broader critique of the show and, furthermore, reveals her positioning of Shane (and, therefore, androgyny) with non-femininity. Shane, as with the other characters, is temporarily positioned here as inauthentic because she is not androgynous enough. In this sense, it is clear that androgyny equals authenticity for the Stomper group, at least in this interactive moment.

From line 10, the women begin to recognise the character of Shane. In line 13, Sam concedes that Shane is a character who looks somewhat like a lesbian: 'she's the only one who looks vaguely like a dyke, actually'. In doing so, she aligns herself with my earlier stance that Shane looks like an authentic lesbian but also clearly hedges her statement through the qualifying adverb 'vaguely'. In doing so, she suggests that this androgyny is to a limited extent. It is her use of 'dyke' which is most telling here, however. Sam could have chosen 'lesbian' in this moment – this is the term that had been used up until this point. That she did not do this indicates that 'dyke' means more than simply 'gay woman', here; it is used by Sam to distinguish Shane from the other characters who are supposedly gay yet who embody the hegemonic ideal of femininity. In this sense, we can see that Dyke has some meaning of 'non-femininity' or, in the context of Shane specifically, 'androgyny'. In line 15, this analysis is supported by Sam's claim that Shane being typically found to be most attractive is logical – 'she's the only dykey one'. Here, a group-specific, momentary ideal is constructed: non-feminine women are more attractive to lesbians.

This claim is not challenged as the topic moves on, revealing perhaps that this suggestion is simply accepted as fact by the other women. Though not responded to in this interaction, the implication of Sam's claim does deserve further consideration as, essentially, she positions feminine women as being unattractive to lesbians. Given the earlier discussion of Shane as somewhat androgynous and therefore somewhat dykey, it is apparent that Sam's claim positions non-androgynous women as non-dykey. Given the context presented earlier in this chapter, it is logical to suggest again that this positions Dykes as authentic lesbians. The stance that Dykes are more attractive may be explained by a consideration of what non-Dykes represent – ideological femininity. By rejecting traditional feminine styles, Sam may also be said to be rejecting the heteronormative style of womanhood that – as lesbians – the Stomper group do not present any desire to share. Furthermore, in suggesting that these styles are not attractive to lesbians, Sam may be said to be rejecting that which is ideologically attractive to heterosexual *men*. As Inness (1997: 31) argues, feminine lesbians are often viewed as unbelievable in mainstream culture – for a woman to desire other women, it is presumed that she must be masculine in some way (see Section 3.3 for a discussion of this). Furthermore, of course, heterosexual male culture may prefer to believe that the style of woman that they desire – ideologically, a 'feminine' one – would also be attracted to them rather than other women. In this way, it may be argued that feminine lesbians are not often an authentic part of lesbian culture either; a woman who exhibits traits associated with male desire is more likely to hold a less authentic status as a lesbian (as 'bi-curious', for example). It appears that this ideology is invoked by Sam in her brief comment about Shane being dykey if she is most attractive to lesbians – she is the closest in the show to a butch lesbian and, therefore, the furthest away from heteronormative womanhood.

The CoP-specific formulation of androgyny as authenticity is clearly facilitated here by wider, macro-level understandings of sexuality, style and identity. The Dyke persona is meaningful only in relation to the group's understanding of butchness as legitimacy, but also in relation to their knowledge of wider binary structures of gender. In this way, it is clear that the Dykey persona is not unique and is not constructed in isolation from broader sociocultural ideologies, not least those which suggest that homosexual people must be somehow gender inverted. The persona, therefore, is partial – it is produced in relation to both 'contextually situated and ideologically informed configurations' of lesbianism (Bucholtz and Hall 2005: 606). Through the construction of this persona, the women in this interaction also engage in their own identity work. In debating Shane's legitimacy as a lesbian (in response to my claim that she is androgynous), they express their own legitimacy simply by implying that they have the authority to do so. In other words, the women engage in an authenticating tactic of inter-subjectivity (Bucholtz and Hall 2005: 601) – they insinuate that their own legitimacy as lesbians allows them to judge Shane's. Importantly, though it is not explicitly outlined, the construction of the Dyke persona in this interaction is apparently achieved through the women's rejection of non-butch traits, or heteronormative femininity. In other words, the existence of the Dyke persona exists because of the non-dykey traits that other lesbians may hold. As analysts, it is useful to explore the identities that are rejected or avoided by speakers in order to better understand the identities that are actively claimed, and it is therefore worthwhile considering the construction of the Stompers' rejected persona. As shown below, this rejected persona was that of a Girl.

5.2.2   Girliness as antithetical lesbianism

As indicated above, the women often described that which they viewed as inauthentically lesbian as being 'girly'. In the interaction which follows, the Girl persona was established, negotiated and then rejected. It occurred during a meal at Jill's house, where all of the core Stompers (with the exception of Marianne) were present and spent the evening in casual conversation. The topic shown in the extract below was raised by Eve and then discussed briefly by the other women. Eve mentioned a study that she had read about which supposedly linked finger length to sexuality. There had been some popular discussion in the British media about this experiment (such as Radford 2000), and Eve had recently heard about it – the experiment was originally carried out by researchers at Berkeley University (Williams et al. 2000) and suggested that a high level of testosterone in the womb led to a person's ring finger being longer than their index finger. The study included lesbian women who, along with heterosexual men, were found to have longer ring fingers (and therefore to have been exposed to more testosterone during pregnancy). This topic was introduced following a conversation that had taken place about a recent television documentary looking at homosexuality in twin siblings, making it relevant for Eve to introduce a topic concerned with the debate around whether sexuality is biologically preordained or a result of cultural context and upbringing.

Interaction 5.2 'The finger test'

Claire (C), Eve (E), Marianne (M), Hannah (H), Sam (S), Author (L)

```
1   E    You know that thing about trying to tell whether you're a lesbian 'cause
```

```
2   S                                           Oh [it's-]
    E    of the size of your- which finger is it?   [One] being longer than the
```

```
3   S                       [er::]
    E    other?                           [Which is] to do with the level
    L         It's you::r [this] it's first finger [isn't it]
```

```
4   E    of testos[terone that was in your-]
    L             [If you if your index fin]ger is long- no if your ring
```

```
5   S                                        Yeah
    H                                        Which is your ring and which
    L    finger's longer than your index finger.
```

```
6   S                                           [Course] mine is.
    E                       Wedding [ring finger.]
    H    is your index?                         [that that] that's-
    L                           [That's your ring.] (.) [and that's-]
```

```
7   S                                                      [No
    C    Mine's not is it?
    E                                           Oh [that's
    L                   Yeah that's your ring and that's your index
```

```
8   S    you're just-]                              [@(2)]
    C                                               [See that I'm
    E    it you're] still other @(1)
    J                                        And [what's got
    L                           On the other hand I think
```

```
9   S                                           No but mine-
    C    a-] I'm a real [gi::rl]
    J    to be?]
    L               [It's gotta] be longer than your index finger.
```

```
10  S    [mine is]
    C             [I'm a proper gi::rl]
    H    [Oh it is]
    E           [Well there you go.]
    J                           What does that mean?
    L                                      It's something to do
```

```
11  E                   [It's all to do with] how much [testosterone] [there was-]
    H                                                  [<@ more @>]
    L    with biology and [the genes and stuff]      [testosterone]
```

```
12   E                    It's [testosterone in your mother's] wo::mb.
     H    [testosterone]@>      [@(2)]                              (.)Honestly?/
     J                                                                        /Well
     L    [testosterone]
--------------------------------------------------------------------------------
13   S                                      [Yes that's] [[that's it that's it]]
     E                                                   [[You're obviously
     J    it's longer on my left hand but not [my ri::ght]
--------------------------------------------------------------------------------
14   S                                      [Actually my left hand- @ (.)]
     C                                      [@ (1)] Oh my God
     E    [ambidextrous]                    [@ (3)]
     H    [you're bisexual] [@ (1)]         [@ (2)]
     J                     [Yes well] that's right. <[@ That's ok@>]
--------------------------------------------------------------------------------
15   S                            [So you're just-] sorry but you're just not
     C    look at- look how gir::ly I am
     H                                      [@ (1)]
--------------------------------------------------------------------------------
16   S    a lesbian that's it it's proof. [@ (3)]
     H                              [That's the end of that] you're out of the
--------------------------------------------------------------------------------
17   S                                                      [Yes.]
     C          I am s- I am so:: (.) female.          I'm such a [girl]
     H    group.                                                  [Mm.]
     J                                      Ostracised.
     L                                                            You can
--------------------------------------------------------------------------------
18   C              /Yeah I- I'll give up my degree in science [my my second degree in
     E                                                         [Well that completely
     L    no longer-/
--------------------------------------------------------------------------------
19   C    maths.]                          @ (.)
     E    blows] the theory on that one.
     H                                      In a very old fashioned comment here
--------------------------------------------------------------------------------
```

In this interaction, the Girl persona is negotiated via Claire's gradual claiming of it, despite the fact that, as is apparent from the discussion earlier in this chapter, being 'girly' was already recognised as being symbolically non-lesbian in this CoP. It supports Bucholtz and Hall's (2005: 588) claim that identities are emergent in interaction rather than being predefined or somehow inherent, particularly given that Claire clearly constructs an ironic identity position for herself. In claiming the identity of Girl, she enables the construction of the group ideal that those who are Girly are not authentic lesbians – a position which clearly supports the implicature behind the Dykey persona constructed above. Two interesting themes emerge from this conversation; firstly, an ideological binary is invoked through the women's discussion of a Girl as non-lesbian (considered below) and, secondly, bisexuality is also constructed as being inauthentic (considered in the subsequent section).

5.2.2.1   Girl

This first analysis considers Claire's role in the interaction. Claire positions herself as a Girl in order to deal with a paradox which emerges in the conversation, ironically positioning herself as a legitimate lesbian. Claire's claiming of a Girly self emerges in response to Eve's introduction of the finger test which, in itself, reveals much about the values of the Stomper group. It is notable, for example, that no woman admits to not having heard of the experiment that she introduces, perhaps because of her presumptive construction 'you know that thing about ...' (line 2). This reflects the importance of intellectualism and education to the Stomper women. The women's desire to be viewed as authentic lesbians is also apparent, however, in the fact that they engage with the experiment fully, using it as an opportunity to actively 'test' their own sexuality.

Upon realising that her ring finger is not longer than her index finger and, therefore, that she has not 'passed the test', Claire takes the interesting approach of determinedly positioning herself as a Girl. This begins in line 7, as she uses the tag question 'is it' to open an adjacency pair and invite another speaker to evaluate her finding. This is responded to with 'no' by Sam in the same line, whilst Eve refers to an earlier part of the conversation (in which Claire described her feeling of being different whilst growing up to be gay) by joking that Claire is 'still other'. This positions Claire as not only 'other' in heteronormative society, as had been intended by her original use of the term, but as 'other' within the lesbian community as well. In line 9, Claire ignores the opportunity to remove herself from this illegitimate frame (as I suggest that she may be looking at the wrong hand for the experiment) and instead defines herself as a 'real gi::rl'. Claire's desire to make this identity claim clear is apparent as she both lengthens the vowel in 'girl' and uses the intensifier 'real'. This continues in line 10 as she uses another intensifier ('proper') to define herself as an authentic, tangible Girl. In doing so, she does more than invoke the literal meaning of 'girl' as a young female but indexes both the ethnographically salient persona and the wider connotations of the word which relate it to femininity. She seemingly acknowledges that she has failed the test and then takes control of the situation by deliberately destabilising her own identity as a lesbian. This illustrates the agentive nature of identity construction as well as the fact that some identities may be temporarily constructed as 'crafted, fragmented, problematic, or false' (Bucholtz and Hall 2005: 602), as Claire denaturalises the Stompers' idea of a legitimate lesbian.

This 'girly' identity claim intensifies throughout the remainder of Claire's interaction as, in lines 14–15, she demands the attention of the other women: 'oh my God … look how gi::rly I am'. The women begin to align Claire with this category as well, perhaps in response to her rather enthusiastic request that they acknowledge it and, in line 15, Sam cements the meaning behind Claire's identity move by stating that she is 'just not a lesbian'. This is reinforced by Hannah and Jill in lines 16–17, when they playfully tell her that she is 'out of the group' and 'ostracised'. Here, the women are actively involved in constructing the CoP ideal that a Girl is not a lesbian, as well as securing the normative identity of a Stomper and the boundaries surrounding the group. They also authenticate their own status as Stompers through this authorising move.

It is clear, then, that Claire's identity claiming facilitates the collaborative construction in this moment of the notion that Girls are not real lesbians. In doing so, however, she puts herself in what might theoretically be a vulnerable situation – she overtly claims that she is not an authentic member of the Stomper group. As is evident from the remainder of her interaction, Claire uses this to her advantage by emphasising her actual distance from the Girl persona. From line 18, her identity claiming switches from overtly claiming a 'female' or 'girly' identity to indexing ideological masculinity. She does this through the mention of her undergraduate and postgraduate degrees in science and mathematics, suggesting that she would have to give these up if she were no longer a lesbian. In doing so, Claire clearly aligns herself with fields which are, traditionally, part of an androcentric domain (see Bergvall 1996: 186), and contrasts the Girl persona with that of an intellectual. By invoking the idea that these subjects are somehow masculine in nature, Claire constructs an apparent contradiction; she cannot be a (biological) Girl if she also has achievements in a masculine sphere. This again relies on the women's familiarity with ideological binary gender (one is either masculine *or* feminine) and gender inversion ('real' lesbians are more masculine than Girls) and highlights the partialness principle: 'no speaker can ever produce an identity in complete independence from existing identity categories' (Bucholtz and Hall 2005: 606). Though done in jest, this move allows Claire to reclaim her status as a Dyke. Interestingly, Eve (lines 18–19) then rejects the test as inconclusive as a result of Claire's revelations, illustrating that Claire's authenticity was never actually in any doubt.

Claire's claiming of the Girl persona may be defined, here, as a *negative identity position* – an ironic juxtaposition with her authentic lesbian self. This is achieved in this moment only because of her existing (strong) membership of the CoP and her confidence in her own sense of self, and it is this that makes it clear that her identity claiming is, in fact, ironic. Whereas the typical, sincere claiming of a mutually negotiated persona (such as, for the Stompers, a Dyke) may be referred to as *positive identity positioning*, then, negative identity positioning involves aligning oneself with an inauthentic role – one which is oppositional to that which is typical or normative – in order to ironically express authenticity. This notion reflects the negative identity *practices* detailed in Bucholtz (1999), whereby the linguistic and non-linguistic styles indexical of groups from which speakers wish to distance themselves are rejected. For example, Bucholtz (1999: 211) shows how the nerds in her study would avoid current, popular youth slang in order to disassociate themselves from the 'cool kids'. In considering the *paradoxical* claim-staking of a persona which is ideologically oppositional to that which is considered good or authentic within a CoP, however, the term 'negative identity *position*' is distinct from Bucholtz's negative identity *practice* as it concerns stance-taking *towards* a recognised label or category. This is in contrast to the construction of oppositional personae through the use of the nerd girls' distancing styles. As with Bucholtz's use of the term 'negative', however, my use of it here also refers to what speakers are *not* (Bucholtz 1999: 211). Claire's alignment with the inauthentic persona of Girl in order to emphasise her claim to an authentic Dyke position therefore illustrates the ironic nature of negative identity positioning in this moment, one which may only be understood with an awareness of the relationship between these two categories.

The discussion surrounding Claire's apparent inauthenticity in this moment demonstrates the ease with which the women link the Girly persona with femininity and with heterosexual womanhood. It is neither questioned nor challenged that this (inverted) link between gender and sexuality exists, and it is further naturalised by the use of a scientific experiment involving testosterone to construct lesbian authenticity. The finger test provides the women with the opportunity to claim a legitimate lesbian self by linking higher testosterone levels with both lesbianism and maleness. The experiment's finding about lower testosterone being typical in females (rather than males) also conflates femininity and heterosexuality in women. It is therefore the experiment itself that positions femaleness in opposition to lesbianism, but it is Claire who begins the construction of the CoP-specific persona by describing this as 'girly'. In doing so, she extends the notion that one is either a lesbian or a straight woman to imply that one is a Girl *or* a Dyke, femme *or* butch, essentially constructing the ideal that one cannot be a femme Dyke or a butch Girl.

By suggesting, in line 17, that she is 'so female' because she is apparently not a lesbian, Claire also seems to imply that lesbianism is associated with masculinity and even maleness. However, the Stompers identified as women and as feminists, and at no point in my ethnography did they overtly claim a male identity. Given this, it seems plausible to suggest that Claire's use of 'female' is ambiguous here. The cultural ideologies drawn upon by the women so far in this interaction have dictated that authentic lesbians are not Girly and that being Girly is about being stereotypically female. 'Female', in this sense, is synonymous with 'femininity' and, consequently, Girliness. The women are unable to claim a 'female' identity, therefore, due to its association with femininity and, specifically, heterosexuality. Far from revealing some rejection of femaleness in its most literal sense, then, conflating it with heterosexuality suggests that the Stompers' version of (Dyke) womanhood is intrinsically lesbian whilst the mainstream 'female' is reserved for the (Girl) heterosexual. Furthermore, this moment does not necessarily reveal some claiming of a masculine or male identity – it once again expresses a desire to eschew *femininity*. In this moment, Claire rejects femininity, deconstructs what it means to be a woman, and positions an authentic lesbian in a specifically queer frame. A fuller discussion of how 'femininity' was made meaningful within the Stomper CoP, through their rejection of it, is provided in the following chapter.

5.2.2.2   *Bisexual*

In addition to revealing the problematic nature of femininity and the Girly persona, this interaction also illustrates the difficulty of accounting for bisexuality in the system put forward by the Stompers. If one is either a Dyke or a Girl and, therefore, a lesbian or a heterosexual woman, bisexuality quite literally has no valid place. This issue emerges in lines 12–13, as Jill announces that her ring finger is only longer on one of her hands. Whilst her turn is short, as Claire quickly regains the floor, this moment does allow the women to temporarily place Jill in a negative identity position, one which they *assume* is ironic. Following Jill's announcement that she only 'passes' the test on one of her hands, Eve steps in and assumes the role of evaluator, joking that this must mean that Jill is ambidextrous. However, Hannah successfully takes the floor at this moment with the more contextually relevant joke that this must mean that Jill is bisexual (line 14). Though Hannah laughs at her own joke, nobody else does, perhaps reflecting the potentially face-threatening nature of it.

To understand why a claim of bisexuality might be threatening in this moment, one must again consider the ethnographic context. Whilst interviewing Marianne, I discussed with her the meaning of the Sapphic Stomper group. Marianne told me that she felt comfortable in a group of gay women as it felt like a safe space, and went on to say that the Stompers are 'very strongly a lesbian group ... quite strictly ... and, you know, even women who define themselves as bisexual aren't strictly meant to be part of the group'. Though bisexuality was not a concept that I addressed with each individual member, it seems reasonable to suggest that this was a group norm given that bisexuality implies some sexual contact with men and, therefore, some engagement with heteronormative practice. As Hughes (2012) has illustrated, lesbian culture often positions those women who have never had sexual relationships with men as more authentic, or as 'gold star lesbians', because they have not been 'contaminated' by men, and by heterosexuality. The derogatory way that bisexuality was thought of in the Stompers, of course, is also highlighted in the rejection of 'bi-curiousness' earlier in this chapter. In this sense, for Hannah to position Jill as bisexual in this moment rather goes against the constructed values of the group. This may explain the lack of laughter at Hannah's comment until Jill herself laughs in line 14, when the other women apparently felt secure in sharing the joke. That this was more tentatively done than when positioning Claire as a Girl also, perhaps, reflects Jill's relative newcomer status. In response, Jill makes a crucial identity move in line 14. She appears to accept and acknowledge the bisexual label by saying 'that's ok'. This could be interpreted as an admission of her sexuality to the group, or as a coming-out moment. If this was her intention, however, it was unsuccessful. Whilst it is significant that Jill presents herself as comfortable with her designation of bisexual as an *individual*, at a *group* level it is assumed to be a joke because it is not a legitimate way to construct the Stomper version of 'lesbian'.

Telling jokes has been found to be a common form of group-based interaction and to be particularly useful as a tool for dealing with contradictions or tensions between interactants. Eggins and Slade (2004: 157), for example, argue that speakers can use joke-telling in order to 'simultaneously expose and cover up' contradictions between them. In this sense, it is quite likely that the other women assumed that Jill's comment was intended to be a humorous, ironic challenge to the negative identity position that she had been assigned. This would fit with the sarcastic nature of Claire's identity work in this interaction, but also indicates that it would not occur to the women that she might, in fact, identify as bisexual. Irrespective of whether they doubted her lesbianism or not, however, Jill's alignment with this position (as with Claire's alignment with the Girl persona) is rejected by her interlocutors in order to suppress this potential difference and to maintain the group's shared sense of self as gay women. In this way, the women downplay that which is potentially 'damaging to ongoing efforts to adequate' the Stomper group (Bucholtz and Hall 2005: 599). By putting forward a bisexual category and then rejecting it, the women are able to emphasise the inauthenticity of it. That Jill's individual difference from the Stomper norm is erased in order for the women to collectively negotiate a shared group identity once again, then, reveals the rejection of any self which is in any way connected to heterosexuality (as with the Girl persona, above).

5.3   Concluding remarks

In the description of interactions occurring during my fieldwork and emerging from recorded conversations with the Sapphic Stompers, this chapter has revealed the significance of the two personae salient to this group's identity construction: Dyke and Girl. If considered within the indexical framework presented by Bucholtz and Hall (2005), it is apparent that each of these ethnographically significant personae was negotiated through various moves and stances on the interactional level to index broader categories associated with lesbian culture on an ideological level (namely 'butch' and 'femme'). These categories may be interpreted as rather essentialist and reductive, but it must be remembered that the interactions illustrated here reflect the women's engagement as a CoP. In other words, it reflects their desire to construct a meaningful, shared sense of self. The women's identities in different contexts would be likely to reflect different aspects of themselves, perhaps often with no reference to their sexuality, and indeed as individuals they had varying views on how important their sexuality was to the group. However, due to their shared sexual orientation and the significance of lesbianism to the CoP, it is unsurprising that their identity manifested itself in this way in these moments. In addition to their hiking, their presumed shared lesbian orientation united them and, given that they knew one another primarily (often solely) as Stompers, it is also unsurprising that they drew on broadly accessible ideological identity categories associated with lesbian culture. In doing so, they were able to construct a sense of sameness and engineer a group identity, despite a lack of intimacy or real knowledge of one another as individuals.

By addressing cultural stereotypes and engaging with them through their interaction, it could be argued that the women's use of Dyke/Girl and butch/femme were a kind of parodic reappropriation (Butler 1990: 166), allowing the women to express a culturally resonant identity whilst reworking existing stereotypes for their own gain. Indeed, the claiming of an authentic lesbian identity through rather abstract means, such as having a degree in mathematics or science, or a particular haircut, would suggest that the women may have been using these stereotypes ironically. That is to say, they did not necessarily believe in all that they projected at that moment but, instead, were aware of the stereotypes and used them to reappropriate the – often homophobic – discourses which surround lesbian culture. The women's reworking of the negative epithet 'dyke' seems to illustrate this, as well as demonstrating that the Stomper identity was one which embraced queerness. As Butler (1993: 229) argues, it is necessary for minority groups to lay claim to the discourses which exist to marginalise them because, in doing so, it is possible to reverse and refute them. Certainly, for the Stompers, the use of broader ideologies enabled them to articulate a positive lesbian identity – the Dyke persona, informed by various stereotypes from within lesbian culture – in contrast to that which is ideologically 'femme' – the Girl persona, rejected (literally, in the case of the finger test) for its relationship to heterosexual femaleness.

The following chapter expands upon this argument, revealing moments whereby the women explicitly rejected that which was heteronormatively feminised. In doing so, it will be argued, the women were able to rework the expectations of femaleness, recast traditional ideologies associated with womanhood as specific to *heterosexual* women, and thus formulate their own ideals and norms about *lesbian* women's styles, practices and behaviour. Through the consideration of the women's rejection of styles and practices associated with being a Girl, the following chapter provides an in-depth exploration of the Stompers' construction – and rejection – of various 'femme' styles and practices.

6
Negotiating Authentic Style and Practice

As illustrated in the previous chapter, the Stompers were able to construct an idealised 'authentic' identity, through a range of interactive tactics, by positioning themselves (or others) in line with or against two core personae – Dyke and Girl. In doing so, the women were able to project their knowledge of the group norms and practices and, accordingly, to index an authentic lesbian self. An important aspect of this identity work, therefore, was their construction of an oppositional structure in which Dykes and Girls were binary; in this way, they were able to position a Dyke as authentic and a Girl as inauthentic. This chapter considers this concept by presenting the women's clear rejection of feminised, Girly practices. The relevance of opposition in the women's construction of authentic lesbian identity (where an *in*authentic identity must exist and be rejected in order to highlight that which *is* authentic) is explored in depth, here.

The use of binaries, Baker argues, is a typical part of identity construction, since identities typically acquire meaning only when they are cast 'in opposition to something else' (2008: 121). Men may position themselves as being fundamentally different from women, gay people from straight people, young people from old, and so on. Furthermore, as Baker shows, it is typically the case in an ideological binary that one side is more valued than the other. In gender, for example, women are often considered to be deviant from men (who are usually defined as neutral and normative). For the Stomper women to not only construct a clear binary, but to also evaluate one side of it as positive and the other as negative, is therefore not an unusual method of identity construction. Indeed, it represents the broader ideological structures of society. Furthermore, it is clear that their knowledge and understanding of binary structures were directly influenced by their experiences as gay women, a status which, one might argue, automatically positioned them on the 'negative' side of the heterosexual/homosexual dichotomy. The women seemingly responded to the heteronormative world in which they were placed, therefore, by constructing a normative identity for themselves as a minority group. Koller (2008: 18) supports this point, arguing that lesbian discourses exist in relation to broader sociocultural factors rather than in isolation; they are 'embedded within a host culture that is organized in diametrically opposed terms'. As women, the Stompers constructed a specifically female identity but, as lesbians, they rejected that which was heteronormatively so.

This chapter will reveal that, at times, this identity construction occurred in a rather predictable way; the women rejected that which was traditionally and broadly salient as symbolic of femininity, such as lipstick. It will also show, however, that at times certain 'feminine' practices were not collectively agreed upon as being indexical of lesbian inauthenticity. By virtue of the fact that not all of the women were identical in every aspect of their style and behaviour, yet endeavoured to mutually construct a shared identity as lesbians, the Stompers had to continually negotiate and redefine what the personae of Dyke and Girl actually meant in order to accommodate their individual differences. Through ethnographic accounts and the analysis of one long extract, this chapter argues that the two oppositional personae were constantly redefined in order for them to remain clearly distinct from one another.

6.1 Rejecting Girly practices

For the Stompers, there were certain clear markers of lesbian inauthenticity. Typically, as shown in Section 5.1, these revolved around styles such as hair length or signs of vanity. Practices which the women perceived as being Girly were often positioned by the Stompers as being inauthentic, as shown by a lesbian couple in Section 5.1.1 who were delegitimised because of their clothing, hairstyles and use of make-up. Make-up, in particular, was typically perceived as being non-lesbian due to its close association with heteronormative ideals of femininity and attractiveness. I was particularly conscious of this because, unlike the other women, I usually wore a little make-up. At times, this positioned me as 'other', such as at a daytime birthday party for one of the Stompers, where I found myself talking to a woman who was a fairly regular hiker with the group. Although we had briefly met once before, this particular woman did not remember me. Upon telling her that I had been on a walk some weeks earlier, at which she was also present, she said 'I don't remember meeting you. Were you wearing all this make-up then?' The delivery of this question was aggressive and clearly implied that it was unusual, if not inappropriate, for a woman on a Stomper walk to be wearing make-up. Furthermore, the implication was clear – the amount that I was wearing ('all this make-up') was excessive. In pointing out that I had flouted the norms of the group, this particular Stomper acted to define and, therefore, to regulate the group's expectations.

On another occasion, Marianne, Sam, Claire and I were in conversation, talking about the times that they had recently been mistaken for men while in public toilets; this is a common, frustrating and upsetting experience that many lesbian women face (see Halberstam 1998: 20 for an account of 'the bathroom problem') and was one which the other Stompers shared. I commented that this was less likely to happen to me due to my adherence to more feminine styles, such as my wearing of make-up. This led to a discussion of make-up and, more specifically, lipstick, which was described as 'horrible' and 'unattractive'. In this conversation, the women worked particularly hard to distance themselves from make-up and to position it in a negative way; it was very clear that it was symbolically antithetical to the identity that they worked together in constructing: the real, butch lesbian.

Instances such as these made me consider why, beyond this apparent symbolism, many of the group members were so against the use of beauty products and cosmetics. An interview with Sam indicated that it was not make-up specifically that could be positioned in a negative way, but rather all products designed to enhance one's femininity, as she commented that she could not 'understand why anybody would want to wear scent'. Whilst not a beauty product per se, perfume has clear associations with femininity, which I suspected to be at the root of the women's rejection of such beautifying products. As Talbot (1995: 144) argues, the clothing and cosmetics industries repeatedly position femininity as ideal for women in such media as lifestyle magazines. Women are frequently advised on what make-up to wear to give an impression of seduction and perfection, and heteronormative discourses certainly position cosmetics as a way of appearing more attractive to the opposite sex. When the specifically heterosexual nature of this is considered, it is perhaps logical that the Stompers would place the wearing of make-up as antithetical to their concept of authentic lesbianism. Furthermore, as already indicated in Section 1.1, Stomper identity was frequently associated with feminism. In the 1970s, a decade which most of the core Stompers experienced, feminist discourse typically positioned 'all fashion and cosmetics [as] simply tools of sexual objectification and therefore instruments of male oppression to be discarded' (Craig 2003: 20). By rejecting heteronormative ideals of femininity, then, the women arguably also rejected a patriarchal approach to womanhood by rejecting traditionally feminine styles and practices.

Typically, the women mutually constructed the meanings of the various styles that they rejected, as they did with the positioning of a Dyke as authentic and a Girl as inauthentic. However, this was not always a clear-cut process. Whereas it was relatively straightforward to adopt a position in line with or against the two personae by, for example, literally claiming embodiment of the label, the practices and styles which were classed as indexical of each persona had to undergo considerable negotiation. This is because, as women, the Stompers were likely to embody some traits which others might well interpret differently – as being Girly, for example. Often, differences that emerged in an interaction would simply be erased by the women, but it was also common for them to consciously articulate these differences and contemplate their meaning within the group setting. In the interaction which follows below, for example, the women are shown to engage in shifting stance-work to support varied physical styles that those present claim or project. In this way, the individual differences between the women are adequated (see Section 2.4) and negotiated in order to maintain a homogeneous Stomper identity in the moment.

6.2   Negotiating Girly practices

The conversation transcribed below follows a story that I had been telling about a teenage boy at a recent family event. I described him as being visibly bored and restless with nothing to do, which led to the topic of childhood games that we all used to play. The interaction took place during dinner at Jill's house, a short time after the discussion of 'the finger test' (see Section 5.2.2), and the extract begins at the point at which I mentioned a game played when I was a child. In this game, an ironing board was used as a make-believe surfboard. In response to my introduction of this game, Eve comments that she had 'never tried that', joking with the group that she would like to try it now:

Interaction 6.1 Ironing, skirts and shaving

Claire (C), Eve (E), Hannah (H), Jill (J), Sam (S), Author (L)

```
1  E (.) never tried that/              /I could try that now. <To Jill> Have
   H                  /[Cool]
   L                  /[When] I was little/
```

```
2  S                              [No don't no] no no no no]]
   E you got an ironing board?    [Actually I-]
   L                  I wouldn't recommend it.[I had very] flexible bones]]
```

```
3  S I've spent enough time at [A&E this week] thankyou
   H                       [An ironing board?]   {<to Jill> Oh yes.} No self-
```

```
4  E                            Well that's buggered me then.
   H respecting lesbian has a bloody ironing-board @(.)
```

```
5  S                         Sheets? You don't iron your sheets?
   E I can't bear not having ironed sheets.
```

```
6  S [That's] anal.
   E [Mm]        No no it's beautiful when you get into a perfectly [ironed-]
   L                                                    [I don't]
```

```
7  S              [Ironed shee::ts?] God where do you find [the time?
   H                                                 [Ironed
   L I don't own an iron [let alone an ironing board]
```

```
8  S You're not working] hard enough @(.)
   C                           I can't remember the last time I
   H sheets?]               That's sad.
```

```
9  C actually got my [iron out of its box I don't] think I've got it out in
   E                 [It's a good way of airing them.]
```

```
10 C two years let's put it that way./
   E                     /Oh I have. {Jill returns to the table}
```

```
11 S                               @(.)
   E                            @(1)
   H                                     Mmhm
   J                  <*Oh god no.*>
   L Do you iron bed-sheets Jill?            So you're not as
```

```
12 S                                        How does
   E    [No she's not that bad. Shirts have to be done though.]
   J   Only [shirts and trousers (.) and skirts] that's all]
   L bad.
```

```
13 S this (.) link in with Asperger's then [this ironing sheets]
   C                          [Well you see you have] to [think] it
   L                                             [Skirts?]
```

```
-----------------------------------------------------------------------------
14  S                                        [@ (.)]
    C  probably-
    E                                         [You've got ski::rts?][@(.)]
    H      I was gonna say [that] ski::rts? [You've got ski::rts?]    Have you
    J                                                          [Yes]
    L                        [Ah::]                            [@(.)]
-----------------------------------------------------------------------------
15  E [Skirts]                    [<Can you] match [this> with last time] I wore [a
    H [got skirts?]                                                          [When
    J             Yes I've got [ski::rts.]
    L                                       [And do you wear them?]
-----------------------------------------------------------------------------
16  S                         [Why do you] wear them is- @(1)
    E dress]                                        [they are cool]
    H d'you] wear them?
    J                 Well I have to [admit that-]          [Because in]
-----------------------------------------------------------------------------
17  S                          [That's no exc-]
    J summer they are considerably cooler [than trousers or] shorts (.) I have
-----------------------------------------------------------------------------
18  S            [That's true]
    E                                     [Cos] it's been bloody cold
    J  to say I [have not] worn a skirt this summer.
    L                                      [I-]
-----------------------------------------------------------------------------
19  C                           O::oh get you./    [I don't-]
    E   hasn't it/                                          [[You're
    J                                  /But [certainly] in [[hot
    L          /I wore a skirt in Croatia.
-----------------------------------------------------------------------------
20  E bragging]] there
    S                        [That's true yeah]
    C                        [Do you own a sh-] skirt? I don't own a
    J   weather]] I will always wear skirts
-----------------------------------------------------------------------------
21  S      No [I haven't got one now]
    C skirt.
    E         [I haven't owned one since] I was twenty-one.
    H                                           [[I haven't got one.]]
    L                                    I [[wouldn't wear one]]
-----------------------------------------------------------------------------
22  S                              [I could probably find one of
    E                              [What in case people noticed?
    L (.) in this country but it was much much-
-----------------------------------------------------------------------------
23  S those wrap-around things.]
    E A::h it's Lucy she's got a skirt] on.
    H                                   I'd wear a [wrap-around one on
    L                                             [But in Croatia where
-----------------------------------------------------------------------------
24  C                           [@ (1)]
    E                                 [Was this when] you shaved your
    H holiday]          I've got one of [those.] [That was a s-]
    J                                   [@ (1)]
    L no-one] knew me
```

```
----------------------------------------------------------------------------
25 E legs or not?
   L                   Oh I- that's that is the one time that my legs will be
----------------------------------------------------------------------------
26 L seen by the public (.) the one time I wore a skirt is in a foreign place
----------------------------------------------------------------------------
27 C                                             /Why do you not sha::ve
   J                     /Do you never wear shorts?/
   L where no-one knows me./
----------------------------------------------------------------------------
28 C then? <Tut> [God you are a] real proper butch aren't you?
   H                                                   [@ (.)]
   E       No:: [can't be bothered]                    [@ (1)]
   J                                                         Do
----------------------------------------------------------------------------
29 C                                             God I'm [th-
   E               Yes. Occasionally.
   J you wear shorts?
   L                             Last time I wore shorts       [a
----------------------------------------------------------------------------
30 S                                         [[What do you]]
   C I'm getting a re::al]   [complex] now about I- I'm a [[real gi::rl]]
   L number of people] laughed [at me]
----------------------------------------------------------------------------
31 S shave your legs?           [Why::?]
   C               Yeah [why not?]          @ (.)
   J                         [Do I what?]    I shave my legs.
   L                   [Do you] Jill?
----------------------------------------------------------------------------
32 C [Cos they're better] that way./
   H [Shave my legs?]
   J                       /Course they are. They're much more
----------------------------------------------------------------------------
33 S                         [I'm not no::.] I mean I- I do it
   C                 /They a::re.
   H                             I [shave my legs.]
   J attractive shaved./
   L                             Yeah.
----------------------------------------------------------------------------
34 S sometimes but on the whole I prefer::            [natural.]
   H                                 I do I haven't [for some time]
----------------------------------------------------------------------------
```

In this conversation, the women discuss a number of practices which
are in some way related to heteronormative femininity – ironing,
wearing skirts and shaving their legs. These three practices may be seen
as symbolic of femininity on a broad cultural level: ironing, a house-
hold chore, has traditionally been viewed as 'women's work' due to the
role of women in the home; skirts and dresses are used as cultural cues
to a person's sex, with the silhouette of a woman in a skirt often used
to denote female toilets in public spaces; and women are culturally
expected to be hairless, whereas body hair on men is typically associated

with masculinity or virility. Given the clear connection made between ideologically feminine practices and the (inauthentically lesbian) Girl persona, it is clear to see that these three practices are symbolically illegitimate for the Stompers. Despite this, each one is highlighted and challenged during this interaction as the women negotiate their way around the presumed norms of the group and, at times, subvert the expected identity construction of a Dyke. The following analysis firstly explores the delegitimation of practices deemed Girly, before the issue of heterogeneity in the group is addressed.

6.2.1   Delegitimation of a Girly practice

It is interesting to note that, in this interaction, Hannah tends to initiate or be the first to draw attention to the topics which are most logically incongruent with the Dyke persona. In doing so, she may be seen as using the tactic of authorisation, that which involves 'the affirmation or imposition of an identity through structures of institutionalized power and ideology' (Bucholtz and Hall 2005: 603) to assert her legitimacy as a Stomper lesbian. In turn, this allows her to illegitimate the practices mentioned in the conversation; she presents herself as aware of prevalent ideological practices for the group and therefore authoritative enough to manage the boundaries of these ideologically non-Dykey practices. She initially achieves this through her partial repeat of Jill's comment ('an ironing board') with a questioning intonation in line 3. Through the claim that 'no self-respecting lesbian has a bloody ironing board', Hannah determines what is 'self-respecting' and simultaneously constructs a new norm: real lesbians do not iron. This positions the idea that Jill might have an ironing board as ludicrous and Jill herself, therefore, as a 'self-respecting lesbian'. Her use of the expletive 'bloody' allows her to express shock at the idea of Jill owning such a thing, though the laughter and use of this relatively inoffensive swear word indicate the humorous, light-hearted nature of her statement. Nonetheless, the indirect indexical relationship between ironing and Girliness (via its direct indexical link with heteronormative, patriarchal roles for women – positioned as non-lesbian by Hannah, here) serves to reproduce the shared notion of Stomper authenticity as non-Girly.

Eve challenges Hannah's statement in line 4 by arguing that she could not 'bear not having ironed sheets'. By strongly aligning herself with this statement (using the emotive 'bear'), Eve both challenges Hannah's stance and simultaneously places herself in a negative identity position – one which conflicts with the norms of the group. Interestingly, perhaps in mitigating this negative identity move, Eve's preceding comment (line 4: 'well that's buggered me then') uses an expletive. This correlates with Hannah's use of 'bloody' in line 4 as, again, this is an expletive which is relatively inoffensive (see Allan and Burridge 2006: 108). Nonetheless, to swear is ideologically unladylike (see Lakoff 1975) and may therefore serve to distinguish Eve from this Girly persona. Furthermore, she goes on to suggest that ironing one's sheets is func-tional, as it is 'beautiful' to get into freshly ironed bedlinen (line 6). By assigning ironing a practical use, Eve attempts to remove it from a purely Girly frame (one which such practices as wearing lipstick would inhabit, for example) as her reasoning for engaging in this ideologically 'feminine' activity is not for vanity or appearance; it is for comfort. Whilst her use of the 'empty' adjective 'beautiful' (Lakoff 1975) could arguably be seen to index a feminised category and to contradict her typical persona as a Dyke, therefore, Eve's turn here also illustrates her reworking of the concept of 'authentic lesbian' in this moment. Indeed, her focus on ironed *sheets* as beautiful as opposed to ironing more gen-erally allows her to again remove herself from an inauthentic identity position. This move may be interpreted as her exploiting the tactic of denaturalisation, whereby 'the authenticity of an identity is challenged or questioned because a rupture of that identity has been perceived' (Bucholtz and Hall 2004: 501). In challenging and reworking the indexical meaning of ironing – from being domesticated to practical – Eve highlights the temporal and shifting nature of the Girl persona. In doing so, she is able to admit her preference for ironed sheets without going so far as to claim a negative identity position (see Section 5.2.2.1), simply suggesting instead that the meaning of ironing is multifaceted rather than directly indexical of femininity.

Irrespective of her tactical reworking of ironing as – for her purposes – an authentic practice for a lesbian, Eve's admission still temporarily places her in an inauthentic frame. Interestingly, the other women remark primarily on the items that Eve claims to iron rather than the act of ironing itself, with Hannah mocking her in line 8 by saying '<u>sheets</u>? That's <u>sad</u>'.[1] By repeating the word 'sheets' (lines 5 and 7) and accusing Eve of being anally retentive (line 6), Sam also criticises Eve, perhaps taking the opportunity to belittle a woman with whom she has an awkward relationship and to position herself as comparatively authoritative; she uses a questioning intonation to suggest some regulation over what is acceptable or normative. Though her challenge appears to be made light-heartedly, accusing Eve of being 'anal' implies concern with the trivialities of life, a characteristic of stereotypical femininity evident in misogynistic accounts of women (and implied by

Lakoff 1975: 8). When rebutted by Eve, Sam alters her attack and targets her professionalism by suggesting that, in order to have enough time to do this, she must not be 'working hard enough' (lines 6–7). To imply some laziness directly challenges Eve's authenticity not as a lesbian, specifically, but as a Stomper more generally – the Stomper women were all well-educated professionals, and this often seemed to define what they had in common.

In response to this challenge, perhaps, and in line with Hannah's initial construction of a 'self-respecting lesbian', Claire and I aim to position ourselves as Dykes by shifting the topic away from sheets, specifically, and back to the practice of ironing. My turn in line 7 ('I don't own an <u>iron</u> let alone an ironing board') achieves this and facilitates Claire's claim that she has not taken her iron out of its box for a couple of years (line 9). In this moment, Claire uses vague and non-committal phrases such as 'can't remember' and 'don't think' to express the lack of importance that ironing has in her life, clearly indexing a Dyke identity by rejecting that which is ideologically opposed to Stomper authenticity (a negative identity practice). This is a more predictable identity move, one which overtly rejects that which is Girly in order to claim an authentic persona. It is upon Jill's involvement in the conversation, however, that the Girl and Dyke distinction becomes less clear. She suggests (in line 12) that, whilst she would not deign to iron her sheets (thus positioning herself in direct opposition to Eve), she would iron various items of clothing, including her skirts. This leads to a broader discussion of various practices which are more directly (and less controversially) aligned with the Girl persona – wearing skirts, and shaving.

6.2.2   Heterogeneity within the Stompers

The partialness principle is particularly apparent at this point in the conversation, as the women are only able to position themselves as authentic in relation to what else happens in the interactive moment. Though partialness has been shown so far to relate to the broader ideological structures which constrain the women's reproduction of a butch/femme dichotomy, it is also the case that the women's identity construction can only ever be partial due to its reliance on interactional constraints. Therefore, whilst the women begin by taking stances invoking a Dyke persona in this moment – specifically against skirts and shaving – they do not become mutual for the group as a whole due to the challenges made by those present. This is particularly clear in the case of Jill's justification of wearing skirts (see below). My own engagement in the group's interaction is foregrounded in line 13, as

I consciously direct the conversation towards Jill's mention of her skirts. My stress on the word 'skirts' shows my use of the tactic of illegitima-tion, as I highlight the contrast between ideologically Dykey practice and this stereotypically feminine style. My awareness that skirt-wearing contravenes the presumed normativity of the authentic Dyke, typically adhered to by the group, influences my interruption of Claire in order to highlight it. In part, this was my role as a participant, interacting with the group in line with Stomper norms, but my role as researcher may also have led me to alter the direction of the conversation in line with a potential topic of significance. Either way, as Jill had already brought this to the attention of the group, and since Hannah suggests in line 14 that she was 'gonna say that', it seems that my turn here does not overly influence the spontaneous responses of the group.

The ideologically problematic nature of Jill's claim is revealed firstly by her pause before stating 'skirts' in line 12 and, secondly, the drama-tised and synchronised responses of Eve and Hannah whereby they claim incredulity: 'you've got skirts?' (Eve and Hannah, line 14). Jill's response to this follows the syntactic construction of the question (line 15: 'yes I've got skirts'), achieving a clear and definite response. Despite this, the rhetorical pattern created between me, Hannah and Sam: 'do you wear them?' (Author, line 15); 'when do you wear them?' (Hannah, lines 15–16); 'why do you wear them?' (Sam, line 16) creates a need for Jill to justify her skirt ownership. The clear contrast between skirt-wearing and authentic Stomper behaviour, and thus the denatu-ralisation of Jill's identity at this moment, is mutually constructed by the three of us here, though Jill's justification of this practice challenges that position. As with Eve's explanation of ironing sheets as being practical, Jill's argument that skirts are preferable to wear in the sum-mer (line 17: 'they are considerably cooler than trousers or shorts') is based around a logical, reasoned argument. One might claim that such logic and reason are themselves indexical of maleness, which serves once again to challenge the feminised image with which the accused is being aligned. However, the Stomper identity revolved around the activity of walking and, as such, tended to be focused on practical styles (such as sensible, waterproof clothing). As such, in the context of the Stomper group, wearing skirts for the purpose of outdoor comfort may arguably be an acceptable anomaly.

Though this reasoning is not immediately accepted by Sam, who begins to argue that this is no excuse (line 17), she concedes that it is true that they are cooler in line 18, supporting Eve's comment of agreement in line 16. This leads to the admission of the other Stompers that they occasionally wear skirts, with Hannah (line 24) and me (line 19) suggesting that we might wear a skirt if on holiday (mitigating our claim and positioning this skirt-wearing as non-normative behaviour – this allows us to reduce the threat to our Dykey identity). The next significant move is from Claire (line 20), who asks whether the other women wear skirts. That it is even thinkable for her to ask this question demonstrates a clear shift in the typically firm boundaries around feminine styles. Her question suggests some surprise that this is now a possible style for the group, and includes her own immediate rejection of skirts: 'do you own a skirt? I don't own a skirt' (lines 20–21). Following this is a reluctant admission of skirt-wearing from the remaining Stompers, as each woman mitigates their claim by suggesting that it was some time ago; Sam uses the temporal marker 'now' in line 21, while Eve claims that she had not done so 'since [she] was twenty-one'. Although the boundary between what is Girly and Dykey has been made flexible in this moment, then, it is clear that the women's typical alignment with more normatively authentic (i.e. butch) practices reveals their concern to still be positioned as Stomper-identified lesbians. For instance, when Sam refers to a sarong in line 23, where she also presents the concept as odd by using the word 'things', she aligns herself with the group-specific notion that butch styles are more authentic, but also with the momentarily relevant norm that Dykes might *sometimes* wear skirts. This demonstrates the women's reluctance to distance themselves from dominant ideologies in favour of the ever-changing rules and norms of the group, illustrating again the relevance of both local norms and wider ideological structures.

The conversation quite inevitably and naturally moves at this point to the final topic discussed in this interaction: shaving. After assuming that I shaved my legs, Eve is asked by Claire whether she does the same thing (line 27), though the syntactic construction of Claire's question 'do you not shave then?', whereby the qualifying 'then' is used to question Eve's *not* shaving, positions not shaving as more unusual than shaving. When Eve's emphatic 'no' is received, Claire labels her as 'a real proper butch' (line 28). This exchange reflects an interesting contradiction about which of these practices – shaving or not shaving – were expected and normalised. The persona of Dyke, in its typical rejection of heteronormative femininity, could logically be aligned with not shaving, as shaving is a practice associated with the ideologically feminine desire to appear hairless. In this instance, though, Claire positions it as an acceptable practice simply because she does it herself. Through the use of the intensifying 'real' and 'proper' to premodify 'butch' here, Claire suggests that it is possible to go above and beyond the styles that she associates with butchness. It also implies that one can still be butch yet also engage in an ideologically feminised practice; a Dyke may shave her legs but she is more authentic if she does not.

This is similar to Hannah's earlier (lines 3–4) construction of a 'self-respecting lesbian', whereby the category of 'lesbian' may exist without the pre-modifying 'self-respecting'. In this sense, one can presumably be a self-disrespecting lesbian or a lesbian who does not match the Stomper norm of what is authentic and Dykey. Both Hannah's and Claire's construction of the broader category of lesbian implies, therefore, that one can be an *actual* lesbian without being a *proper* (i.e. authentic) lesbian. This may be seen to directly contradict the positioning of two personae in binary opposition to one another, whereby nothing may exist in between (as constructed in the previous chapter), illustrating yet again that identity construction is only ever partial, as it varies in accordance with the requirements of the interactive moment. On the other hand, however, it suggests that a 'Girl' is *not* necessarily a hetero-sexual woman, as the binary between an 'inauthentic' and 'authentic' lesbian has so far been perceived. Instead, being inauthentic may be seen to be highly specific to what the Stompers themselves do – they position their own styles as the most authentic, but acknowledge that not all lesbians adhere to the same practices as them. The women can be seen to be engaged in identity work, here, which allows them to renegotiate the boundary between the two oppositional personae typi-cally constructed within the group; they claim that styles which would ordinarily be positioned as Girly are temporarily indexical of a Dyke. This allows them to save face and ensures that their own authenticity as a Stomper lesbian remains intact.

This latter part of the interaction also seems to suggest that leg-shaving is less iconically feminine than wearing skirts or ironing. This may be explained, perhaps, due to an increasing association of grooming with men as well as women and, therefore, that broader cultural norms (placing grooming as more gender neutral than hyper-feminine) are being reworked to fit with the group's interaction. On the other hand, it is clear that the indexical relationship between not shaving and butch lesbianism remains prevalent in this interaction, as Claire then goes on to invoke the oppositional personae of the group in line 30. She presents herself as a Girl (continuing from her earlier alignment with the persona in the previous chapter) in direct opposition to the butch persona that she attributes to Eve. In doing so, she overtly positions 'butch' as a positive, authentic model to achieve, and Girl as a negative and illegitimate way of being a Stomper woman; indeed, she expresses her concern for being Girly by claiming that she is developing 'a complex' about her femininity. That this emerges as a result of her shaving her legs makes it clear that this practice maintains its Girly connotation, and leads to Claire's alignment of herself with this negative identity position once more. Furthermore, Claire uses the expressive 'God' before labelling Eve 'a butch' in line 28 and herself 'a girl' in line 30, emphasising the significance of both labels in comparison to one another by using them as concrete nouns rather than adjectives. This allows her to personify herself (as 'a girl') and Eve (as 'a butch') in these two different identity positions, reproducing the group's normative notion that being a Girl and a lesbian is an antithetical notion.

Although leg-shaving has clearly been constructed as indexically Girly in this moment, the fact that it has also been put forward that one might still be a 'butch' even if one is not a 'real, proper' butch creates the opportunity for the other women to move from their typical antifeminine stances. Though it is clear that shaving is Girly, for example, Claire's admission that she engages in it means that the other women (who, like Claire, are already legitimate Stompers) may also maintain their authenticity whilst admitting to an 'inauthentic' practice. This illustrates the reworking of a clear normative ideal, and is specific to this interaction. In shifting the boundaries of acceptability about what is legitimate, Claire engages in the tactic of denaturalisation, violating the accepted norms of the group and highlighting her own deviation from Dykey practices. In doing so, she disrupts the group's notion of normative Dykeyness and presumed sameness.

This is apparent from Sam's turn in lines 30–31, as she asks Claire to clarify whether she shaves her legs and then questions why she would choose to do so, clearly constructing her stance in line with the 'real, proper butch' of Eve rather than Claire's 'Girl'. Claire's weak assertion that shaved legs are 'just (...) better that way' (line 32) is salvaged by Jill's supportive stance alignment which states that shaved legs are more attractive (lines 32–33). This positions leg-shaving as authentic within a desire-based frame; by characterising it as more sexually attractive, it is given more value as a lesbian practice. Though lesbianism is, at least in part, defined by some aspect of sexual desire and behaviour, it was unusual to see this referred to explicitly in a Stomper interaction. Indeed, the lack of intimacy between the members made it unlikely that they would discuss personal preferences in this way. Jill's comment carries weight, however, because it highlights something fundamental about their engagement together – they fact that they are all attracted to women. It is for this reason, perhaps, that she is not challenged on this point.

After the subsequent discussion between Jill and Claire, whereby it is established that Jill also shaves her legs, and Hannah follows this by acknowledging that she also engages in the practice, Sam's initial stance against shaving begins to falter. Once it becomes clear that the majority stance at this moment is in favour of leg-shaving, Sam's shifting position begins to reveal her desire to position herself as authentic. In line 33, her self-correction indicates her insecurity, with 'I mean' marking her shifting stance from 'I'm not' to 'I do [engage in the practice of leg-shaving]'. Her use of the temporal marker 'sometimes' to suggest that it does happen on occasion again demonstrates alignment with a practice as a momentary norm of the group. It also shows Sam's reluctance to engage with it fully due to its clear departure from established norms. This is, perhaps, indicative of the fact that Sam had only relatively recently come out; she – more than all of the other women in the interaction – maintains a distance from the potentially Girly index. This move is then followed by Hannah, who alters her previous stance in line 33 ('I shave my legs') to say that she has not for some time, again using a temporal notion to qualify the truth of the statement and aligning herself with the stance of Sam.

The need for homogeneity is evident, here, as Sam and Hannah both engage in the tactic of adequation by modifying their stances to align with the emerging majority stance. In doing so, they erase the heterogeneity that has emerged in this moment. The complexities and tensions of temporarily constructed norms are apparent from this extract, as individuals decide between alignment with practices which have clear ideological links to the established authentic Dyke persona, and potentially conflicting norms which are constructed in the moment. What can clearly be shown from this is that it is the mutual production of these norms which enables meaning to be attached to particular practices. Furthermore, individuals may choose to align or disalign themselves with those practices if they wish to attempt to change the parameters of the group. In this sense, authentic practice is constantly negotiated and reworked in the moment-by-moment interaction of a CoP.

6.3   Concluding remarks

Though the partialness principle was shown in the previous chapter to relate specifically to broader ideological structures and local, ethnographically salient personae, the women's interaction in the moment detailed in this chapter demonstrates that identity construction is also partial due to its reliance on interactional constraints. The women in the extract presented here have been shown to actively negotiate the indexical meaning of specific practices in a way which does not necessarily reflect their typical engagement with the dichotomy of butch and femme. Whilst the women may construct individual stances which index Girliness due to the ideological, direct indexical meaning of a practice (such as skirt-wearing indexing femaleness), the alternative meanings of the direct indices (such as skirt-wearing actually indexing practicality) must be negotiated before the practice can indirectly index the Girl persona itself. In other words, femininity itself does not necessarily index Girliness – it is contextual and therefore negotiable.

As argued by Bucholtz and Hall (2005: 598), indexicality is fundamentally intersubjective and based on sociocultural context for its meaning, and this is particularly evident in the extract presented in this chapter. It remains the case, however, that even in those instances where the boundaries between Dyke and Girl became blurred and the women took stances which contradicted the Stomper sense of self, the dichotomy between the two personae was continually reproduced and reinforced. The women may have reworked the meaning of specific practices in order to achieve their own authenticity, but they did not claim an overtly Girly identity in the process. Instead, they played with boundaries, shifted meanings and constructed new versions of their own reality to fit with the group. The fact that they constructed the additional personae of a 'self-respecting lesbian' and a 'real, proper butch' demonstrates that the women were, essentially, making up roles which best suited their need to negotiate what was authentic. The fact that no group of people are ever homogeneous in terms of their idiosyncratic styles or practices outside of a given CoP makes it highly likely that they will constantly rework and renegotiate the framework they use in constructing an authentic, group-specific self. If they did not, they would be forced to pretend that they matched all of the traits of the group and, therefore, would be at constant risk of exposure and deauthentication.

The relevance of gender dichotomy is once again clear in this chapter, from the points at which the women cooperatively rejected stereotypically feminine styles such as make-up, to the moments where they justified why their own ideologically feminised practice did not equate to their being a Girl. It has been suggested that many of the moments whereby the women rejected that which may be perceived as Girly are tied into the women's relationship with feminism – they rejected that which may be interpreted as a patriarchal tool in the oppression and objectification of straight women. However, the very fact that the women used such a gendered dichotomy as Dyke/Girl arguably invokes an interpretation of femininity which is, fundamentally, anti-feminist; the qualities afforded to the more 'feminine' persona were belittled as irrelevant, weak and vain. As Martin and Lyon (1972) and Johnston (1974) claim, reproducing a butch and femme distinction in this way may actually reproduce harmful patriarchal structures, meaning that the Stompers' apparent aim to eschew traditional femininity may have resulted in a rather misogynistic approach to traditional womanhood. However, by rejecting that which is feminine and indexing a more masculinised Dyke persona, the women arguably subverted gender norms themselves since, as women, they engaged in non-normative practice. In doing so, the women's embrace of butch styles may be seen – as both Case (1993) and Nestle (1992) argue – to be revealing the very performative and ideological nature of gender. It is arguable, then, that the women endeavoured to challenge patriarchy itself by their adoption of non-feminine styles and practices (a claim supported by Newton 1984: 557).

Whether or not the women's authenticating tactics in the moments detailed in this chapter and in Chapter 5 represent their desire to make a political statement, they do reveal the accessibility of gender ideologies within lesbian culture. It is clear that the Stompers' need to construct an authentic self within the group was intrinsically tied to that group's lesbian focus, and therefore draws upon broadly accessible ideologies reworkable between women who rarely engaged with one another outside of their CoP. By drawing on broader ideologies of gender and sexuality, the women ultimately achieved a sense of sameness, albeit one which required constant redefinition, as in the extract detailed in this chapter. The following two chapters reveal how these women collaboratively constructed other aspects of Stomper authenticity, those not always directly associated with lesbian culture yet intrinsically tied to the norms presented here. In the next chapter, specifically, the role of politics and awareness of queer culture to the women's membership is explored.

7
Indexing Authenticity via Cultural Knowledge

The Stomper women have so far been shown to position certain styles and practices as 'authentic' by taking stances in line with their own, group-negotiated norms. These norms have been illustrated as emerging in particular interactive moments, such as in a discussion of television characters or choices made about clothing. Key moments such as these have been selected so far in order to illustrate the co-constructed, mutually negotiated way in which Stomper norms are established in the group, and this analysis has focused until now upon the women's rejection of Girly practices and their embrace of butch or Dykey styles. This chapter, in developing the profile of the Stompers further, will detail aspects of other constructed Stomper norms which are associated with their shared interest in women's and gay rights. The two analyses which follow reveal how the constructed norms of the group, whilst linked to the Stompers' experience as lesbian women, did not always directly index their sexuality. As shown in Section 1.1.1, not all of the Stomper women viewed their sexuality as being of primary importance to them, and this chapter reflects that. In contrast to the moments of interaction presented in the previous chapters, the extracts here illustrate a less playful use of stereotypes as the women align themselves with clear ideologies associated with certain political stances.

7.1 Feminism as normative

It was common for the Stomper women to make presumptions about one another's political beliefs as a result of their shared experiences as lesbian women. Most notably, it was often assumed that the women all identified as feminists, with remarks frequently being made which took for granted a certain inclination towards this perspective. For example, the very first time that I met Jill – on a walk with Hannah, two other regular Stompers and one newcomer – she made a comment which clearly indicated that she had assumed that we were all feminists. As we walked through a field at the beginning of the hike, we passed a cow, its body bulging and distorted due to a heavy pregnancy. A number of the women remarked on the sight, commenting on how uncomfortable the cow must be and wincing empathetically. Jill then said '... not that it's politically correct to be concerned about our appearance, of course, but I'm glad I'm not that shape!' The other women present laughed and the topic ended there due to a query about the next direction to take on the walk. It was telling, however, that Jill went to some effort to qualify her statement 'I'm glad I'm not that shape'. She justified this by first suggesting that she was aware that she ought not to refer to appearance in this way because of 'political correctness'. By articulating an awareness that it was not an entirely appropriate stance to take, Jill both asserted this awareness as a norm and positioned her stance as out of character, or exceptional. Her use of the term 'political correctness' is notable, here, as it typically refers to the avoidance of language or practices deemed discriminatory or offensive to minority groups. In this sense, her use of the phrase seems to show her avoiding offending feminists, indicating her presumption that the women around her identified in this way. The inclusive pronoun 'our' also seems to be used to presuppose the other women's joint engagement in this idea, and her turn suggests that she understood a need to express her awareness of, if not consistent adherence to, feminist principles.

Later, towards the end of the walk, the women were discussing a television programme some of us had seen the previous evening. Jill again justified her eventual statement by preceding it with an awareness of feminism: 'Not that we feminists should be worried about shallow things like appearance, but that woman on TV looked awful with her hair a mess and her dress like something that's been in a charity shop for ten years!' Here, Jill again suggested how she *ought* to be behaving before flouting her own rule. This time, however, she referred to feminism directly and clearly aligned herself with it. More importantly, perhaps, she again used an inclusive personal pronoun in the form of 'we', directly referring to the other women on this particular walk (two of whom she had never met before – myself and the other newcomer) as feminists. That this was not contested suggests awareness amongst the women present – irrespective of how well they were or were not acquainted – that feminism holds some symbolic currency for lesbian women of this generation and social class. As Koller (2008: 41) argues, the main agenda within lesbian discourse during the 1970s – the period of time that most of the Stomper women came of age – was to conflate it with feminism, but that this second-wave feminism was very much a discourse which spoke to white, educated, relatively privileged women – the sort of women that the Stomper women typically were. Jill's assumption that middle-class, lesbian women in their middle age were feminists, then, is perhaps not particularly surprising.

What is interesting from these comments by Jill, however, is not only the political implication behind them but also the very fact that the assumptions were made and drawn upon in order to bring those present together. Her language constructs a sense – albeit one which is assumed – of homogeneity between the women. She constructs this in line with a broader ideal, reflecting the use of stereotypical identity categories demonstrated already in earlier chapters. As Queen (1998: 206) argues, the desire for some aspect of community based on a defining characteristic such as sexuality is bound to utilise broad hegemonic ideals in order to find some common ground. Whilst the previous chapters have demonstrated the use of broader *gendered* ideals for this endeavour, then, the assumption of feminist identity reflects Jill's *political* expectations about these women. As Chapter 8 will reveal, such expectations were not unusual and, indeed, were shared by many of the other Stompers, yet the notion of a 'feminist' still underwent constant negotiation.

What follows in the current chapter, however, is an account of the women's politics more broadly. Two moments of interaction are analysed below, during which the women take stances to position themselves as politically aware. In addition to feminism, focused on in more detail in the following chapter, it is shown here that Stomper politics were related to gay and lesbian issues. The women's experiences as lesbians and their ultimate rejection of heteronormative ideologies clearly had some influence on the politicised aspects of their identities; as shown already in Section 1.1.1, most of the women that I interviewed claimed that they identified with feminist and gay rights movements. Marianne, for example, claimed that her identification as a feminist was crucially connected to (and indeed influenced by) her sexuality, stating that 'my understanding of the world as a feminist partly led me to be a lesbian'. Jill similarly identified primarily as a feminist and had been involved with campaigns for gay rights and equality in the 1960s and 1970s. Like Marianne, Jill saw sexual orientation and political awareness as going hand in hand, arguing that she felt 'despair if a woman who's also gay can't get her brain round sexual politics'. The extracts dealt with in this chapter reflect this perspective and reveal that there was a clear expectation that the women present had some association with sexual politics.

7.2 Political awareness as an authentic Stomper stance

7.2.1 Intellectualism

All of the core Stompers, with the exception of Claire, had been in their teens or twenties during the 1970s. They were all well-educated professionals and, as indicated above, tended to assume a certain political (specifically feminist) orientation. Claire's age difference was occasionally an issue which led to her holding differing views from the other women, as will be shown in Chapter 8, but, despite this, part of the group's practice was to talk about current affairs from a left-of-centre political perspective. These conversations would often revolve around issues of gay equality, such as the debate around civil partnerships,[1] and it was important that the women could show an understanding of the issues and have something to contribute to the conversation. In this sense, intellectualism and political concern were very important to the Stomper ethos.

This is particularly evident in the following extract of conversation, which demonstrates a moment whereby the value of this political intelligence was overtly constructed. It occurred during dinner at Jill's house and took place between Jill, Claire, Sam, Hannah, Eve and me. As mentioned earlier, Jill had been active in feminist and gay rights groups in her youth, and she produced a pamphlet at this dinner from a 1974 meeting of a women's movement in which she was involved at the time. She produced this pamphlet because, she said, she thought that I might be interested in it (reflecting her interpretation of my research into lesbian culture). Feeling that I ought to demonstrate interest in this and share it with the group, I read out a section from it and then – in jest – suggested that the women discuss it.

Interaction 7.1 Gender fucking

Eve (E), Hannah (H), Jill (J), Sam (S), Author (L)

```
1  L  It says {<reading from pamphlet> a central part of the gender role is sexual
```

```
2  L  orientation (.) masculine equals fucks women feminine equals fucked by men
```

```
3  L  (.) homosexuality and bisexuality as sexual orientations are thus a
```

```
-----------------------------------------------------------------------------
4  E                                    Oh dear I [knew I'd got wrong]
   L  betrayal of a key element in the role.}        [Discuss @ (1)]
-----------------------------------------------------------------------------
5  S                          [I spent- I think] I'd have to read it (.)
   H  I didn't understand that
   J                      @[(2)]
-----------------------------------------------------------------------------
6  H                               /Derr:: [@(3)]
   J  {<in 'Northern' accent> You wha::t?/
   L                                      [I think it's-] it's saying that-
-----------------------------------------------------------------------------
7  E                          It's a::ll to do with penetration Hannah
   H                  [@(1)]
   J  What did you sa::y?}
   L                  [@(.)]                                        It's
-----------------------------------------------------------------------------
8  E       /Do [you penetrate] or are you penetrated?
   H                                        (1) Oh I see. @(5)
   J          [@(1)]
   L  saying/
-----------------------------------------------------------------------------
9  S                     thankyou for that elucidation @(.)
   L  No it's s- it's/                        it's saying that that
-----------------------------------------------------------------------------
10 E                                              And therefore
   H                           Oh [I see]
   L  that gay that gay people    [gender] fuck. (.) Essentially.
-----------------------------------------------------------------------------
11 E  it [doesn't fit.]              [because it doesn't fit.]
   L     [They mess with] the system [because they don't fit] yeah.
```

The use of the tactic of authorisation is particularly clear in this brief interaction, as some of the women aim to position themselves as intellectually superior to the others. Eve is active in this identity work, immediately aligning herself with the symbolically powerful academic register in which the text has been delivered (though this was potentially influenced by my use of the verb 'discuss', connotative of academic assignments). In line 4, Eve responds to the reading by sarcastically suggesting her 'failure' to live a heteronormative lifestyle. In doing so, she demonstrates both her comprehension of the text and the importance of showing this. The essay-style question that I give to the group provides them with the opportunity to overtly articulate their knowledge of issues associated with feminist and queer discourses, though Jill's approach to this is to construct a clear opposition between herself (who, as owner of the pamphlet, has already established her authenticity in this context) and Hannah.

Jill begins by openly laughing at Hannah, following this with a face-threatening act;[2] she positions her as ignorant through the voicing of a stereotypical 'Northern' accent, pronouncing 'you what?' as /jə wɑː/ rather than /wɒt/, which would be closer to the Southern English accent that both women typically used. Trudgill and Giles (1978) hypothesise that speakers evaluate particular accents dependent on the social connotations that they have and, in using this accent, Jill seemingly indexes a lack of sophistication and intellect which is stereotypically associated with Northern speakers. As Wales (1999) argues, the 'North/ South divide' in England is highly pervasive in most native speakers' minds; there are clear and fixed stereotypes attached to 'Northerners' and 'Southerners', which she attributes primarily to the industrial revolution in Britain. Northern accents, Wales suggests, are culturally synonymous with working-class mining communities and lower educational standards, whereas Southern accents suggest intelligence and middle-class occupations. Certainly, the implicature of Jill's comment seems clear, as Hannah immediately responds with a sound representing her gormlessness or stupidity ('derr', line 6).

The use of this Northern accent to index lower intellectual status highlights the shared social norms of this group in terms of their age, geographical origin and social class. The majority of the women came from the South of England, and using the Northern pronunciation here to imply stupidity allows Jill to construct herself in opposition to this as a Southerner (therefore removed from both the accent and its index). All of the women in this interaction, except for Claire, have a Southern accent and, though it seems unlikely that the contextually specific indexical link between ignorance and the Northern accent is a direct attempt to offend Claire, this may partly explain why she takes no turn in the conversation despite being present at the table during the recording. In constructing a negative identity position (see Section 5.2.2) by drawing on a shared ideology of intellectualism in the group, Jill positions Hannah in a role which is inappropriate for a Stomper member. Her use of the tactic of illegitimation is apparent here, as she draws on an ideological system of class-based status and education in order to assign Hannah this identity position. By literally putting words in Hannah's mouth in line 7 ('what did you say?'), again with this Northern accent, Jill also effectively delegitimises Hannah's role by preventing her from expressing herself. In doing so, Jill positions herself as comparatively intellectual.

That Jill's identity work is achieved through comparative means is worth remarking upon; by 'ventriloquating' Hannah (Bakhtin 1981), Jill positions herself as knowledgeable and authentic and Hannah as less so, not only marking out intellectualism as indexical of authenticity in the Stomper group, but presenting herself as relatively superior (and thus *more* authentic). This may be seen to reflect the tactic of distinction (Bucholtz and Hall 2004: 495), the process whereby speakers may show how other social groups are separate or different from them in order to affirm their own group identity and positively evaluate what they do in comparison to others. In this instance, however, Jill's mocking actually disrupts any homogeneity in the group by positioning Hannah as an outsider for her own gain. Although Jill makes herself distinct from Hannah in order to articulate her own authenticity as a group member, this is not a tactic used in order to create a shared social identity, whereby the group as a whole is distinct. In contrast, it appears to be an individual tactic to distance herself from one member who has shown herself to be temporarily illegitimate. Even when a consequence of such identity work is to reassert the shared norms of a CoP, then, this does not mean that it will necessarily be done collaboratively.

In line 6, having been laughed at openly, Hannah seemingly accepts her fate. She self-deprecates in line with Jill's framing of her as ignorant and laughs openly and loudly at herself in this moment. This may be seen as a face-saving move, one which allows Hannah to align herself with the majority view rather than dispute her ascribed position and risk making herself more vulnerable. This analysis is supported by my experience of Hannah as a relatively timid personality who rarely spoke up or made a point of something which she thought or knew to be false. During my fieldwork, for example, I noted her tendency to mitigate much of her speech and to be the first to concede defeat in any situation where opinions might be voiced. For instance, when a wrong turn was about to be taken on a hike that Jill was leading, she once said ' I think it might be that way', pointing in a direction different from that being taken by Jill, but then accepted Jill's route immediately when it was presented (incidentally, Hannah was correct, and we were going in the wrong direction). Although this was, to some extent, a level of politeness expected of the group members, in other situations non-leaders pointed out errors to the leader in order to ensure that the hike went smoothly for all engaged in it. Hannah's acceptance of the temporary role of 'stupid Northerner' in this moment, therefore, seems to reflect her typically passive engagement with the group.

Hannah's positioning is further constructed by her reaction to the face-threatening act of being 'taught' about the meaning of the text (lines 7–12). This imposition on Hannah is administered primarily by Eve, taking the role of teacher and thus positioning herself as an intellectual. Through the use of this teacher role-play, Eve positions Hannah as unknowledgeable – crucially, again, this allows her to position herself as comparably intelligent. By appearing to ask Hannah the question (in line 8) 'do you penetrate or are you penetrated?', directing it at her rather than presenting it as a rhetorical question, Eve threatens both Hannah's negative face (as her contribution requires a response), and her positive face (as it requires her to reveal something that she might be judged for). It was also highly unusual for any sexual or intimate knowledge to be shared or asked about in this group of women, which makes this a rather intrusive and shocking question. The challenge also has the effect of simplifying the text that I read out, making it easier for Hannah to understand and, in doing so, patronising her by placing her again in a subordinate or ignorant role. On a later occasion, Sam told me that she was irritated by Eve's comment about penetration, as she felt that it was deliberately provocative. Sam and Eve's relationship (as illustrated in Section 1.1.1) was tense, and this might also explain Sam's sarcastic jibe at Eve in line 9: 'thank you for that elucidation'. Her comment seems to imply that Eve's contribution was inaccurate or unsuitable, though her use of the high-register 'elucidation' also allows Sam to present *herself* as intellectual as well. In doing so, Sam is able to challenge the uniqueness of the role that Eve has created for herself and, at the same time, index a persona which is clearly being constructed as valuable and authentic in this moment. In contrast, Hannah's desire for the conversation to be over is apparent from her claim to have understood the text (as a result of Eve's provocative explanation) in line 8: 'Oh I see'. This is then repeated in response to my own explanation of it, yet delivered *before* the crucial verbal element is spoken ('gender fuck', line 10) – this is the part of the clause which explains what gay people were seen to be doing 'wrong'. By claiming her comprehension before the explanation has been given, Hannah reveals her desire to appear knowledgeable, irrespective of how well she understands what has been said. This indicates her concern to be removed from the 'learner' role in which she has been positioned, and highlights the inauthentic connotation of this role.

It is evident that Hannah's temporary inauthenticity here provides a negative identity position against which the other women are able to oppositionally locate themselves and, as a result, claim a legitimate Stomper self. By positioning themselves as authentic in comparison to Hannah, the other women in this interaction also produce a normative political intellectualism in the group and construct this as indexical of Stomper identity. This illustrates that the women's construction of authenticity was achieved throughout their interaction in ways which did not always index the personae of Dyke or Girl, as suggested in the previous chapters. Instead, another valued persona is produced in this moment: that of the intellectual woman. It is clear from this interaction that intelligence was symbolic of Stomper authenticity, but also that this intelligence could be displayed through a specific, valued knowledge: of sexual politics.

7.2.2   Awareness of sexual politics

It has so far been suggested in this chapter that the women valued intellectualism and that they positioned this – alongside a feminist orientation – as an aspect of authentic Stomper identity. This section explores the role of sexual politics, shown in Interaction 7.1 to have symbolic relevance for the group, in the construction of an authentic identity apparent during a hike between me, Claire, Marianne and Sam. In this moment, which is transcribed below, the women positioned themselves as authentic by positioning me as ignorant; this has clear parallels with Hannah's experience, above. Given that I had not been born until the early 1980s, there was an inevitable cultural difference between myself and the other Stomper women (typically born in the 1950s or early 1960s). As discussed in Section 4.2.2, they tended to treat me as an apprentice, and this included telling me about cultural events and phenomena that occurred in their youth or which I was less familiar with due to my age. One such moment emerged as a result of our conversation about *The L Word* (detailed in Section 5.2.1). Following our discussion, we began to lament the lack of lesbian-specific shows available in the mainstream media. Marianne's response to this was to begin to tell us about *Two in Twenty*, a feature-length lesbian film from the 1980s, styled in the format of five episodes of a soap opera. The phrase 'two in twenty' alluded to the phrase 'one in ten', a term popularised by Alfred Kinsey's claims about 10 per cent of the population having some degree of homosexuality. This exchange reveals the value placed upon knowledge of gay culture in this CoP, as the women endeavoured to position themselves as informed and familiar with the study (Kinsey et al. 1948). Furthermore, Marianne's mention of the 1980s *Two in Twenty* allowed her to demonstrate her engagement with lesbian culture over a prolonged period of time, as the opening line reveals below.

Interaction 7.2 Two in twenty

Marianne (M), Sam (S), Claire (C), Author (L)

```
1 M Yeah <inaudible> (.) there was something but I can't remember if it
```

```
2 M was really he::re or it was only that I saw it in a film later and it
```

```
3 M  was it was called Two in Twenty that was a soap a lesbian soap
```

```
4 S               I [didn't see that]
  M                 [Mmm Two in] Twenty 'cause one in ten sounds so <@ lonely @>
  L  Oh really?
```

```
5 S  [@ (6)]                        Oh [that's nice]
  M  [@ (6)]                           [It was really] funny it was really
  C  [@ (6)]
  L  [@ (2)] (.) Oh that's ridiculous
```

```
6 S      Sounds good.
  M  good.                                      Yeah that's what
  L              Why (.) is it meant to be one in ten?
```

```
7 S      [Well that's the] kind of base line [isn't it with gays number of gay
  M  they [used to say yeah]                  [some people say it's less
```

```
8 S  people]
  M    now] <inaudible> some surveys make it less now
  L                                          I remember being in
```

```
9 S  [Depends where you draw [[the line on]] the-]
  C  [You must you(.)you you [[must know]] where] one in ten comes from
  L  [c-]                    [[@ (.)]]
```

```
10 M                             [Mmm]
   C  surely.                    [Yeah]              <@ doing
   L      (.) Where one in ten comes from?   What d'you mean?
```

```
11 S      [It's to it] [was Kinsey who it wa- Kin[[sey] that put]]
   C  yo::ur[ PhD? @>]                          [[It's from the Kinsey report]]
   L        [What th- that there's one in ten-]
```

```
12 S  that out there first yeah
   C                    Who who did and it's only for ma::le homosexuals
   L                 Oh ok
```

```
13 S  [It's only for males]
   C  [as well]         and it weren't even gay it was just homosexual experiences
```

```
14 M                                            [Some surveys-
   C  one in ten men [had ever had] homosexual experiences    [so that were
   L                 [One in ten right]             Very low
```

```
15  M  have a]low[er]
    C  at 1960s] [but] that's where it comes from (.) from 1965  so it's probably not
    L                                                      Ok
```

```
16  M                                 [probably (.) one in a half of ten now]
    C  really very accurate but (.) you [probably want to mention Kinsey]
```

```
17  S                                              [@ (5)]
    M                                              [@ (2)]
    C  somewhere in your-/[@ (2)]                  [@ (2)]
    L                     /[No I do] know who Kinsey is    Thanks:: <sarcastically>
```

Marianne's joke in line 4 – in which she gives the byline of the film *Two in Twenty* – is immediately responded to by the other women present in this moment. In laughing along with Marianne, the women clearly place her contribution in a humorous frame and indicate that they understand her joke. My lack of understanding is revealed, however, in line 5, as I comment: 'that's ridiculous'. This response was a result of my desire to evaluate the joke and have something to say, but not having the cultural knowledge to do so accurately. This is particularly evident in line 6, as I respond to Sam's positive stance towards the joke with a question; I reveal that I am not familiar with the phrase 'one in ten'. This leads the other women to take on a 'teacher' role, and also facilitates their competing to demonstrate their own cultural knowledge (of the gay phrase) and intellectualism (through their understanding of its implications).

From line 6, the women engage in identity work which allows them to present themselves as being knowledgeable, framing my relative ignorance in comparison with themselves. To begin with, Sam and Marianne jointly construct a direct answer to my question. Marianne's immediate response begins with 'yeah' in line 6 and follows with the declarative statement 'that's what they used to say'. Sam then overlaps with this in line 7, taking the floor and demonstrating her own knowledge, taking on the role of educator at this moment by beginning her turn with the evaluative 'well'. By interrupting Marianne, Sam competes with her to present herself as knowledgeable, demonstrating the symbolic value of this move in indexing her understanding of gay culture. Sam continues to hold the floor as Marianne attempts to regain it by talking over her. The competitive nature of this interactive behaviour demonstrates the perceived importance of the content of the women's talk as they both actively endeavour to present themselves as knowledgeable and as able to teach me something new. This reveals the value of this act of positioning, given the typically polite nature of the group's discourse.

Interestingly, although Sam and Marianne adopt a 'teacher' role which, inevitably, positions me as less knowledgeable (and therefore less authentic as a Stomper), they also endeavour to reduce the extent of my inauthenticity in this moment. They assume that I have a certain level of understanding about the phrase 'two in ten' by using the tag question 'isn't it' (Sam, line 7), for example. This provides me with the opportunity to save face, implying that I already had this knowledge and that Sam was simply reminding me of it. Similarly, the fact that neither Sam nor Marianne directly refer to Kinsey in this moment assumes my knowledge of the origins of the phrase. The information that 'one in ten' refers to the number of gay people in the population is absolutely crucial to an understanding of the phrase, but both women assume that I already know this. The information is presented as logical and obvious, therefore, which demonstrates the women's interpretation of me as a fellow intellectual (as they interpret it). In this sense, their interactive tactics serve to authenticate me. My turn in line 8, where I begin to change the subject, marks a move on my part to confirm that I have the relevant knowledge (despite the fact that I do not) and to reduce the extent of my inauthentic positioning. This is challenged directly by Claire, however, in line 9. From this point onwards, a more competitive display of knowledge occurs, again foregrounding the authentic status of an intelligent, informed persona.

Claire's challenge begins with a clear floor-taking move, where she begins to talk at the same time as Sam (who is about to continue demonstrating her knowledge by further evaluating the statistic). At this point, I end my own turn, and Sam does the same once Claire raises her voice with the words 'you you you must know', successfully holding the floor by accentuating her point. The emphasis Claire places on 'you' seems designed to accentuate the fact that I should be aware of the Kinsey report due to my research focus ('doing your PhD', line 11). In one sense, this positions me in an authentic role due to my presumed intelligence and knowledge of gay culture – Claire's assumptions about my PhD focus suggest this. On the other hand, though, to directly challenge my knowledge is a clear face-threatening act, especially given the importance that this evidently has for the Stomper CoP, and Claire's turn requires a response. In this way, Claire tests me, and my response in line 10 ('where one in ten comes from … what d'you mean?') indicates that I do not have an answer. That Marianne then joins in with Claire's test of my knowledge in line 10 (by aligning herself with the challenge through the minimal response 'mmm') indicates that the women are jointly creating an opposition between myself and them, based upon culture-specific knowledge. In doing so, they emphasise the significance and value of knowledge of gay issues and position me as temporarily inauthentic. Once again, they position themselves as authentic in comparison.

Once the answer to my question – 'it was Kinsey' – is given by Sam in line 11, the requirement for me to directly respond to the challenge is temporarily removed, with the women instead all competing to get across the key points of the report. Interestingly, whilst competing in this display of knowledge, the women also collaboratively construct their interpretation of the validity of the report. For instance, Claire points out in line 12 that it was just 'male homosexuals', a point which is then mirrored immediately by Sam (in line 13) with 'it's only for males'. The value of displaying this knowledge is most clearly demonstrated by Claire in line 15, where she moves from the general '1960s' to the more spe-cific '1965' after an apparent pause for thought to, presumably, ensure accuracy. Claire effectively positions herself in the role of 'expert' at this moment, and succeeds in taking the floor from the other women through her articulation of this high-level knowledge. Through the use of the epis-temic adverbial 'probably' to suggest the inaccuracy of the report in line 15, Claire takes a new stance in relation to it, one followed by Marianne who evaluates it as of less significance in the present day (line 16).

My concern to save face in this moment is apparent from my sarcastic contribution in line 17, which the women interpret – as intended – as a humorous turn. My desire to fit in with the group and be seen as equal often led to such awkward interactions as this one, as I often found myself trying to seem older, wiser and better informed about the issues that mattered to these women. Though I engaged with them over a long period of time, learnt about their values and the meaning of their various practices and identity moves, and began to be accepted as 'one of them', the cultural chasm between us because of my age was often highly apparent. Far from disrupting the cohesion of the group, however, it is clear from this interaction that the women used this to their advantage, taking stances which allowed them to display their knowledge and experience. In this way, it is clear that CoPs can sustain heterogeneity within them, so long as the shared and valued ethos is both prevalent and maintained.

7.3   Concluding remarks

It has been made particularly clear in this chapter that, by positioning others in a negative identity position, the women were able to align themselves with an authentic persona and to therefore index a Stomper identity. It was apparently an accepted part of this CoP's practice for members to illegitimate one another for their own individual gain. In this sense, the women were not consistently cooperative, and often acted in ways which served their authenticity as a group member at the expense of others, or which required them to employ an aggressive or competitive style. Nonetheless, their identity work in such moments served to foreground relevant aspects of the group's ethos. Importantly, it has been illustrated here that the construction of a lesbian-based identity need not always be directly related to sexual behaviour or desire; an authentic self, in the moments presented in this chapter, may also be fundamentally tied into shared backgrounds, interests and beliefs on a broader level.

As indicated at the beginning of this chapter, feminism was one of these shared beliefs, and had a rather assumed symbolic status for the Stomper women. In no small way, this was a consequence of their shared age and class experience, and symbolic of the Stomper identity was their presumed interest in political and cultural issues associated with women's and gay rights (as highlighted by the two interactions detailed above). Intellectualism and political awareness were unmarked and presumed, yet any interactive move which suggested that a Stomper woman did not share these traits was likely to be highlighted and scrutinised. In this way, the women were seemingly able to manage the boundaries of what was expected practice and to reinforce the ethos of the CoP.

Though some apparently uncooperative or antagonistic turns have been shown in these two interactions to take place, it has also been shown that they were typically humorous and that they existed to enhance the group's understanding of their shared ethos. Typically, this ethos was understood and recognised by the women – such as the value of gay culture – and they could index an authentic persona in a relatively straightforward way as a result. Yet it was not always the case that the women jointly indexed such cultural or politicised stances without some evaluation or clarification of their meaning. As with the personae of Dyke and Girl, what it meant to be politically aware was also actively negotiated by the women. Interestingly, whereas a Dyke or Girl may be quite logically constructed in line with the various stereotypes and pervasive ideologies which exist in lesbian culture – with women free to align themselves with or against each persona fairly easily – the idiosyncrasies in the group really came to the fore when the women actively negotiated the meaning of a 'feminist'. The next chapter demonstrates that the *assumption* often made by the women, and outlined at the beginning of this chapter (that their typical class, age and background meant that each Stomper was a feminist), was not necessarily accurate. It focuses quite specifically on Claire, a character in the CoP who has already been shown to have played a considerable role in the construction of meaning in the group, but who has also been shown to differ from the other women in key ways. The analyses in Chapter 8 show the meaning of feminism to the Stompers as a whole and to Claire as an individual, revealing how meaning-making may still occur even when the essence of sameness holding a CoP together has been disrupted.

8
Political Difference and Maintenance of Shared Identity

The data analysed in this book so far has indicated that the Stompers, whilst idiosyncratic in their interactive style and not always cooperative in their stance-taking, nonetheless tended to mutually negotiate the meaning of core aspects of Stomper identity. In constructing what it meant to be a 'real' lesbian, for example, the women jointly engaged in positioning a Girl as inauthentic and those traits associated with Dykes as legitimate. Though they sometimes prioritised their own, individual, identity work at the expense of others in the group, the interactions presented so far have illustrated a shared ethos, one relying not only on lesbian culture but on the women's expectations of one another's experiences as middle-class, middle-aged gay women. The previous chapter began by illustrating the expected significance of feminism to the group, before going on to describe the importance of knowledge, intellectualism and understanding of queer politics and culture. In this way, it indicated that not everything that the women did, as members of a lesbian group, necessarily indexed their sexuality in a direct way. This chapter will return to the relevance of feminism, specifically, to the Stomper women. It will also reveal moments whereby the women, rather than engaging in a friendly or bantering style in order to gain individual legitimacy, explicitly disagreed with one another's stances and took on differing personae within the same interactive moment. In this way, it will explore how the women managed the disruption of their idealised homogeneity and maintained a coherent group identity.

8.1 Deconstructing feminism

As shown in the previous chapter, the individual Stomper women often identified as feminists and typically assumed that the women that they walked with would do so as well. As has been detailed already throughout this book, the typical age of the women engaging with the Stomper walks meant that many of them had, in some way, experienced the second-wave 'women's liberation' movement of the 1970s. Furthermore, many of the women – Marianne, Jill, Hannah and Eve in particular – explicitly identified as feminists. This was undoubtedly a factor in the typical rejection of Girly styles; since feminism can be defined, in part, as a challenge to the system of norms and expectations that control, subjugate and judge women according to their appearance (Grogan 2008: 75), it is unsurprising that a group of women who typically identified as feminists would also reject traditional symbols of femininity and use this in the oppositional construction of their own (queer) womanhood.

There is a clear ideological link between lesbians and feminists, of course, which extends beyond the fact that many of these women happened to come of age during a crucial time in the women's movement. The category 'feminist' has been ideologically associated with lesbians since separatist groups grew in number in the 1970s and many women made a choice not to engage in heterosexual relationships, viewing them as reproducing broader patriarchal power relations. Given that, as has been illustrated so far in this book, the women often drew on broader stereotypes associated with lesbian culture and identity in order to construct a meaningful identity for themselves, it was likely that they would also draw on feminism as a way of creating temporary homogeneity. The fact that many of the women viewed themselves as feminists outside of the group (such as Jill who, as shown in Interaction 7.1, still had pamphlets relating to feminist activism from the 1970s) clearly contributed to the relevance of this political movement in their identity construction as lesbians.

This chapter deals with two final interactive moments between the women. The first of these, below, shows that feminism was assumed to be relevant by most but – crucially – not all of the Stomper women. Despite the prevalent stereotypical links made between lesbians and feminists in broader culture, and despite the relevance of feminism to lesbian culture and experience more broadly, this interactive moment reveals that a significant factor in the Stompers' reliance on the political movement was, in fact, the *typical* age of the women making up the CoP. It shows a conversation between me, Sam, Marianne and Claire, in which Claire positions herself as an outsider due to her relative youth and, therefore, reveals exactly how significant the women's shared age was to the assumed norms of the group. The conversation follows from our discussion of Kinsey, shown in Section 7.2. Marianne had pointed out that I was younger than the others present and that I might not be so aware of studies that were meaningful to them because 'things have changed'. This led to her lamenting the fact that feminism was less of an issue for young women in the twenty-first century than it was for her generation, when every young woman was presumed to be a feminist and would own copies of key feminist texts. In response to this, I named a scholar that I was aware of – Lillian Faderman. The resulting conversation is presented below:

Interaction 8.1 Too young to be a feminist

Marianne (M), Sam (S), Claire (C), Author (L)

```
-------------------------------------------------------------------------------
1 C:                    Yeah (.) The Love that Dare not Speak its Name I don't
  L:[Lillian Faderman]
-------------------------------------------------------------------------------
2 C:thi- I can't remember what it's called [that]                    that's
     L:                                    [Surpass]ing the Love of Men
-------------------------------------------------------------------------------
3 M:      Oh that [yeah]                    [[No:: I never read that properly
  C:the one      [I never] read I haven't   [[read any of these things(.)I'd
-------------------------------------------------------------------------------
4 M:I've had a look at it]]
  C:like to just say for]] the tape I was never like (.) a feminist
  L:                                                   You were never
-------------------------------------------------------------------------------
5 S:                                      <@too young to be a feminist@>
  C:        I- I'm too young to be a feminist.
  L:a feminist?
-------------------------------------------------------------------------------
6 S:                         [[It's]] come back though hasn't it
  M:[Oh you are still a feminist you just [[weren't]]
  L:[I'm a feminist (.) and I'm younger than you]
-------------------------------------------------------------------------------
7 S:[(0) there was a kind of]              [It but it went out [[of
  M:[involved in that time]                            [[I don't
  L:               It hasn't come back  [no-one no-one cares
-------------------------------------------------------------------------------
8 S:fashion]
  M:think it has] I don't think anybody c- I don't think it's arou::nd
-------------------------------------------------------------------------------
9 M:anymore        The issues are just not there anymore which I don't
  L:     No-one cares
-------------------------------------------------------------------------------
10 M:understand in the years                         [yes.]
   L:                  Well the issues are there it's just [that]
-------------------------------------------------------------------------------
11 S:                        [Well we have actually-]
   M:nobody's addressing them anymore (.) [you know pornography's]
   L:no-one's
```

```
12  S:          [we have achie::ved a- an awful lot it hasn't just gone]
    M: on every [computer screen and nobody seems to give a damn anymore]
    L:                                                                 You
```

```
13  S:     I mean it has moved on I mean when feminism kicked off women were
    L: what?
```

```
14  S: le::gally very much second class citizens (.) [so an awful lot's changed]
    M:                                               [Some things have moved on]
```

```
15  S:                                  (.) Yeah (1) well some of us
    M:and some things have moved in a negative way
```

```
16  S:have just kind of gone underground.
```

In this interaction, two main stances are taken in order for the women to construct their identities as group members in line with the category 'feminist'. In contrast to their usual engagement, whereby the women typically sought a sense of homogeneity, this extract reveals difference between the women, fuelled by Claire's disalignment from Marianne and Sam. In this moment, Claire appears to reject the category 'feminist' in order to construct her own individual identity, whilst Marianne and Sam differ as they compete to claim the most authentic feminist persona. Claire's disalignment from feminism is considered, below, followed by a close examination of Sam and Marianne's efforts to actively construct feminism as a valued Stomper norm.

8.1.1   Feminism as a generational experience

Claire's rejection of feminism comes after our collaborative discussion of the work of the feminist writer Lillian Faderman. After I volunteer the name, she responds positively in line 1 with 'yeah' and, up until line 4, seems to articulate her knowledge of feminism. Her awareness of the value placed on (relevant) political knowledge in this CoP (as illustrated in the previous chapter) is apparent in line 1, as she pauses before offering 'the love that dare not speak its name',[1] the pause suggesting that she may fear that she might be inaccurate. This is followed by an immediate self-repair of 'I don't thi- I can't remember what it's called' (line 2). Moving from positioning herself as having no knowledge ('I don't think') to having the knowledge but being unable to recall it, complete with the affirmative 'that's the one' in lines 2–3, suggests a concern to show awareness of Faderman and, therefore, to index feminist knowledge. Ultimately, this contributes towards her construction of an authentic Stomper persona, given the symbolic currency that feminism has for the group's shared sense of self. However, in line 3, Claire then begins to shift away from this articulation of feminist knowledge towards a defensive stance against feminism itself; she claims that Faderman's book is one of many 'things' that she has not read. Claire effectively reduces the importance of the book itself here (as does Marianne in line 4, claiming that she has only 'had a look at it') but, by grouping it into a genre, also reduces the importance of feminist texts as a whole. This differs significantly from my own conscious move: to express my knowledge by providing the title of the book, performing a feminist persona in order to recover from my earlier loss of face for not recognising the work of Kinsey (Interaction 6.2). Claire, by contrast, begins to overtly reject the label 'feminist' at this point, albeit 'for the tape'.[2]

Claire's overt distancing of herself from the category 'feminist' takes place from this point onwards, in line 4, as she argues that she 'was never like (.) a feminist'. Her use of the past tense verb 'was' appears to immediately establish what feminism means to her, placing it as a historic concept, something which – even if she *had* been involved in it – was in the past and is not relevant now. In doing so, she aligns feminism with the 1970s, a time the other core members had experienced and which she had not – as a woman in her forties, she was a child in this decade. Whilst Claire's use of the filler 'like', followed by a brief pause, seems to downplay the strength of her stance against the feminist category by functioning as a hesitancy marker (Brown 1977: 121), her subsequent claim that she is too young to be a feminist illustrates a clearer determination to distance herself from the category as she perceives it as being meaningful to the group. It is apparent from the falling intonation at the end of her turn in line 5 that she is staking an overt claim to non-feminism, and that she is doing so in order to differentiate herself from the other (older) women. The silence which follows this turn functions to remove her completely from the interaction, in which the identity category of 'feminist' is newly constructed (detailed below). Silence may operate as a powerful strategy (see Jaworski 1993) and, in this instance, it seems to allow Claire to avoid taking another stance and removes her completely from the interaction. In this way, she is able to avoid association with the prevalent identity category which contradicts her view of herself.

Claire's stance-taking away from the feminist identity category may show more than a straightforward rejection of feminism in this interaction, however. Given that she made an error in referring to Faderman's text as 'the love that dare not speak its name', it seems logical to argue that her rejection of feminism functions as a face-saving device.[3] This is evident in her shifting stance-taking; she begins by presenting herself as knowledgeable and interested in lines 1–2, and ends by constructing an unconcerned and apathetic stance in lines 3–5. This shift suggests that Claire begins by aligning herself with a concept that she understands is of symbolic value to the group. Indeed, her earlier mocking of me for not being familiar with Kinsey (Interaction 7.1) demonstrates both her historical knowledge of gay culture and politics and her ability to express Stomper authenticity through her shared understanding of the CoP ethos. Upon accidentally referencing the wrong moment of queer history and revealing herself to be less knowledgeable than she might have wished, then, Claire may be seen to have made a move which will protect her positive face, or her desire to be approved of (Brown and Levinson 1987: 62). By actively rejecting feminism after stumbling in her identification of it, claiming that she is too young to be a feminist allows Claire to present herself as nonchalant or simply unconcerned with that concept. This turn, therefore, allows her to justify her apparent lack of awareness of feminism.

   Claire's stance here may seem unusual; CoPs are typically thought of as consensual in nature, a site whereby those who can articulate the general shared stance of the group are seen to have established their authenticity and 'right' to engage with it and thus be seen as members (Eckert and Wenger 2005: 584). In consciously and deliberately claiming to be distinct from the other members, therefore, Claire potentially places herself on the periphery of the group and jeopardises her full membership. However, the significance of her stance, with regard to her age, cannot be underestimated. Her claim that she is young serves to remind her interlocutors that she, unlike them, was not present during the women's movements of the 1970s, and to disassociate herself from their experiences at ten years (or more) her senior. Whilst Marianne would have been in her late teens and Sam in her twenties during the 1970s, a crucial decade for the development of both second-wave feminism and the politicisation of lesbian identity, Claire did not reach this coming of age period in her life until the late 1980s. Indeed, the emphasis that Claire places on her youth in this moment was relatively typical of her engagement with the Stomper group. As discussed in Section 1.1.1, when comparing themselves to her, the other Stompers often made self-deprecating jokes about the menopause or collecting their pensions, referring to themselves as 'old' in comparison to Claire (or myself). Similarly, Claire often played up to her role as the youngest core member, jokingly complaining that I had taken her place since arriving in the group, or mocking the other women by suggesting that they were old enough to be her grandmother. In this sense, Claire's marked age difference from the other women was never erased, but rather was exaggerated and stressed.

Similarly, whilst Claire's occupation and education as an adult placed her squarely in a middle-class bracket, her background differed from that of the older women in the group in that she was from a local, working-class family. In combination with her youthful status, this factor may help to explain her resistance to the category 'feminist'. Many lesbians in the 1980s saw themselves as marginalised because they did not connect their sexuality with politics, and these groups began to critique white, middle-class, lesbian culture for its focus on feminist issues. Non-white and working-class lesbians in the UK, in particular, had begun to feel excluded by this decade and, in reclaiming lesbianism as an identity which defined them, rejected lesbian feminism (see Koller 2008: 86 for an excellent account of this). It was during the time of this cultural discourse that Claire came of age and, as such, her view of feminism may have differed considerably from Marianne's or Sam's.

Claire's disalignment with feminism due to her relative youth, however, is worth considering in more depth. Rather than claiming that she is from an alternative political generation or taking a third-wave perspective on feminism, whereby as a 'younger' feminist she may be pitted against 'older' feminists (see Denfeld 1995 for an example of this phenomenon), Claire's turn here serves simply to construct the category of 'feminist' as an older person. In turn, she is able to claim a 'young person' identity. Her articulation of herself as 'too young', therefore, allows her to project a persona which marks her out as fundamentally different from the other women. In addition to her declarative statement that she is 'too young to be a feminist', Claire's earlier turn in line 4 (whereby she claims that she 'was never like (.) a feminist') contains interesting use of the discourse marker 'like'. An alternative analysis of this feature, other than that it is used as a hesitancy marker (see above), is that it functions as a highlighting device, or focuser (Romaine and Lange 1991: 244). The fact that it appears immediately before a brief pause and the term 'feminist' itself, which was bound to be controversial within this setting, suggests that it acts as a kind of subtle, linguistic, drum roll, foregrounding the statement that Claire is about to make. Importantly, though the use of 'like' in this way was typical of Claire's language use in the recordings that she was a part of, it tends *not* to be aligned with people of her generation. Research such as that by Dailey-O'Cain (2000) and Tagliamonte and Hudson (1999) has found this to be a feature likely to be used by younger speakers (in the UK and Canada), whilst perceptual dialectology has shown that 'like' tends to be associated with youthfulness (Dougherty and Strassel 1998). Since the feature may be broadly viewed as symbolic of youth and was not a feature found in the language use of any of the other (older) Stomper members, and given that Claire's age was frequently marked in other areas of the women's discourse, it is feasible to suggest that her use of 'like' in this moment contributes to – and makes more convincing – her stance-taking towards a youthful persona.[4]

Given that, as detailed above, Claire often felt that she was somewhat peripheral to the group due to her age, and considering her usual interest in feminist issues, it may be argued that her primary objective at this moment was not to reject an identity category which she simply felt did not apply to her, or which had caused her to lose face. Instead, she appears to be utilising a mainstream stereotype (of feminism as meaningful to women in the 1970s rather than those in the current time) in order to position the other CoP members in one group and herself in another. Claire's stance-taking against a concept which is symbolic of the group as a whole allows her to mark herself out as different, or as *indifferent* to this part of the group's sense of self. It is not clear whether Claire wishes to reject feminism as a whole but it is apparent that, in this moment, she wishes to move away from the ethnographically salient Stomper identity which is informed partly by feminist thought. Irrespective of Claire's motives – whether she does or does not identify as a feminist – it is apparent that the category is tangible and ideologically salient enough for her to reject in order to make a firm identity claim. In this sense, feminism may simply be the tool used to construct her difference, given its relevance in accentuating her relative youth (the reason why she sometimes felt excluded from the group). The category of 'feminist' itself, therefore, may be somewhat inconsequential. Nonetheless, Claire's complex rejection of the category within this interactive moment creates a need for the other women to redefine 'feminist' in an age-specific way, as considered below.

8.1.2   Feminism as normative

The mutual construction of the category 'feminist' begins, in line 6, with Marianne's challenge 'Oh you are still a feminist you just weren't ... involved in that time', and my own comment that 'I'm a feminist (.) and I'm younger than you'. In these turns, the correlation between age and feminism is rebuked in an attempt to encourage Claire to identify with this category. Indeed, Sam simply laughs at the idea that Claire would not be a feminist, suggesting that the notion was unthinkable to her. By delegitimising Claire's claim that one could be 'too young' to be a feminist, Marianne and I attempt – and fail – to adequate her with the rest of the group. It is in the following discussion, however, in which the relative success of feminism in the current time is debated, that the other group members begin to play an active role in constructing a feminist persona in line with their own experiences and values.

The knowledge and understanding that Sam and Marianne have of the symbolic value of feminism in this CoP are apparent from their discussion in lines 7–16, whereby the social implications of Claire's claim are considered and the women actively construct the meaning of the category 'feminist' for themselves. In response to Claire distancing herself from the label, Sam claims that feminism is still relevant by suggesting that it has 'come back'. Sam's use of the tag question 'hasn't it' (line 6) is responded to firstly by me with the dialogically mirroring statement 'it hasn't come back' and then by Marianne co-constructing this stance in arguing 'I don't think it has'. This reveals a potentially threatening move against Sam, in which we question her knowledge of feminism. Her response to it reveals much about the significance of feminism to the group; she aligns herself with the category of 'feminist' by using the first-person plural 'we', describing this collective group as active feminists who have 'gone underground' (again using the first-person pronoun 'us'). This allows her to construct the 'feminist' category in a specific way, using phrases from the semantic fields of fighting and activism (such as 'kicked off' in line 13 and 'underground' in line 16), whilst simultaneously authenticating herself through her clear alignment with that category. Sam's construction of 'feminist' and her overt stance-taking in line with it thus allow her to perform a persona of 'activist'. In this sense, she shifts the focus from books read and positions herself as a 'true' feminist in contrast to me and Marianne (redefining the category away from intellectualism and towards action). Furthermore, by claiming an active involvement in the cause, Sam both reauthenticates herself in line with the contextually specific value system of the group and claims an extreme position which extends beyond mere subscription to feminist views, clearly positioning herself in opposition to me and Marianne by claiming that she is an *active* feminist. This is a move also seen in Section 6.2.2 with Claire's categorisation of Eve as a 'real, proper butch' for not shaving, as it serves to define a 'more than' feminist.

Importantly, it is evident from line 11 of this extract that Sam and Marianne have differing views of what feminism means. Whilst Marianne focuses on issues reflecting misogynistic trends in society ('pornography's on every computer screen and nobody seems to give a damn', lines 11–12), Sam focuses on the equality of men and women (with women no longer being 'second class citizens', line 14). Clearly, both women raise these issues with the joint purpose of illustrating the problematic way in which women tend to be treated in society and, in this sense, have clear feminist views. The ways in which they interpret 'being a feminist' clearly differ, however. These two aspects of feminist concern may reflect a difference in the ages of the two, with Marianne in her fifties and Sam in her sixties, as 'women's liberation' (that which Sam seems to be arguing has succeeded) did focus primarily on equality as opposed to issues of misogyny, which were addressed later (perhaps in a period with which Marianne had more direct engagement). Had the conversation continued, it is possible that the women would have come to a jointly negotiated definition of feminism by agreeing on key aspects of it, but the walk ended at this point and the topic changed. Indeed, in line 13, Marianne began to concede Sam's point that 'some things have moved on', suggesting that their views on the important aspects of feminism are fundamentally similar (namely, the place of women in society). Though the women disagree over the details, perhaps also reflecting their awkward relationship and desire to be distinct from one another, they each construct a persona which indexes an aspect of the Stomper ethos, making claims to their legitimacy in the group and thus verifying their identities. These are key aspects of the tactic of authentication (Bucholtz and Hall 2005: 601) and, once again, reveal the CoP's ability to house difference.

The identity under construction in this moment is specifically feminist and, though clearly indexical of the Sapphic Stomper group, again has no *direct* link to the women's sexuality. The women do not lay explicit claims to their sexual orientation in these moments, for example, rather focusing on their identities as feminists (or not). Yet if we revisit the examples offered in the previous chapters – where the women positioned others as less authentic for not understanding queer culture (Chapter 7) or as more authentic for not engaging in heteronormatively feminised practices such as shaving their legs (Chapter 6) – it becomes apparent that the role of feminism in the group was intrinsic to the women's version of lesbian identity. It is clear that feminist thought is intertwined with the women's desire to queer the version of womanhood presented in mainstream society, rejecting Girly practices and authenticating the Dyke persona because, as well as rejecting heterosexual versions of womanhood, the women rejected the roles laid out for them by a patriarchal, objectifying society. Though not all of the women necessarily fell in line with this perspective at all times, it seems that they were all aware that this was a fundamental part of the group's ethos. In this sense, it appears to be the women's typical experiences as feminist women that inform their stance against femininity, as well as their experiences as lesbians. This is not to suggest that the two aspects of the Stomper identity are mutually exclusive, but to argue that they are intimately connected and that, together, they shape the sociocultural context which informs their temporal stance-taking and interactive tactics.

To view the links between sexuality and politics in this way – as intertwined and fundamentally connected within the group's concept of authentic lesbian identity – is convenient, yet (as the final extract of data dealt with in this book reveals, below) it was not a perspective shared by all of the Stomper members. As has been clearly illustrated already in this chapter, Claire did not always seem to share the women's feminist views. Although she may not have subscribed to this perspective, however, it seems reasonable to suggest that Claire was aware of lesbian culture which, in and of itself, is intertwined with feminist discourse. The final extract presented in this book, below, explores Claire's attitudes towards feminism, particularly in relation to the salient ideology of inherent homosexuality.

8.2 Constructing (in)authentic lesbianism

As indicated in the data presented so far, much of the Stomper women's interaction was playful, with challenges to or claims in line with lesbian authenticity often being presented in a humorous frame. They used stereotypes to index often exaggerated lesbian personae, aligning themselves with butch stereotypes despite their individual differences or justifying their adherence to femme practices through often tenuous means. In this sense, as suggested in Chapter 5, one could argue that the women parodied the ideological lesbian in order to find something coherent to engage with, as a group with sexual orientation in common. As a CoP, they worked at constructing an authentic lesbian persona, one that was butch, intellectual, professional, politically minded and feminist (though, as shown above, Claire did not always adhere to this latter point), and they typically engaged with the ideology of 'naturally' inverted gender in gay people). Yet there was also heterogeneity within the group, such as in how the women oriented to the label 'lesbian', whether they viewed themselves primarily as a feminist or as a lesbian, and so on. The women typically reduced these differences by constructing and aligning themselves with a coherent Dyke persona, and did so irrespective of their individual variation. In other words, they did not have to identify as a Dyke outside of the group or on a personal level, but performing the persona within the CoP context allowed them to stake a claim as a legitimate lesbian within Stomper parameters. This meant that they could use wider stereotypes in order to construct a relatively playful persona, rather than get into intimate or complex detail about their perceived sexualities.

It has also been shown that, during their interaction, the women could express individual differences which placed them outside of the legitimate Stomper frame, or temporarily placed them in a negative identity position as a Girl or as an uninformed or uneducated person, yet each could maintain her own group membership by virtue of her legitimacy as a regular Stomper and her presumed sexual orientation. In this sense, the CoP was flexible and ever-changing. However, on one particular point, there appeared to be less freedom: the ideological link between sexuality and biology. As shown by the finger test in Section 5.2.2, an assumption was commonly put forward that the women were in some way 'naturally' (biologically) lesbian. The women's conversation below, which immediately follows the finger test over dinner – a conversation in which testosterone and lesbianism were clearly conflated – reveals the salience of this theory for the Stompers. This quite naturally led to a discussion about whether sexuality is biologically preordained or a choice, with Hannah introducing the topic. She begins by positioning the latter view (sexuality as a choice) as 'old fashioned':

Interaction 8.2 Political lesbians

Claire (C), Eve (E), Hannah (H), Sam (S), Jill (J), Author (L)

```
-----------------------------------------------------------------------------------------
1  C                            @ (.)
   E   theory on that one.
   H                               In a very old fashioned comment here but (.)
-----------------------------------------------------------------------------------------
2  H   some people may have (.) also considered the consequences of (.) their
-----------------------------------------------------------------------------------------
3  S               [Oh yes certainly]
   E          Mm
   H   sexuality  [In terms of lack] of contraceptive and things like that.
```

```
-------------------------------------------------------------------------
 4  E  (.) What I wanna be a lesbian 'cause I don't get pregnant when I [(.)] fuck
    H                                                          [@ (.)]
-------------------------------------------------------------------------
 5  E  other women?              It has a certain logic to it <@ but I
    H              <@ yes yeah @> yeah.
-------------------------------------------------------------------------
 6  S                     [Mm]
    C                              [[But that was all that like]] those- (.)
    E  don't know @> how much [that's] [[really a dri::ver]]
-------------------------------------------------------------------------
 7  C  those political lesbians that I heard about @ (.)
    E                                              [Politic]al lesbians?
    L                                              [And who-]
-------------------------------------------------------------------------
 8  S               [[Well yes there was there were [<inaudible>]]
    C                                                    The
    J  [Well] there [[are political lesbians aren't [there]]
    L  [@ (.)]
-------------------------------------------------------------------------
 9  S  [There was a it was a sixties] and seventies things wasn't it
    C  [ones I he::ard about]                            [Yea::h]
    J                                                    [There] were
-------------------------------------------------------------------------
10  S                        [[Yes there were.]]
    C         [I did- I didn't] [[know any of them]] personally obviously being
    J  a lot in [the seventies.]
-------------------------------------------------------------------------
11  S            [Mm]           [@ (1)]
    C  a (.) small [child] then that [@ (1)] you would you would you would re::ad
    H                               [@ (2)]
    L                               [@ (.)]
-------------------------------------------------------------------------
12  C  about them and and think (.) yeah   political les- that's the same
    H                                 @ (.)
-------------------------------------------------------------------------
13  S                                       [Yeah]
    C  thing isn't it/                     [I am] [such] a feminist
    H               /but there were political lesbians [yeah]
    J                                                  [Yeah]
-------------------------------------------------------------------------
14  S                                    [mm]
    C  I- I (.) am [gonna be a lesbian]                        And and
    H            [reject men and-]      [mm]
    J                                   [whether they] are or not
-------------------------------------------------------------------------
15  C  they're all straight now obviously aren't they because you know you
-------------------------------------------------------------------------
16  S              [<@ That's not tru::e @>]
    C  can't really [you you can't fa::ke it] No you can't fake it if
-------------------------------------------------------------------------
17  C  the only reason you were were a [lesbian]
    E                                  [Course you can fake it darling @ (.)]
    L                                  [It's not is it about is it is it about]
-------------------------------------------------------------------------
```

```
-------------------------------------------------------------------------------
18  C                                                      Well
    H                                                            sticking to
    L  faking it or is it about just (.) making a choice and (.)
-------------------------------------------------------------------------------
19  S                        [Some people think you can make a] choice
    C    pe::rsonally (.) [I wouldn't wanna be like you know]    no (.) havi-
    H  it
-------------------------------------------------------------------------------
20  C  having had no choice (1) I would be horrified to think that somebody had
-------------------------------------------------------------------------------
21  C  chosen
    E                                                      [It's just
    H         But some people might think I don't want to be:: [in this role
-------------------------------------------------------------------------------
22  E  choosing (.) it's your choice.]
    H  (.) and everything that society] says that goes with it    that it
    J                                                      Yeah
-------------------------------------------------------------------------------
23  S                              Mm
    E                              Well I-/
    H  imposes upon me by being this.        /And therefore I'm going to be
    J                              Mm
-------------------------------------------------------------------------------
24  H  lesbian and therefore I don't have to go along with [the::se]
    J                                            [Yes] but conver::sely
-------------------------------------------------------------------------------
25  C           Yeah I would [love to have-]                  [I would
    H  [entrapment]
    J  [there are]              [there are women] who who have perhaps [been
-------------------------------------------------------------------------------
26  C  love to have been] straight
    J  attracted towards lesbianism] and then backed off because they knew of
-------------------------------------------------------------------------------
27  H                                                          [True]
    J  all the social pressures that would be involved in that I mean I'm [su-]
-------------------------------------------------------------------------------
28  C                                                          Yeah
    E                        [[I think that]] works [out] the other way too
    H  [the other way]                              [Yes]
    J  [I've certainly] known [[women like that]
-------------------------------------------------------------------------------
29  C                        If I had a straight cell in my body I would
    E  [You can stay in the closet]
    H  [It works the other way yeah]
-------------------------------------------------------------------------------
30  C  be strai::ght I mean why would-/
    J                                      Life is much much
    L                        /Life would be easier
-------------------------------------------------------------------------------
31  S           [Mm]    [Mm]                      Mm
    C  [you bother] [@(.)] [go]ing to all this effort?
    J  [easier]                              Yeah (.) much
-------------------------------------------------------------------------------
```

```
-----------------------------------------------------------------------
32  C          /so the thought that somebody would like give up that easy life
    J  easier/
-----------------------------------------------------------------------

33  S  (.) but they did                        [[and actually-]]
    C                  [yeah but I don't-]
    L                  [But but then but] then [[some people]] b- but some people
-----------------------------------------------------------------------

34  L  see it much more as a choice than others don't they some people genuinely
-----------------------------------------------------------------------

35  L  see it as     (.) as it was it was a it was a choice or or or- or:: or that
-----------------------------------------------------------------------

36  L  or that they have an option that they don't have to make a choice or::
-----------------------------------------------------------------------

37  S  [yep my-]                                                    My ex
    L  [it wasn't] a choice so I think it probably varies for everybody.
-----------------------------------------------------------------------

38  S  regarded it as a choice.                                   [@ (3)]
    C                                                             [@ (3)]
    E                           I think it's a natural (1) talent.
    H                                                             [@ (3)]
    J                          Mm.                                [@ (3)]
    L                          Mm                                 [@ (3)]
-----------------------------------------------------------------------
```

Given Claire's results in the finger test, it is perhaps understandable that she is so active in constructing a normative lesbianism here, one which she plainly endeavours to align herself with. Her stance is most evident in line 29, where she refers to having not one 'straight cell' in her body. She clearly implies, here, that her (homo)sexuality is biological and predetermined, and directly contradicts the category that she adopted in her earlier alignment of herself with the labels 'Girl' and 'female', based upon her supposedly biological heterosexuality (see Interaction 5.2). The difference between her previous construction of self and that which she creates in this moment (only a few minutes later) is characterised by her shift from mock distress ('oh my God, look how girly I am': Interaction 5.2, lines 14–15) to the more serious style used here in establishing a new persona: the 'political lesbian'. As with the construction of the personae Dyke and Girl, and even the identity positions 'self-respecting lesbian' or 'proper butch' (Interaction 6.1), this temporally specific persona is made real in this moment as it allows the group to align themselves with or against it. In doing so, they may engage in identity work and project (through negotiation and definition of that persona) an authentic Stomper self. Whilst Hannah introduces this concept in order to tentatively align herself with the persona, Claire's role in this extract is to deauthenticate it and construct a normative lesbian in opposition to it. This reveals much about the conflicting ideologies surrounding homosexuality within the group, as well as the dynamics within the CoP. Below, the construction of a normative lesbian is considered in relation to the emergence of the coherent persona 'political lesbian', before Claire's self-positioning and construction of authenticity in relation to this persona are analysed in more depth.

8.2.1   Constructing and deauthenticating the 'political lesbian'

From the beginning of this interaction, it is clear that the concept of choosing one's sexuality, introduced by Hannah, is contestable and taboo. This is evident from the mitigation preceding her assertion, which she describes as a 'very old fashioned comment' (line 1). This alludes to Hannah's age and implies that her comment may be irrelevant to some at the table; although she was no older than Sam, Eve or Jill, she *was* of an older generation than both Claire and me. This seems to justify her making a statement with which others may disagree, and also allows her to distance herself from the remark. This highlights the controversial nature of her statement, as does the use of 'some people', the third-person 'they' and the hedging of 'may have' (line 2). The result of this distancing serves to protect Hannah's alignment with the rest of the Stompers, but also requires the women to ascertain what sort of 'people' she is referring to.

Before Claire begins to take the floor, Eve challenges Hannah's statement in line 4. By this point, Hannah's claim that some people might have chosen their sexuality based on practicalities such as contraception has been supported by Sam ('oh yes certainly', line 3). Eve challenges this notion by ventriloquating the persona through the use of the first person: 'What, I wanna be a lesbian 'cause I don't get pregnant when I (.) fuck other women?' The rising question intonation and the use of 'what' to construct the turn as an interrogative illustrate the sarcastic and doubting nature of Eve's turn, and the use of the expletive 'fuck' (unusual in the CoP, as implied by Eve's pause before saying it) shows this to be a challenge. The use of sarcasm and taboo language creates a provocative, combative and direct question which is challenging to Hannah's positive face (as it threatens the credibility of her statement) and negative face (as she is required to respond). The laughter in Hannah's affirmative response and in Eve's subsequent rejection of the notion as unlikely (lines 5–6) creates a more light-hearted tone, however.

At this point in the interaction, Claire supports Hannah by suggesting that such women did exist, using 'but' to contradict Eve (line 6) and describing them as 'political lesbians' (a term mirrored as a question by Eve in line 7). Jill and Sam then take the opportunity to position themselves as authoritative Stompers by articulating their knowledge of lesbian feminists in line 8, competing for the floor and (as in Interactions 7.1 and 7.2) revealing the value behind the expression of such knowledge. This is evident from the fact that both women use the evaluative 'well' at the beginning of their turns in line 8, indexing a knowledgeable persona. Both also show an interesting use of tag questions (Jill: 'well there are political lesbians, aren't there', line 8; Sam: 'it was a sixties and seventies thing wasn't it', line 9). The use of a tag question here reduces the dogmatic tone of their turns and thus reduces the threat to Eve's positive face, as they both essentially position her as, compared to them, lacking in knowledge. As with data which has been used by Moore and Podesva (2007), these examples seem to illustrate the conducive function of tag questions. In line with Hudson's (1975) analysis of tags as carrying the sincerity condition of both a declarative and a question, Moore and Podesva (2007: 458) illustrate that tag questions not only prompt interlocutors to agree but also encourage a response in line with the stance of the speaker. The apparent function of Jill and Sam's turns is not to challenge Eve, therefore, but to allow her the opportunity to articulate some agreement with them and therefore show a shared knowledge of the subject. This illustrates the Stompers' concern to maintain cohesiveness and sameness through the adequation of that which contradicts it.

The positioning of 'political lesbians' as a concept from the past (as opposed to the present day) is cooperatively achieved through Jill's mirroring of Sam's stressed word 'seventies' in line 10, and Sam's subsequent mirroring of Jill's past tense 'there were' with the affirmative 'yes there were'. It is clear that the concept of 'political lesbian' has been coherently constructed and given a meaningful definition (a woman who made a feminist-oriented choice to be a lesbian) by this point, and it is at this moment (from line 13) that Claire begins to take this in a specific direction, one which serves to deauthenticate the persona. The Stompers' construction of authentic lesbianism as matching the cultural ideal of a gender-inverted woman is taken to the extreme at this point, as Claire implies that a 'political lesbian' is an improbable and ultimately illegitimate phenomenon. By premodifying 'lesbian' with the adjective 'political', given that 'lesbian' can stand alone as a concrete noun, Claire (who, of course, first presented this as a definable persona) positions the lesbian in question as merely partial, as *defined* by her politics. Rather than adding an extra quality to the noun, by stating that the lesbian was also political (already an expectation in the Stompers, as shown in the previous chapter), Claire's premodification here constructs this as a person who is a lesbian *because of her politics*.

In line 11, Claire contrasts the persona with the first person in order to present herself in opposition to political lesbians, seemingly reflecting her desire to mark out her age difference (evident by her claim that she was a 'small child' during the 1970s, line 11). This is supported by her use of oppositional personal pronouns in line 10, whereby she sets up a clear contrast between 'them' and her (via her use of the pronoun 'I'): 'I didn't know any of them personally'). Stressing the word 'personally' also clearly places her as different and unconnected to these political lesbians. Her motivation in doing this becomes clear from her turn in line 15, where she claims that 'they're all straight now obviously'. Though Sam contradicts Claire in line 16, she does so in a way which implies that she does not believe that Claire is being serious; she laughs throughout the declarative statement which challenges Claire ('that's not true'). Claire's shift from hedging ('you know', 'really') in lines 15 and 16 to a firm, declarative statement that 'you can't fake it [lesbianism]' by the end of her turn in line 16, however, illustrates that she is not joking or being sarcastic. At this point, the tone of the interaction seems to shift from jokes about Claire's youthfulness and humorous alignments of political lesbians with unrealistic, hypothetical figures, to a serious account of whether one *can* be a lesbian by choice.

Eve's humorous comment that you can 'fake it' in line 17 attempts to make light of Claire's claim; alongside the use of 'darling' to index a superficial or false character, she presents the idea that one cannot be a lesbian for political reasons (because one cannot pretend to have a given sexual desire or orientation) as laughable – one *can* pretend. At the same time, Sam, Hannah and I attempt to cooperatively construct the notion that it *is* possible for a woman to choose to be a lesbian (lines 17–19), directly engaging with this idea. It is noteworthy that, at this point, the idea of choice is in the present tense, as the position of the 'political lesbian' has moved from being a 'seventies' phenomenon to a person who may currently make the choice to be a lesbian. At this point, we see Claire refusing to accept that this might be a possibility; she uses her own personal experience, which she positions as being normative, to engage in the tactic of illegitimation, deauthenticating the constructed persona in line 20 by claiming that she 'would be <u>horrified</u> to think that somebody had <u>chosen'</u> to be gay. By not only using emotive language to express the shock that she would feel at such a discovery (indicating the non-normative nature of it) but also using a conditional structure to imply that it was something that *might* happen rather than *does* or *has* happened, Claire clearly positions the notion of sexuality-by-choice as directly oppositional to her own sense of reality, and of her identity. Furthermore, she articulates her own interpretation of her sexuality most vehemently in line 29, positioning it as biological when she argues that, if she had a 'straight cell' in her body, she would choose to be heterosexual rather than gay.

At this moment, the very notion of authenticity as a Stomper has shifted entirely. Typically in the women's interaction, ideological notions of lesbian normativity were constructed based on changeable practices and styles. The women could choose whether or not to wear make-up, shave their legs, drink pints or half-pints or use an iron, and in this sense the Stomper category that the women usually indexed was based on authentic *practice*. What Claire invokes here, however, goes beyond CoP or individual styles. It clearly positions sexuality as a product of nature. Whilst this is an individual stance to take (as illustrated by her second use of 'personally' in line 19 and description of *herself* as 'having had no choice' in line 20), the women's reaction to it, detailed below, reveals much about the possibility of contradictions and challenges in this group as well as the circumstances under which individual variation may be erased for the sake of homogeneous stance.

8.2.2 The construction of homogeneity

Up until line 19, Jill and Sam make a particular effort to distance themselves from the persona of 'political lesbian' by using the third person to refer to 'them', but nonetheless offer an alternative perspective to that put forward by Claire, justifying the existence of such women. Once Claire remarks that she would be heterosexual if she felt she could be, however, the women shift from arguing that such a phenomenon exists to ultimately agreeing with Claire that it would be easier to be this way, with Jill echoing my comment in line 30: 'Life would be easier' (Author); 'Life is <u>much</u> much easier' (Jill). At this moment, the interaction shifts to align with Claire. Though not overtly mirroring her views and agreeing that 'political lesbians' are in some way inauthentic, it is ultimately agreed that life would be less complicated if one matched the heteronormative ideal. My own turn in lines 33–37 demonstrates an attempt to articulate a compromise between the view of Claire and (what I suspected to be) the views of Jill and Hannah. Despite the fact that both Jill and Hannah described themselves as political, and appeared to express understanding with women whose sociopolitical experiences had led to their identification as lesbians in this interaction, at no point in this interaction did either woman overtly align *herself* with the 'political lesbian' persona. This would seem to be a direct result of Claire's negative evaluation of it, as to align oneself with it would be to take on an inauthentic role within this moment.

Though it has already been suggested, through the analyses in this book, that one may take on a negative identity position and yet maintain authenticity (such as Claire in the finger test, for example), it is clear that to align with the political lesbian persona in this moment, given the way that it had been constructed, would have been impossible. This is apparent from Hannah's ceasing talk and Jill's abandoning of her defence in lines 29–30. At this point, it seems that a dichotomy has been created whereby one is either biologically lesbian *or* has chosen to be lesbian, and to align with the political lesbian persona would be to remove oneself from the opposing (unspoken) category of 'biological lesbian'. This is evident from Claire's repeated construction of 'them' in comparison to herself, who has no 'straight cells' in her body. This foregrounds the meaning behind the mutually constructed Dyke. The Stompers' authentication of culturally prevalent lesbian styles was based on the way in which they rejected traditional femininity, invoking cultural notions of inverted gender and reinforcing this through their articulation of what it meant to be a Dyke as opposed to a Girl. Furthermore, it has been shown that this is a consequence of the women's construction of authentic lesbianism in opposition to heteronormative femaleness. To be biologically 'different' would tie into broader cultural notions of gender inversion, and to have been born homosexual would clearly be the most authentic type of lesbian; it directly opposes a woman who has the ability to choose (to be lesbian or, presumably, to be straight). As with the rejection of bisexuals for engaging in heteronormative acts in Section 5.1, a woman who *could* be straight should inevitably be classed as illegitimate within this ideological system.

In addition to the logic that emerges as a result of the women's broader interaction together as a CoP and their shared construction of authentic Dykeyness, another reason that the political lesbian persona cannot be positively aligned with at this point is because of the weight behind Claire's assertion. Claire is the only member of the group at this moment who defines her own experience and sexual orientation, and it appears that this contributes to her more powerful position. Her stance is not shaken or altered throughout the interaction, whereas the other women abandon their own agendas in light of it. Claire's assumption about her interlocutors' personal definitions of their sexuality is striking; by insinuating that it is abnormal and wrong to have a lesbian lifestyle due to some political belief, Claire creates a situation whereby any woman actually orienting to this definition would have to either take a combative stance or remain silent. Despite their attempts to justify and explain the existence of such lesbianism, the distancing tactics and lack of personal identification with the persona that the other women are defending leave Claire ultimately unchallenged in her claims about political lesbians in this interaction.

It is interesting, however, that it is only Claire that overtly negatively evaluates the political lesbian identity. The other women's decision not to do so suggests that they might, in fact, view the 'ideal' Dyke and her corresponding butch styles as merely ideological and culturally constructed – as socially situated rather than biologically preordained. Claire's difference from the rest of the group is starkly illustrated in this moment as a result, as her view seems to become dominant due to her personal identification with it. The nature of Claire's stance, the weight behind the notion that butch styles are more authentic, and the emotion that is displayed in this moment seemingly combine to prevent Claire's stance from being challenged. This illustrates that stances may sometimes come to index a CoP identity in a way which has less to do with mutual or cooperative negotiation, and more to do with the authority or power behind the person who has made it. It was also unusual to see the women talk so personally about their own feelings or about something which defined their sexuality; as has been outlined throughout this book, the women's shared sexuality was usually assumed rather than directly articulated. Claire's forthright assertion about her own sexual orientation, therefore, may explain the other women's decision not to directly challenge her stance, and to ultimately find a way to show some agreement with her. In her analysis of two speakers constructing their respective ethnicities through their interaction, Schilling-Estes (2004: 183) demonstrates that awkward moments in conversation may be 'smoothed over' via the use of linguistic or discursive devices which show similarities between the speakers. This is evident here; the moment at the end of this extract, where Jill, Sam and I agree with Claire's claim that heterosexuality would be an 'easy life' (line 29), illustrates our desire to accommodate her views by aligning ourselves with an aspect of them with which we could agree. This also illustrates the tactic of adequation, as the differences potentially damaging to the group's sense of homogeneity are erased (Bucholtz and Hall 2005: 599).

Though she is the only one to strongly articulate her stance against the 'political lesbian' persona, Claire's distinctive view is also more relevant to the CoP ethos, as discussed above. Had Claire's view *not* linked to the general ethos of the group, it may have been *her* sole stance, rather than that of the other women, that was adequated in order to create a shared view. This reveals that, whilst similarity and agreement are presented as an imperative for CoP membership by critics of the concept, who argue that it cannot allow for difference (see Davies 2005: 576, for example), an ethnographic understanding of a CoP may reveal, as this analysis has done, that not every stance must be engaged with and agreed upon by every member. Rather, all group members must understand and relate to the general ethos of the group (in this case, that lesbians are *different* from straight women and that femininity marks out this difference) and mutually negotiate their way around the other important facets of the value system without damaging an individual's status irreparably. The complex range of stances and the construction of an inauthentic persona within this interaction illustrate that a group identity must be constantly renegotiated in light of new ideals which are presented, and that this may involve the erasure or adequation of individual differences.

8.3   Concluding remarks

Although their interactions are clearly governed by definable boundaries related to the gendered binary of Dyke and Girl, the last two analysis chapters have demonstrated that the Stomper women's mutual negotiation of a coherent identity also revolved around their relationship with feminism. Furthermore, they have shown that the Stomper construction of shared authenticity did not necessarily negate their ability to construct an *independently* authentic self. This has been shown to be dependent on their level of engagement with the group. For example, divergence from a constructed and mutually negotiated norm was apparently acceptable in this group only if that divergence could be justified within the boundaries of the Stomper ethos. In this sense, a woman taking stances towards a negative identity position, even one which was temporarily so, must have shown a clear understanding of what it meant to be a member of the CoP by claiming identities which did *not* detract from its core philosophy at other times. Furthermore, an individual Stomper evidently *could* be removed from the authentic persona under construction by expressing their difference on some more fundamental level, transcending the CoP boundaries, but would only maintain *authentic* status as a Stomper if they were already an established member. The data above has shown that CoPs must embody differences and, at times, negotiate their way around them – their members are individuals with idiosyncratic views, practices and ideas, and these may be accommodated as well as challenged.

This chapter has shown that Stomper identity was continuously renegotiated through the redefinition of identity positions within the group. Members contributed to the construction of new or alternative meanings within the CoP by drawing on that which bound them together. In the cases presented above, it has been shown that their assumed experiences as middle-aged, middle-class lesbians led to the women's use of feminism as a symbol for the construction of their identity. Typically, Claire has been shown to have been the anomaly in the group's definition of authenticity with regard to their relationship to politics; her difference in terms of her age has been foregrounded as the main reason for this. Without her disruption of the women's construction of a feminist-related identity, it seems feasible to suggest that the Stompers may have had less reason to negotiate the meaning of personae such as 'political lesbian' and categories such as 'feminist'. Her conflicting roles in the interactions above, however, highlight the fact that broader categories do not have the same meaning for all people; they are reproduced in interaction and are, therefore, continuously redefined.

An understanding of the context in which the interactions presented in this chapter occurred has once again been shown to be crucial for an in-depth analysis. The significance of feminism to some of the women (because of their shared history or presumed engagement in the women's movement due to their age and sexual orientation) and its lack of relevance to Claire (reflecting her coming of age at a different moment in time) have been outlined in order to explain their conflicting perspectives on the relationship of politics to lesbianism. Furthermore, Claire's concern to position herself as youthful, illustrated in both interactions in this chapter, has been evidenced throughout this book from her more typical engagement with the women, whereby she regularly positioned them as comparatively old. Fundamentally, however, the importance of the Stompers' overall rejection of heteronormative femininity has been shown to directly impact on the success of Claire's lone stance in the final extract; without an understanding of why anti-feminine, butch styles were so intrinsic to the authentic Dyke persona, it would be difficult to interpret the other women's erasure of their own, initially opposing, stances as anything more than an eagerness to appear homogeneous. As it is, the women's mutual rejection of heteronormative womanhood and their embrace of a queer identity rather inevitably led to their rejection of a lesbianism of 'choice'.

The following chapters will consider the implications of the analyses presented in this book on how we understand CoPs, in terms of their membership and the identities which are formed within them. In Chapter 9, the Stomper group will be considered from the perspective of the CoP approach, with the prevalence of broader cultural ideologies on their local stances and interactive roles outlined in relation to sociocultural linguistics – the theoretical framework which has shaped the discourse analysis in this book. In Chapter 10, the significance of the women's use of gendered personae and their negative evaluation of roles traditionally associated with womanhood will be considered and evaluated in relation to our understanding of language and sexuality. In particular, it will aim to deal with the potential contradiction that can be viewed in a group which is typically defined as 'feminist' yet also rejects femininity and ultimately reproduces binary gender.

9
Understanding Communities of Practice

In the analyses presented in the previous four chapters, the local cultural context within which each interaction occurred has been outlined and positioned as central to the reading of the various interactive moves made by the Sapphic Stomper women. The conversation taking place at that time, the relationships between the women present and the significance of the topics raised and views expressed have all been considered in order to explain the indexical meaning of the stances taken. In this way, the necessity of an ethnographic framework for the analysis of interactive constructions of identity has been demonstrated. The CoP described and explored in this book was one with its own norms, values, ethos and expectations, and making sense of how its members attached meaning to its practices has required an understanding of each of these aspects of the group. In order to understand why the Stomper women evaluated such practices as wearing make-up or skirts in a negative way (as in Section 6.1), for example, or why they positioned bisexuality as somehow inauthentic (such as in Section 5.2.2.2), or what subtle indexical links were made to broader queer culture through the claiming of the label 'Dyke' (see Chapters 5 and 6), it was essential to also understand what it meant to be a Sapphic Stomper. Through the ethnographic methodology described in Chapter 4, an insight into this was achieved.

Viewing a group such as the Sapphic Stompers as a CoP (rather than as simply a collective or a network) has also enabled the analyses presented in this book. Interpreting the Stomper women's regular engagement together as a vehicle for the construction of shared, meaningful practices has allowed for a clear view of what is authentic in the group. This is considered in depth in this chapter, alongside a consideration of how this particular CoP may differ in its structure and organisation from those observed in previous sociolinguistic research, in order to evaluate the CoP approach in light of the experiences with the Stompers detailed in this book.

9.1   Authenticity in a community of practice

The analyses presented in the previous chapters are based on inter-pretations made whilst in the ethnographic field, and in this sense represent just one perspective. Yet the perceptions made have been facilitated by participant observation, a role which requires an under-standing of how one should take part in key CoP practices, and they carry value as a result. In the case of this research with the Stompers, my status as a participant led to a complex process whereby I went some way towards gaining 'authentic Stomper' status. As a participant in the activities that the core members of the Stomper group engaged in for a 15-month period, one could argue that I also became a member of the group. Certainly, as argued in Section 4.2.2, I was encouraged to lead a hike (a core Stomper activity) and my attendance at Stomper events was facilitated by the other women. To some extent, therefore, I became an apprentice in the CoP, learning how to be a Stomper through my engagement in Stomper practices. In this way, I observed how meaning was made and identities negotiated, and acquired an understanding of what mattered to the women (and, more importantly, what they presented and perceived as mattering to them). In this sense, I had some validity, beyond my status as a researcher, to be present during Stomper meetings. On the other hand, however, my agenda as an ethnographer meant that I could not engage with the group objec-tively and that they were unlikely to view me as an impartial member of the group. It is highly likely that there were events that I was not invited to, discussions I was not privy to, and that my apprenticeship had certain conditions that I was not aware of. Though I may not have been truly *equal*, however, I was certainly exposed to the typical prac-tice of the group for a long enough period to enable me to learn how to project a Stomper identity, and what that identity entailed. In other words, I was able to perform a level of authenticity shared, recognised and negotiated by the Stomper women. I was able to take stances which reflected the typical ethos of the group towards concepts which I knew to have particular ideological resonance with the women, either in terms of their own CoP-specific group norms and ideals, or in terms of their demographic as middle-class, politically oriented, middle-aged lesbians. I could, therefore, perform a Stomper identity. Whether or not this meant that I could be truly 'authentic', of course, is a more complex issue.

As discussed in Section 2.4, authenticity – rather than referring to some innate trait or characteristic which makes one 'real' – is perhaps best equated with the concept of 'legitimacy'. To be a legitimate member of a CoP, one might argue, a participant must engage convincingly in practices which are recognised and valued by CoP members. This reflects the concept of legitimate peripheral participation as provided by Lave and Wenger (1991: 29), who argue that those on the periphery of a CoP become full members of it (gain legitimacy) by engaging with, thus participating in, the practices of the group. For Lave and Wenger, this concerns the learning of knowledgeable skills, but for the purposes of identity construction, we may reinterpret this as the learning of how to project a 'real' CoP-specific identity. In the case of the Stompers, this has been shown to encompass the negotiation of what is a 'real' lesbian, a 'real' hiker and a 'real' feminist. In other words, the negotiation of what *counts* is what enables the negotiation of what is *legitimate* within the group, in turn facilitating the construction of an *authentic* Stomper self. By moving from the status of a peripheral member – as I began, not yet able to engage in practices and styles thought of as legitimate by the group – to that of a full member who does engage in legitimate practice, one is able to gradually perform identities which are meaningful and recognisable to that particular CoP. Perhaps most important in this process, as will be considered in more depth in the following chapter, is the development of an understanding of what the CoP is *not*. In the case of the Stompers, for example, understanding what a 'real' lesbian was to them – through their embrace of the Dyke persona – required an equal understanding of why and how the group rejected the Girl persona. The process of authentication often occurs in contrast or opposition to other recognisable identity positions and, in this sense, a CoP identity may be made 'real' via the construction of someone or something else as 'artificial'.

For a CoP member to acquire authenticity, then, they need to learn about what is inauthentic. This can only be achieved through their engagement with the CoP, their informed interpretation of their practices, and their understanding of what other CoP members are doing. However, this presupposes that an individual has access to a given CoP (such as the Stompers) and can, therefore, engage in the construction of an authentic persona (such as a Dyke). Without this, they will be unable to engage in authentic identity construction. The potential restrictions and issues in the CoP approach which are associated with this issue of access are considered, below.

9.1.1   Doing authenticity in a community of practice

In order to achieve membership of a CoP which, in turn, allows the construction of an identity which is recognised as authentic and legitimate within that group, it has been argued above that one must engage in the practices of the CoP. By doing so, one will gradually learn the meaning of those practices and, therefore, what is valued by the other members; one will gain legitimacy as a peripheral participant, and then gradually become a full member. This enables the performance of a salient identity. It has been shown in the previous chapters that such Stomper practices ranged from hiking with specialised, expensive equipment to avoiding taboo language; these practices could be quickly adopted upon being observed. The practice of appropriate stance-taking towards particular core ideologies was more complex and took longer to develop an understanding of, but again was accessible to those who shared some fundamental demographic aspects with the typical Stomper (such as sexual orientation or age) and who engaged regularly with the group in their hikes. In this sense, the CoP framework, whereby one may learn to project a specific social identity as a result of mutual engagement in shared practice, is reflected in the Stomper group.

It has been argued, however, that the CoP is not a framework which can accommodate the analysis of speakers that do not fit the mould. Gee (2005: 590), for example, argues that some predetermined match must be made between a potential member and the CoP they wish to join, and that in this sense the CoP cannot explain how speakers who do not match the demographics of a group can develop the tools required to construct a CoP identity. Yet, as has been shown to be the case throughout this book, every woman in the Stomper group was assumed to align with the lesbian identity category irrespective of their personal orientation outside of the group or their individual style. In this sense, a woman who did *not* match the typical demographic of the group could still participate in it, so long as they could perform an appropriate identity initially. It may be argued, as a consequence of this, that a CoP is fundamentally dynamic and that all identities associated with it are performative – this includes the 'type' of person expected to join it. Rather than view potential and actual CoP members as a homogeneous unit, therefore, the CoP ought to be perceived as able to cope with diversity and heterogeneity (as will be discussed later in this chapter). This is not to suggest, however, that simply anybody has the opportunity to join any CoP – clearly, there are restrictions. For the Stompers, a potential member was expected to be female-bodied and gay, as the group was exclusively lesbian. One could argue that this fact meant that this group was restrictive, as men and heterosexual women were prevented from being a part of it, but those with any desire to join the group (who, one would assume, would be lesbians) *would* be able to become a peripheral member relatively easily. In much the same way as a CoP of musicians would only welcome musicians, or a group of cyclists would only welcome those interested in cycling, a community such as the Stompers have to have some prerequisites in who joins them. Indeed, this reflects the order and structure of society; we are categorised and categorise ourselves according to that which we have in common.

If we assume that individuals approach CoPs which are relevant and desirable to them, the next question is one of how the process outlined above – whereby initial engagement allows status as a legitimate peripheral participant – actually occurs. Certainly, Davies (2005: 567) argues that the current, available explanation of how non-members become members is insufficient. She posits that non-members cannot learn the meaning behind CoP engagement unless they have access to the practices of a group, but that they cannot gain access to those practices unless they understand their meaning. In this sense, being a peripheral participant does not necessarily enable the acquisition of practices unless an individual is granted some legitimacy and provided access to them (2005: 569). Though Davies's point suggests that, in order to become a peripheral member of a group and thus begin to make sense of the practices within it, one must be *awarded* legitimacy, with the Stompers this was not the case. Fundamentally, if a woman was homosexual in orientation, she had the right to join the group, at least as a peripheral member. This *right* is the legitimacy referred to by Davies and, in the Stompers, came about as a result of, firstly, their motivation to join the CoP and, secondly, a degree of commonality between an individual and the other Stompers. A peripheral participant of a lesbian hiking group would need to identify and position herself as a lesbian who was interested in walking, thus matching the basic criteria of the CoP (as indicated above). To move from this status towards full membership, she would then need to refer to wider lesbian culture in order to make sense of the practices with which she was beginning to engage, and then play a role in reproducing or reworking prevalent discourses from within that culture. Simply put, there would be nothing to prevent her from joining the group and engaging in the same practices as the other members, but the desire to be a part of that group would motivate her choice of whether she moved to full membership, and her ability to do so would depend on the appropriateness and relevance of the CoP to her. If an individual does not engage with the broader cultural context associated with a CoP, they will not be able to produce the shared identity of that group. Just as an individual needed to be a student at Belten High in order to be a Belten High Jock or Burnout (Eckert 2000), so a legitimate Stomper needed to engage with lesbian culture. 'Legitimacy', therefore, should be considered as an agentive concept; it is not *awarded*, it is established via the seeking out or finding of a *relevant* CoP and the *projection* of a core identity, an identity which acts as a prerequisite for joining the group such as, in this case, being a lesbian. To jointly construct a meaningful identity as a *group*, on the other hand, is a more nuanced process, one which is fundamentally collaborative and which involves the negotiation and reworking of both local and global norms and ideals. A discussion of this process, in relation to the Stompers, is provided below.

9.1.2   Authenticity as a negotiated concept

The analyses provided in this book have shown that the Stompers typically reworked cultural practices stereotypical of lesbianism in order to index the lesbian category via two personae – one which was inauthentic (Girl) and one which was authentic (Dyke). The women have been shown to have negotiated their way around a range of stereo-types specific to lesbian culture, assigning some a 'real' status; Hannah's positioning of Eve as a 'real, proper butch' in Section 6.2.2 is an example of this. Furthermore, on occasion, they ultimately permitted some practices which could initially be classed as Girly and thus inauthentic due to their links with heterosexual womanhood (such as the wearing of skirts in Chapter 6). This illustrates that authenticity as a Dyke was not static, and that new interpretations could contradict old ones if the consensus of an interaction required it. The constant renegotiation of the Dyke and Girl personae, and the Stompers' ability to align with both authentic and *in*authentic identity positions, therefore, reveal the fluid nature of their identity construction.

What is apparent from the continuous, flexible negotiation of authenticity shown in the Stomper group is that the process of identity construction must be viewed as dialogic; one individual alone cannot create a norm or an identity position. Indeed, jointly established patterns of engagement are considered to be staples of CoP membership (Holmes and Meyerhoff 1999: 176), and it is clear from the data presented here that a CoP must mutually construct their shared ethos and the stances which index their membership (and, therefore, the authentic identities which emerge from it). However, it is also apparent that the practices used to do this may vary. For example, it has been shown here that CoP members can construct the same aspect of group identity (such as a persona) through a variety of different interactive tactics, indicating that it is the meaning constructed rather than the tools used to attain that meaning that must be shared and mutually understood by CoP members. As argued by Bucholtz and Hall (2008: 406) and shown in the chapters of this book, a focus on the momentary dynamics of language use or stance enables an understanding of this. In Section 7.2, for instance, the women used a range of interactive tactics to present themselves as intellectual and politically aware. Whilst Jill was mocking of Hannah, for example, Eve was provocative through the use of explicit terminology such as 'penetration'. In this sense, different means may be employed in order to achieve the same identity goal.

The negotiation of meaning by CoP members has also been shown to occur in unpredictable ways through the data and analysis provided in this book. In addition to the Stomper women's employment of multiple tactics which allowed them to construct personae which they then aligned themselves with or against through stance-taking, they have been shown to frequently engage in unpredictable identity practices. For example, the use of negative identity positioning, whereby interlocutors place themselves or others in an ironic position which is recognised within the group to be inconsistent with what is typically recognised as authentic, has illustrated that authenticity is never static. Instead, it is a changing, constructed notion which reflects that which is valued by a CoP. For a speaker such as Claire, in Section 5.2.2.1, to adopt a persona (a Girl) which is fundamentally opposed to that which is typically constructed as authentic (a Dyke) in the group, yet still maintain her authenticity as a CoP member, it is evident that – at least in the case of the Stompers – what is authentic in a CoP is not necessarily set in stone. Though, in this particular example, this ironic move did lead to the claiming of a more predictable, authentic identity, it nevertheless reveals that the means by which such a persona might be achieved can be playful, and that the ideologies being invoked may be parodied. In this sense, identity construction should be viewed as an agentive process, rather than as something which is predefined or which, in and of itself, constrains an individual. It also reveals that identity is a performance, and highlights the importance of understanding the intersubjective nature of interaction. These issues will be considered in more depth in the final chapter.

In addition to the varying methods used in negotiating and constructing what is 'authentic' in a CoP, the data in this book has also revealed the ways in which a CoP can manage a lack of consistency or harmony between its members. The following section will review the Stompers' differences and moments of disagreement in order to demonstrate the ability of the CoP in housing heterogeneity, before this chapter goes on to acknowledge and consider the idiosyncratic nature of this CoP in relation to the broader field.

9.2   Heterogeneity in a community of practice

Whilst Chapters 5 and 6 showed how the Stomper women drew on their shared experiences and expectations about what it meant to be a lesbian, jointly constructing the salient personae of Dyke and Girl and working together to attach meaning to those personae, Chapters 7 and 8 revealed a more complicated system within the CoP. Though the demographic differences between them did not always appear to be relevant, such as the fact of Claire's relative youth, during certain interactions it became particularly evident that the variation amongst the women often had to be addressed. Similarly, when conversations emerged that illustrated the women's alternative perspectives and revealed initially competing stances, such as during the discussion about skirts, shaving and ironing (Chapter 6), the Stompers had to find ways of dealing with this variation. CoPs tend to be hypothetically positioned as reflecting similarity rather than difference and consistently working towards the construction of that similarity, given that they are ultimately constructed through collective styles which alter in line with the contribution of its members (Eckert and Wenger 2005: 584). In this sense, it may be assumed that CoP practices alter in order to fit the individuals within that group, and that CoP members will do all that they can to adequate any variation for the sake of a homogeneous identity. This has been shown to be the case at times in the analyses in this book but, as shown in the later analysis chapters, it was not always possible to erase the differences between the women. The following section considers the ways in which the members of this particular CoP managed the heterogeneity between them by negotiating the boundaries of their difference according to the needs of the particular moment in time.

9.2.1   Heterogeneity: the disruption of boundaries?

Although the women in the Stomper CoP had many similarities between them, typically in terms of their background, at times their interactions revealed a struggle to maintain cohesion due to apparent differences between them with regard to their politics. Far from weakening the CoP structure, differences such as those expressed in Section 8.1, whereby the women debated and defined what feminism was as a result of Claire's claim that she was 'too young to be a feminist', actually reveal that difference may exist within a CoP without directly affecting the overall ethos of the group or the behaviour of others within it. In this sense, individuals will not *always* have an impact on group practices and ideologies. If we consider Claire's claim in this interaction, it is apparent that differences between members may be *absorbed* as well as being simply *erased*. It seems that a consistent understanding of what matters most as a group – in the case of the Stompers, a love of hiking and an awareness of a 'butch is best' ideal, both factors emphasised by Claire in her other interactions – is enough to override moments of disagreement or instability. Though Claire rejected an identity which the other women perceived as being central to the group, in other words, her consistent engagement in authentic identity construction at other moments allowed her to maintain her authentic status.

Claire has been repeatedly foregrounded in the analyses presented in this book, and she has been shown to be, in many ways, the 'odd one out'. She was the only member of the core group from a working-class, Northern background, the only core Stomper not to have experienced the women's movements of the 1970s first-hand, the only woman to dispute the relevance of feminism and the only core Stomper to argue with conviction that sexuality is genetically predetermined. It is particularly interesting to focus on Claire as an example of how heterogeneity within a CoP may be managed, therefore, given the central role that she played in a group of women from whom – in many ways – she differed fundamentally. For example, it was Claire who tended to trigger dispute within interactions. She tended to play a role in conversations which led to the disruption of perceived homogeneity, such as by challenging me to explain my knowledge of Kinsey (Section 7.2) or by insisting that she be recognised as a Girl (Section 5.2), or by disputing the authenticity of a 'political lesbian' (Section 8.2). Her disruptive role demonstrates that the CoP approach, far from being a restrictive model with unchangeable parameters, is dynamic in its make-up.

Because the CoP approach does not assume that certain predefined characteristics or traits define a given group, unusual or extreme stances need not be taken as inherently problematic. Instead, it is possible to view them as a moment of meaning-making, whereby the boundaries of what is 'authentic' or acceptable (according to the group's understanding of broader cultural ideologies) is constantly renegotiated. Indeed, as Eckert and Wenger (2005: 583) argue, CoP ways of doing things are not simply learnt and replicated by new members, but created by the CoP as a whole. In this sense, each interaction that occurs within a group has the potential to allow all members to build upon and alter the local real-isation of broader ideals. This means that apparent dissent or variation can be dealt with in an inclusive and flexible way, with ideals shifting and being adapted according to the needs of the specific interactive moment. Interaction 6.1, whereby the women shifted their stances and reworked the symbolic meaning of shaving or wearing skirts, is a prime example of this. This is not to suggest that all CoPs will operate in this way, but instead to argue that the CoP approach allows us to under-stand local constructions of identity as a flexible, changeable process. Investigating the role of speakers such as Claire, or of interactions where apparently straightforward, inauthentic practices become temporarily authentic, such as wearing skirts, illustrates the developmental nature of the CoP and, furthermore, allows us to understand how and why practices (and their meaning) will shift as time passes and member-ships alter.

Whilst it is useful to view the CoP as an entity which allows for differ-ence and adapts itself moment by moment, however, it is also important to recognise that its boundaries – whilst flexible – must ultimately remain meaningful and in some way representative of the broader ethos of the group. Although variation may occur, and may allow for changing perspectives on what is normative or expected within the CoP, it is also apparent that it can be *through* such variation that a group's boundaries can be reconfirmed. The following section will show that, by drawing attention to what a CoP is *not*, it can be possible to also draw attention to – and reconfirm – what a group really *is*.

9.2.2   Heterogeneity: the reassertion of boundaries and ethos

As indicated above, the heterogeneity that existed in the Stomper CoP was often negotiated by the women, with new norms specific to the interactive moment being constructed in line with the broader workings of the group. The interactions presented in the previous chapters have also revealed that the women occasionally embraced or foregrounded the differences between them. This has typically been shown to be the case with regard to the taking on (or assigning) of negative identity positions. As mentioned above (Section 9.1.3), nega-tive identity positioning highlights the fact that identities are not set in stone but, instead, can change from moment to moment. This kind of ironic positioning also reveals, however, a complex relationship with perceived legitimacy and sameness. If one is to claim an identity that all interlocutors know to be inauthentic within the boundaries of the group, and which those interlocutors perceive to be an affectation rather than a serious claim, it is relevant to consider how that identity position is responded to. In Section 5.2.2.1, for example, when Claire was shown to take on the persona of Girl and to claim it for herself, it was apparent that she was playing with the boundaries of the CoP. Her engagement with the CoP over time seemingly allowed her to take advantage of her knowledge and understanding of the perceived authenticity in the group by taking on a role which directly contradicted that. She did so, in this particular moment, by emphasising all that was antithetical to the idealised lesbian (or Dyke) and claiming it for herself, knowing that her interlocutors would interpret this as an ironic statement. Indeed, by claiming the persona and then emphasising elements of herself which contradicted it (in this case, her degrees in mathematics and in science), she was able to use the negative identity position in order to stress her own contextual authenticity. Claire's apparent embrace of the Girl persona was evidence of the women projecting that which was perceived as inauthentic in order to highlight that which they positioned as authentic. In this sense, one way that they could respond to the heterogeneity that emerged between them – in this case, finger length, revealing the fact that not all of the women were 'naturally' gay – was to highlight that which was different in order to destabilise it and promote that which opposed it. Without a negative identity position such as a Girl, after all, there could be no positive identity position, such as the Dyke persona that Claire adopted as a result of this particular exchange.

It is telling that, despite this tactical use of salient personae and meaningful roles, the women never laid a serious claim to an identity which directly opposed that which they worked hard to construct as authentic and, therefore, as normative in the group. Indeed, although we can see that certain identities could be played with, such as whether one is an authentic Dyke because they do not shave their legs, or a less authentic Dyke because they do (Chapter 6), it is also apparent that not all negative identity positions are available for adoption; the 'political lesbian' (Section 8.2) is an example of this. This persona demonstrates that negative identity positions may not always be adopted and used ironically to emphasise that which is authentic in a group. Indeed, it seems reasonable to hypothesise from this particular extract that certain limitations surround the projection of a negative identity position; in this case, the unusually emotive and personal tone expressed by Claire led to the taboo status of the political lesbian persona. In this instance, although the negative persona was foregrounded and used as a definable concept which was oppositional to that which was being constructed as 'real' in that moment, to adopt this ironically as a negative identity position would be impossible. This instance does reinforce the argument, however, that the members of this particular CoP could emphasise what was normative in their group by foregrounding that which was non-normative. Seemingly, this could be done both through the ironic contradiction of their own rules and boundaries, and the refusal to identify with an inauthentic persona. In this way, the women either actively constructed heterogeneity by assuming a negative identity position, or reinforced their homogeneity by isolating that which was different. That they could maintain a coherent group identity through myriad ways, of course, demonstrates once more that identity construction can only ever be partial; the Stompers were never truly a homogeneous unit, as the stances they took depended on the specific context of the moment and whether they could find agreement between themselves on what, at that moment, 'counted' as authentic. This required some cooperative negotiation and, therefore, typically enabled the Stomper women to reinforce their homogeneity as a group. Yet this was not always the case; at times, the women actively positioned their interlocutors as 'other' for their own gain.

An example of this was shown in Interaction 7.2, when Hannah was positioned as a 'stupid northerner' in order for Jill to authenticate herself via a knowledgeable or expert role. Another occurred in Interaction 7.1, as I was positioned as ignorant in relation to my knowledge of queer culture. As with the highlighting of difference via the adoption of negative identity positions or rejection of personae representing the antithesis of an authentic Stomper, the women in this CoP could take advantage of inconsistencies revealed in their interlocutors' identity construction in order to flag up how they, themselves, were comparatively legitimate and in line with CoP ideals. In this way, it is apparent that not all identity construction and negotiation which occurred in the CoP was strictly collaborative or, indeed, friendly. Though the CoP approach is defined by the joint engagement of its members, then, it is evident from these instances that this engagement does not always need to be done in a supportive way for a coherent value system to be maintained.

This discussion has demonstrated that the CoP as a concept does allow for heterogeneity, and does not presume some artificial similarity within a group of speakers. Indeed, it has shown that heterogeneity may be dealt with in a range of ways; it may be adequated or erased, it may be flagged up and opposed, or it may be ironically assumed as an identity position. By considering that which differed between the members of the Stomper CoP, certainly, an insight into the ideological motivation behind the construction of sameness in the group has been provided. It has been possible for the persona of Dyke and the reasons for its perceived authenticity in this CoP, for example, to be extensively explored and interpreted through an analysis of how its opposing persona (of Girl) was assumed and rejected. The meaning of membership of a CoP is defined by those regular participants within it, and focusing on that which differs as well as that which is apparently similar enables and encourages the researcher to maintain a bottom-up perspective when analysing their data. A micro-focused study of a local context also enables an examination of individuals and, as a result, facilitates a view of how a shared, mutual identity may be constructed despite the diversity that must exist between its members. Such a view, in turn, enables an understanding of how that which is foregrounded and constructed mutually ties into the broader structures which govern the group as a whole.

It has been demonstrated repeatedly in this book that a consideration of both broader ideological structures and local ethnographic norms is vital for an understanding of CoP identity and the meaning behind the various interactive practices used within conversations. The CoP approach has been combined with a sociocultural perspective, in this sense, one which has focused less on broader, generalisable patterns, and more on individuals with differences, disagreements and shifting stances. The following section considers the ways in which the sociocultural linguistics framework used in this book has both enabled and enhanced the CoP approach taken in the analysis of the Sapphic Stompers.

9.3   Sociocultural linguistics and the community of practice

As indicated so far in this chapter, the CoP is an entity which exists despite heterogeneity between its members, in terms of their attitudes, stances and individual idiosyncrasies. Importantly, the CoP has been shown to be a useful way of understanding how speakers create a shared sense of what is real – or 'authentic' – through their regular engagement together in the construction and negotiation of shared norms, and it has been demonstrated that this may occur despite apparent differences between them. The sociocultural linguistics approach has been used throughout the analyses which have revealed this, and has helped to shape the discussion of authenticity as it is created by the Stomper members in two key ways. Firstly, a sociocultural approach has the concept of identity as a performance at its centre, meaning that the CoP identities under consideration here have been repeatedly viewed as temporary and partial. In this sense, heterogeneity between speakers and temporal moments have been analysed coherently. Secondly, the sociocultural framework – as it has been interpreted here – allows a clearer focus on the process of indexicality between a shared practice in a CoP and the 'authentic' identity categories being invoked through that practice. The focus on stance that has been enabled by the sociocultural framework used here has provided a more nuanced approach to indexicality as a result.

A central tenet of a sociocultural approach to sociolinguistics is that identities are emergent in interaction. As Bucholtz and Hall (2005: 587) argue, this principle allows us to move away from 'a traditional scholarly view of identity as housed primarily within an individual mind' and towards the understanding that 'the only way that such self-conceptions enter the social world is via some form of discourse'. In this sense, they view identities as emerging through interactive encounters, within which they are performed by social actors. It has been argued throughout this book (see, in particular, Section 2.3) that ideological identity categories are made real through performativity (Butler 1990); that the repeated stylisation of the self to reflect some broader identity both perpetuates and, importantly, modifies for a local context, the identity category in question. A close investigation into a CoP such as the Stompers allows a clear view of this performative identity construction. The use of a sociocultural framework also allows the interpretation of this identity construction as occurring in layers: an interactive move indexing a locally salient persona which, in turn, points to a broader ideological category. In the case of the Stompers, the women have been shown to perform the category of 'lesbian', for example via their indexing (on a local level, through such interactive moves as stance-taking) of personae such as Dyke. Breaking the identity moves down into these component parts, as the sociocultural framework allows, has therefore also enhanced an understanding of how broad ideological categories are reinterpreted within interaction according to the context-specific ethos of the group, and how the performance of salient personae reflect more than simply a direct reproduction of global ideologies.

In Eckert's (2000) discussion of CoPs, she suggests that we might capture the process of social meaning-making by analysing the level of social organisation where individual and group identities are being constructed. She argues that, by focusing on a level where we can observe the symbolic processes that tie individuals to groups, and those groups to the social context in which they gain meaning, we will be able to understand the symbolic properties of what that group of individuals does through their language (2000: 35). For Eckert, then, the CoP approach should facilitate a focus on local contexts – on how speakers identify as a collective, such as whether they identify with a local Jock persona, and what that persona symbolises on a broader level. By using a sociocultural linguistics approach in combination with this – by focusing not only on local contexts in terms of sociocultural meaning within a given geographical or institutional location, but on individual interactive moments – it has been possible to enhance this understanding of the symbolic processes undertaken by groups of speakers. This enhancement of the CoP approach, provided by the use of a sociocultural linguistics framework, is that identity performance itself – the projection of a salient identity or persona through interaction – may be understood in terms of social *positioning*.

The concept of positioning, as used repeatedly throughout the analysis of interactions presented in this book, has enabled an understanding of how speakers use a variety of techniques, specific to the moment, in order to align themselves with or against a given concept or idea. This extends the concept of performance which, within a variationist approach to the CoP, may be loosely defined as the indexical consequence of a speaker's use of symbolically salient variants. Indeed, Eckert (2000: 214) suggests that speakers' use of specific variants may be viewed as a stylistic process of appropriation of local and extra-local linguistic resources in order to (amongst other things) produce new twists on an existing persona. In this way, a speaker could engage in the performance of a salient persona – one which already has meaning outside of the group, such as a 'nerd' or a 'Burnout', for example – by using linguistic resources linked to that identity. What a qualitative, sociocultural approach (which focuses instead on interactive moments) may offer in extension of this is a more nuanced approach to the analysis of how those personae may be constructed in the moment. By explaining that which a speaker does in order to project a given identity at a particular moment as 'positioning', as in the claiming of intelligence via the positioning of another speaker in a comparatively ignorant frame (as with Jill and Hannah in Interaction 7.2) for example, it is possible to consider not only a range of locally salient linguistic variables as relevant in this process, but to approach the interaction from a bottom-up perspective which considers all aspects of the discursive moment. In this way, a speaker can be viewed as positioning themselves in line with a persona which may only ever be produced once, in that particular moment, but which can be interpreted as having symbolic meaning which relates back to the broader ethos of the group because of the stance taken in relation to it. Stances, in this sense, may be taken once or many times, and may consist of myriad and indefinite numbers of variables or linguistic features. In order to view the performance of a salient persona, therefore, a sociocultural approach looks not only at the linking of that persona with broader ideological categories (through the consideration of how the linguistic variables linking to that persona are salient on a broader level), but at how those personae are constructed in the first place 'on the ground' via the social positioning of oneself and of others. By not restricting an analysis to particular linguistic variables known to have some symbolic meaning, but instead considering stance as a key component of identity construction in interaction, momentary and fleeting personae may therefore also be viewed as being constructed.

It is clear from this that the CoP approach and the sociocultural linguistics framework may naturally coexist together. The advances made within variationist sociolinguistics by the introduction of the CoP (such as the consideration of linguistic variables as symbolic of local personae which are, themselves, indexical of broader categories) have clearly influenced the development of a qualitative approach to identity construction within interaction. In turn, the anthropological underpinnings of the sociocultural linguistics approach (as introduced in Chapter 2) have had a clear influence on the development of the CoP within sociolinguistics, as is evident by the focus on performance, ethnographic context, and the collaborative production of meaning.

This chapter has illustrated that, when viewed from a sociocultural perspective, the CoP may be seen to house heterogeneity, manage conflict and non-collaborative identity positioning, and facilitate the construction of context-specific authenticity. The use of the CoP approach in a qualitative analytical framework has been explored in this book and shown to be of clear value as a result of its comfortable partnership with key principles of sociocultural linguistics. Importantly, this has been shown to be the case despite the fact that the Stomper group did not ideally match the criteria of a CoP as they have been laid out for variationist sociolinguistics. The potential implications and apparent advances to the CoP approach made as a result of its application to the Stomper group are considered in the final section of this chapter, below.

9.4 The Sapphic Stomper community of practice

The use of a sociocultural framework alongside the CoP approach has been revealed, above, to provide a coherent view of the indexical meaning of locally salient practices and stances. By focusing in so closely on just one CoP, as has been done in this book with the Sapphic Stompers, it is also apparent that an advanced understanding of how various practices link to broader ideological categories, via local-level personae, can be achieved. Yet the approach taken in the current study contradicts many of the claims made by those who introduced the CoP approach to sociolinguistics. It contradicts these in two ways; firstly, it does not consider multiple, overlapping CoPs, instead focusing on just one in isolation and, secondly, the CoP under consideration is not placed within an institutional context. These contradictions are highlighted by Eckert and McConnell-Ginet (2007: 28) who, as briefly mentioned in Section 4.2, argue that a CoP is most interesting when it is contrasted with similar CoPs: when considered in comparison to other CoPs, what occurs within one may be contextualised in relation to the institution in which the other groups emerge (2007: 29). In this sense, more than one group is needed to understand their reactions to the context they have emerged from. As Eckert and Wenger (2005: 585) argue, focusing on just one CoP may lead to all that is interpreted from it being specific to just that one local group and therefore may not be translatable to wider society; they argue that the approach should be to look at the links between multiple engagement in multiple CoPs. Eckert (2000: 227) also posits that the institution is, in itself, central to CoP research, arguing that CoPs 'emerge in response to the institution, seeking ways to participate in it, to gain control of it, to avoid it, to find alternatives to it, etc.' As a theoretical approach developed initially for a theory of education (Lave and Wenger 1991), the CoP has been used to understand situated learning within institutional contexts. In this sense, the institution has also been central to its application to sociolinguistics. It has been viewed as untenable to consider a group of speakers who are not responding to a literal structure as constructing a meaningful identity in response to the world around them – this has been a criticism of the CoP approach, in fact (see Davies 2005: 563). Yet the research for this book has demonstrated that the CoP approach may be used for definable groups of speakers existing outside of an institution, and that it may be rewarding to focus on one sole group.

Whilst the existing body of work into CoPs has shown that it is both feasible and useful to consider multiple groups which emerge within the boundaries of an institution since this can show how the identities of these groups are constructed in response to it, to suggest that this is the only way to study such groups may be short-sighted and restrictive. Groups of speakers who regularly engage together and develop shared practices occur in myriad settings, not only institutional ones. Furthermore, the micro-focus of one small group, such as the Stompers, enables a consideration of the most interesting and unique interactional moments whereby *alternative* identities may also be indexed, providing crucial insight into how CoP members are able to subvert their own norms. Though a focus on just one group may make the results from that group non-generalisable, when the aims of an analytical approach are not to draw extended conclusions about patterns of language variation and change across myriad groups but, instead, to examine meaning-making in progress, it is clear that a micro-focus may, in fact, be preferable to the comparative study of multiple CoPs.

The research in this book has illustrated that the most important element of the CoP approach is to relate local practices to a larger, broader context. Though it has been argued that CoPs exist, and should be primarily considered, in response to a definable institutional site, it has been shown here that this broader context need not necessarily be limited to a physical setting. The sociocultural linguistics perspective stresses the importance of defining cultural and ideological levels of meaning before attempting to understand the indexical properties of interactions, and it is clear that this must occur in much the same way as with the literal boundary of an institution. To understand what it means to be a Jock (see Eckert 2000), a Popular (see Moore 2003) or a Norteña gang member (see Mendoza-Denton 2008), for instance, it was crucial for the respective researchers to have an accurate view of the school settings in which the CoPs were placed so that they could understand the ways in which each CoP persona responded to it. The Stompers, in contrast, have been shown to have negotiated their own identities within the ideological setting of lesbian culture – in response to heteronormative and homophobic discourses, for example – rather than within a particular geographical location or institution. Understanding that the Stomper women's interaction was made meaningful through its relationship with broader ideological structures therefore enabled an understanding of their individual stance-taking and the positioning of themselves and their interlocutors. As Bucholtz and Hall (2005: 606) claim in their partialness principle, no identities may be constructed in isolation from broader structures; it is evident here that the Stomper women's construction of authentic identity was fundamentally shaped by ideologies of gender and sexuality and, therefore, that these ideologies themselves functioned as these structures (albeit structures with no physical boundaries). So long as a researcher understands the significance of relevant ideologies to the CoP they are studying, therefore, it is clear that those ideologies themselves can be viewed as the structures in response to which identities emerge.

It is evident from the analyses in this book, therefore, that the language use of a group of speakers such as the Stompers may only be understood if it is linked into the relationship that those speakers have with the wider world. The Sapphic Stomper women have been shown to be concerned with creating salient personae for themselves which reflect a particular orientation towards feminism and queer politics, towards prevalent ideals within lesbian culture (such as butch and femme), and towards the hiking activity in which they regularly engaged. Through the use of a sociocultural linguistics approach, the observations made and data collected in this study have been interpreted through a specific framework which defines their interaction in accordance with the ideologies it invokes and the cultural context of the group. Furthermore, as highlighted above, the CoP approach has provided an ideal base from which to employ such a study. In the following, final, chapter, the sociocultural approach will be examined in terms of its usefulness in exploring the meaning behind the Sapphic Stompers' interactional moves. The chapter will also consider the specifically sexual nature of the Stomper CoP, first revisiting the identity and desire debates outlined in Section 3.3, and then focusing explicitly on what the research presented in this book can tell us about language and lesbian identity.

10
Sociocultural Linguistics and Sexuality

.

This discussion of the Stomper CoP has argued that interactive moves and language usage are indexical of broader, ideological structures. Although, as outlined in the previous chapter, this CoP differed from those typically studied within sociolinguistic research (existing in isolation from other CoPs and being removed from any physical institutional boundaries), the women's engagement together has been shown to facilitate the construction of shared, multifaceted, contextually specific (and therefore changeable) identities. The Stompers' use of prevalent stereotypes and ideologies within lesbian and gay culture more broadly has been revealed, such as their construction of the personae Dyke and Girl via the categories 'butch' and 'femme' and their reproduction of generationally specific ideals around feminism and queer politics. In this sense, they have been shown to create local-level personae in relation to wider sociocultural structures. This book has aimed to explore and understand the relationships between the CoP and the broader ideologies which influenced them and, through the implementation of a sociocultural linguistics framework paired with discourse analysis, it has been possible to do this.

By utilising the valuable insights emerging from the CoP approach within variationist sociolinguistics and translating its key messages onto a qualitative, sociocultural linguistics study, it has been possible to focus on the mutual engagement of the CoP members in this study and to make sense of their identity construction. Yet without the clearly defined principles of the framework put forward by Bucholtz and Hall (2005), the varied and changing ways that the women worked towards this identity construction may not have been so identifiable. This final chapter considers the benefits of not only approaching a research context with the theoretical underpinnings of a sociocultural approach in mind (that identity emerges through interaction, in relation to broader cultural structures and ideals), but of interpreting that approach as a framework through which to understand discursive data. It begins, below, with a discussion of how the Stomper interactions support and enhance the sociocultural linguistics framework, before going on to consider the impact of this approach on the field of language and sexuality more broadly.

10.1   The sociocultural framework and the Stompers' interaction

Fundamental to sociocultural linguistics is the notion that it is entirely necessary to consider interaction in light of its ethnographic and broader sociocultural context. In doing so, we may view identity as a contextually specific, locally produced phenomenon. This has been illustrated and argued in the preceding chapters, both in terms of the ethnographically situated analyses and the discussion of the CoP. More than this, however, the analyses in this book have taken Bucholtz and Hall's (2005) discussion of work taking this approach, in which they identify common themes and define them as key principles, as a workable framework for the consideration of identity construction in action. The examination of the seven separate extracts of interaction between the Stompers considered in this book has illustrated that each of the principles highlighted by Bucholtz and Hall are relevant in the women's identity work. The emergence principle has been evident through their discursive construction of 'Stomper-ness'; without their interaction and mutual engagement in the creation of a meaningful, shared self, there would be no coherent Stomper identity. In this sense, it is clear that the version of identity that the women put forward during Stomper interactions was emergent from their engagement together rather than pre-existing in some way. This 'putting forward' of identity has typically been referred to in the foregoing chapters as *positioning*. This has reflected the performative nature of the Stomper women's identity construction and the fact that they seemed to project a persona which was desirable for a given context. The Stompers have been shown to have positioned themselves in line with global identity categories (such as 'lesbian' or 'feminist'), as well as with ethnographically salient personae (such as Dyke and Girl), and also in respect of those personae which were temporarily constructed in the moment (such as the political lesbian). The positionality principle therefore reflects the findings of these analyses.

The indexical links which the women have been shown to have constructed between such local and global positions, such as between the persona of Girl and the broader heteronormative ideals surrounding femininity, have also been explored in close detail in this book. Similarly, it has been evident throughout the discussion of the recorded data and fieldwork observations that these indexical links are meaningful to the Stompers because of the women's specific engagement with the wider world and, more specifically, lesbian culture. In this way, both the indexicality and partialness principles laid out by Bucholtz and Hall (2005) have been illustrated in this study.

Finally, support has been provided in the preceding chapters for Bucholtz and Hall's (2005: 598) argument that 'identities are never autonomous or independent but always acquire social meaning in relation to other available identity positions and other social actors'. This relationality principle emphasises the importance of understanding the local, temporary nature of identity construction and identifies three pairs of tactics of intersubjectivity. Throughout this book, moments which seem to reflect these tactics of intersubjectivity have been highlighted, some of which are outlined below.

10.1.1   Tactics of intersubjectivity in the Stomper group

The tactics of intersubjectivity introduced by Bucholtz and Hall (2004, 2005) enable an understanding of identity as a concept which is always constructed in relation to something else. As shown in Section 2.3.1.1, they outline three of these relationships. Firstly, they argue that identities are typically constructed in relation to whether they are similar or different from other identities (the tactics of adequation and distinction). Secondly, they posit that identities are constructed as either real or artificial (authentication and denaturalisation), and thirdly they argue that speakers position themselves and others as either legitimate or illegitimate in a given context (authorisation and illegitimation). In the analyses presented in the earlier chapters, each of these relational processes has been highlighted.

For example, given the demographic differences which existed between the Stomper women, it was often the case that they played down any variation between them in order to appear united and, ultimately, homogeneous. Section 8.1 provides an example of what Bucholtz and Hall refer to as a tactic of adequation, as Marianne attempted to minimise Claire's negative identity positioning away from the apparently valued category of 'feminist'. The tactic of distinction is clear from the women's regular rejection of the Girl persona in order to construct an authentic Dyke, though the use of negative identity positioning – such as Claire's labelling of herself as a Girl (Section 5.2) in order to ironically subvert her actual group identification with the Dyke persona – reveals a more complex construction of difference here. By taking on a negative identity position, Claire deliberately destabilised her own identity as an authentic Stomper in order to highlight the illegitimate status of the Girly persona. This may be viewed as an example of the tactic of denaturalisation, given its emphasis on what is false or artificial in contrast to what is inauthentic.

The tactic of authentication, similarly, may be shown to be reflected in the women's occasionally competitive attempts to position themselves as authentic, such as Marianne and Sam's turns in Section 8.1 which allowed them to make similar claims about being feminists. Close attention to this example revealed the perceived importance of this political identity to the group as a whole, and showed how categories such as 'feminist' may be defined and negotiated within interaction. The relevance of political culture for the women was also apparent from the symbolic value that intellectualism and knowledge with regard to feminism and queer culture clearly held for them. In Section 7.2, for example, academia and intellectualism were invoked by members who wished to position themselves in a culturally powerful position in order to evaluate a stance or an identity as legitimate. Whilst Eve authenticated herself as knowledgeable in Interaction 7.2 by using discourse suitable to an academic context, thus engaging in the tactic of authorisation, Jill used a similar approach to deauthenticate Hannah, using an accent indexical of ignorance and, arguably, employing a tactic of illegitimation to position herself as comparably more authentic.

By considering the women's identity work in light of Bucholtz and Hall's proposed tactics, an understanding of the Stompers' identities emerging in relation to positive and negative structures has been enhanced. To be an authentic Dyke, for example, it has been shown that the women typically rejected that which contradicted this idealised identity position. The tactics of intersubjectivity encourage us, as researchers, to examine the ways in which speakers position the self and other in terms of what they are, but also what they are not (see Section 9.1 for a discussion of this in relation to the CoP approach). It has been shown in this book that a focus on stances taken during given interactional moments is one clear way of doing this. The stance approach taken in this book has enabled a localised analysis of how shared meanings are made and, in turn, has enabled a better view of the indexical meanings linking local personae with broader ideological categories.

Through an awareness of the prevalence of relational structures to identity positioning (such as whether a person is authentic or inauthentic, a Dyke or a Girl), it is possible to understand how something meaningful and valued might be constructed. As the tactics of intersubjectivity suggest, we create meaningful selves in relation to one another. This may be through positively or negatively evaluating those groups, people or ideas which oppose what we believe ourselves to be, by playing with what is perceived to be our shared group identity, or even by positioning others in an illegitimate way in order to convey some authority in line with a given, valued persona.

By introducing these three sets of tactics, Bucholtz and Hall develop the commonly held perception that identities are typically constructed as being either similar or different from something else; they suggest that identities are constructed via a much broader range of relations, but that these relations will always involve other sociocultural positions or people (Bucholtz and Hall 2005: 598). My consideration of them here is not an attempt to advocate that these three sets of relations are the only tactics that may exist, of course. It is also not to suggest that the tactics of intersubjectivity which Bucholtz and Hall present should necessarily be a focal point of sociocultural analyses of discourse. As a starting point, they may in fact be redundant; it is first necessary to explore the larger sociocultural and ethnographic context and to understand the indexical relationship between stances taken or linguistic choices made and broader personae or identity categories. Without this contextual understanding, any tactical moves which employ a relational structure, such as those outlined here, may not be accurately interpreted. Furthermore, should these tactics *not* appear within a given body of data, it should not be assumed that identity work, which is dependent on a relationship with other social structures or people, has not occurred. Indeed, a message of primary importance within the sociocultural linguistics framework is that infinite linguistic choices may produce identities in varying, temporal, specified contexts. No doubt the range of relationships drawn upon to construct an authentic CoP identity is similarly countless.

The tactics of intersubjectivity which Bucholtz and Hall introduce do clearly reflect the aims of sociocultural linguistic work, however: to explain the indexical relationships between local practices and broader ideological structures by viewing identity as emergent in interaction. Indeed, the tactics discussed above illustrate some of the most important findings from this research with the Stomper group. They show that identity construction is mutual, yet not necessarily collaborative or cooperative – a speaker might position another social actor in a negative position in order to enhance their own legitimacy within the group. They illustrate that a sense of self as a group is always constructed in relation to other groups, whether that group is perceived, imagined or physically present. They also reflect the theory that identities will vary depending on the context of a given moment, as well as the ethnographic situation. When considered alongside the general principles which have emerged from the sociocultural linguistics work outlined in Bucholtz and Hall (2005), it is possible to interpret the discursive construction of identities in interaction as situated in a given moment, governed by the ethnographic context, and indexically linked to the broader ideological structures which impact upon the group. Close, local-level discourse analysis which does not favour predetermined variables or focus only on one aspect of linguistic usage is arguably best suited for such a task, given the flexibility that is required for such research. This is considered in more depth in the following section.

10.1.2   Sociocultural linguistics and discourse analysis

The theories emerging from work within sociocultural linguistics have been taken as a framework in this book and interpreted in light of three levels of identity construction: interactional, ethnographic and ideological. Through the use of discourse analysis, as indicated above, this study has aimed to achieve a highly nuanced insight into the moment-by-moment interactions of the CoP members in order to consider the links between these local and global levels. As mentioned briefly in Section 9.3, rather than considering how particular variables were used across different moments, this approach has aimed not to generalise about language use but to identify key interactive patterns as they present themselves in a way which is meaningful to the group. In contrast to studies such as Eckert (2000), this investigation has therefore considered how the Stomper members used particular interactive moves (rather than linguistic variants) to achieve different identity goals depending on the context of their interaction. It has been shown that the women employed multiple tactics which allowed them to construct personae, which they then aligned themselves with or against through stance-taking. That they frequently engaged in negative identity practices and positioned others in an illegitimate role in order to illustrate their own authenticity, even situating *themselves* in a negative identity position, highlights the importance of understanding the intersubjective nature of interaction and analysing it at this close level.

The use of qualitative research methods in this study is not to dispute the relevance of quantitative accounts which reveal the overall patterns of language use within CoPs, of course. Rather, it is to highlight the processes through which meanings are jointly negotiated and created by the people producing them (and, indeed, how meanings are disputed or rejected during interaction). To quantify and generalise the use of particular features in a study such as this one would take away from the minute analysis required to explain the different discursive tactics employed by speakers. Tag questions, for example, often occur in the data presented here, yet have held different functions dependent on the context in which they were employed by the Stomper women, being used to facilitate as well as dominate, to express certainty as well as insecurity. Discourse features such as these, therefore, have been analysed here only inasmuch as they are useful to the identity work in progress during a specific interaction, rather than in accordance with their statistical significance to distinct groups within a larger corpus of data. This is, perhaps, the essence of the sociocultural approach, one informed by ethnography rather than a variationist agenda.

A more qualitative approach has been taken by variationist researchers in conjunction with quantitative analysis, of course, and these studies have begun to consider how micro-level moves build up into quantitative patterns. However, a sociocultural linguistics approach such as that taken here must begin with a qualitative investigation of language. In this way, it may account for the features which do *not* occur with statistical significance but which do invoke a category or stance of *ideological* significance. Similarly, a qualitative approach may also capture the various effects that the same move can have in different interactive moments. In Section 8.1, for example, Claire's rejection of the label 'feminist' did not prevent the other women present from continuing to construct this identity, yet in Section 8.2 Claire's forthright rejection of the 'political lesbian' persona led the other women present to neutralise their stances. Such moments make sense only within the context of the CoP, as a consequence of the relationships between the participants and the broader sociocultural context.

From the discussion, here, of the sociocultural framework and its complementary approach of discourse analysis, it is clear that micro-focused studies into groups such as the Sapphic Stompers are both feasible and valuable, particularly to the growing field of language and sexuality. They may provide a view of sexual identity as constructed in relation to both local contexts and broader ideologies of sex and gender, making them relevant to further investigations into how queer (and other) identities are made real in interaction. The following section considers the significance of the findings of this research with the Stompers for the field of language and sexuality.

10.2 Viewing sexuality through a sociocultural linguistics lens

As argued in the previous section, the sociocultural linguistics approach provides a framework which is accessible and applicable to research such as that undertaken for this book. The study featured here has been primarily concerned with lesbian identity and its relationship to broader ideologies of gender and queer culture, and the relevance of the framework to this particular area suggests that it will also be germane for research in the wider area of language, gender and sexuality. As discussed in Section 2.3.1, the field of language and gender has for many years engaged in research from an interactionist approach, one which considers how broader ideologies of gender are reflected and constructed in language use. Aspects of sexuality have increasingly become recognised as intrinsically connected to this, as the likes of Kiesling (2001) and Cameron (1998) have found in their research into young men's constructions of masculinity via articulations of heterosexuality. In a more complex example of how gender and discourses of sexuality may be linked, J. Clark's (forthcoming) research with a young women's sports team finds that, in this context, the construction of female identities which are associated with success and achievement are intrinsically tied to a discourse of homophobia. Studies focused on queer groups remain fewer in number than those focused on heterosexual groups, yet the central theoretical concerns of the broad field of language and gender (such as indexicality and performativity, for example) are also entirely relevant to research which is defined as being focused on language and sexuality. In this sense, it is perhaps logical that research into sexuality should be both supported by, and central to, research into gender identity. The following section considers this point in relation to recent calls to move away from a focus on identity in sexuality research, namely by Cameron and Kulick (2003, 2005).

10.2.1 Argument for continued research into sexual identity

It has become evident within the field that the concept of 'sexuality' is not shared by all those who engage in linguistic research in this area. Despite the apparent coherence between approaches which investigate the construction of gendered identities, and those which investigate the construction of sexual identities, scholars such as Cameron and Kulick have advocated the 'bracketing' of identity, suggesting that researchers should 'leave it behind and forget about it for a while' (Cameron and Kulick 2003: 105). As discussed already in Section 3.4, Cameron and Kulick do not argue that research into language and sexual identity is worthless or uninteresting, but instead suggest that 'sexuality' might encompass more than identification with broader sexual categories such as 'lesbian', 'gay', 'bisexual' and so on. Their suggestion that a focus on a desire-based framework instead of one on identity has largely been influenced by their argument that research into sexual identity may be untenable and predictable, however, whereas this study with the Stompers has demonstrated that a shift away from identity research at this point would be premature. For example, whilst Cameron and Kulick argue that the varying meaning of social categories such as 'gay' and 'lesbian' renders the study of sexual identity difficult to pursue in any meaningful way (2003: 114), the Stompers have been shown to construct meaningful personae by using these very categories as a starting point. Indeed, it is these broad categories, with their connected ideological meanings and symbols, which enable the women to create their own group-specific sense of lesbianism by reworking them.

Similarly, Cameron and Kulick (2003: 105) express concern that a focus on sexual identity in current research may lead to misleading claims about there being just one 'authentic' style of gay or lesbian identity. Whilst it has been made clear throughout this book that one must not attempt to draw any broad conclusions about how 'all' lesbians (or gay people) use language from a handful of studies, it remains worthwhile to investigate the prevalent cultural norms across a number of communities in order to locate salient ideologies which are reworked differently in varying group contexts. Indeed, by viewing what CoPs themselves construct as 'authentic' in line with their own ethos and interpretation of their place within the wider world, it is possible to interpret authenticity as a useful, rather than restrictive, theoretical concept. If we understand what is significant in broader sociocultural terms to varying queer groups, it will ultimately be possible to understand the structures which constrain and shape the realisations of the self which are available to those who identify as a particular 'type' of queer. Indeed, this research with the Stompers has added to the existing studies into language and lesbian identity which suggest that the ideological heteronormative gender binary is likely to have a considerable impact on lesbian identity construction. By engaging in additional research into lesbian CoPs, it will be possible to see whether this is specific to a given generational group, how this might be changing, and to see whether the (potentially harmful) heteronormative cultural context in which these groups engage is changing to enable a more fluid process of identity construction. This is considered in more depth in Section 10.3. Firstly, however, the impact of the sociocultural framework on how we might think about desire is discussed.

10.2.2 Revisiting the desire argument

Cameron and Kulick's argument that desire might be a more fruitful investigation than identity may be reconsidered if we take identity to be something which emerges in interaction in response to broader ideologies, not something which merely reflects pre-existing notions of what sexual identity is. This is not to suggest that desire itself is an untenable approach, but that it may be useful to consider how it may be investigated alongside what evidently remains an important area of research: identity. As argued in Section 3.4.2, desire may be interpreted not merely as that which is erotic or sexually desirable, but also as the expression of what speakers want. Should a speaker's desire in a given moment be to be viewed as an intelligent person, for example, it is feasible that they would employ certain identity moves – those which might be interpreted as tactics of authorisation, for example – to position themselves as comparably knowledgeable. Though this may differ in its execution and intended results from the articulation of erotic desire in a sex club or on a fetishist online message board, for example, it remains similar in that it reveals a want or need to be perceived in a certain way in order to achieve a particular goal.

A number of instances throughout the research presented in this book have revealed the speakers' desires, if 'desire' is interpreted in this way. Throughout the analyses, the women have been shown to have had the desire to be viewed as an authentic hiker, for example. They have shown a desire to position themselves as fundamentally different from heterosexual women via a desire to be viewed as an authentic lesbian because of biological factors such as finger length (Section 5.2.2), a desire to show themselves as being legitimate enough to deauthenticate others (Section 7.2), a desire to be perceived as a feminist (Section 7.1) and the desire to appear youthful (Section 8.1). In each of these examples, the women have wanted to be taken seriously as a particular type of person at that given moment and, as a result, have positioned themselves in ways which could be perceived as meaningful by their interlocutors.

It is interesting, however, and perhaps surprising, that this group of women rarely expressed desire in a more sexual or erotic sense. As a

CoP which, to a significant extent, was defined by the women's shared sexual orientation, it may have been expected that the discussion of sex itself would become a tool in the construction of mutual identity. In contrast, however, lewd jokes or comments were not deemed acceptable in this group and, because of the group's typically unobtrusive and reserved nature, intimate discussions about sexual behaviour or desires would simply not have occurred. In the data collected for this book, only one exception to this emerged; in Section 6.2, sex was alluded to by Jill during a discussion of shaving one's legs. She argued that it is 'more attractive' for women to have shaved legs, an argument which led to the joint negotiation of this particular activity as having some authenticity as a lesbian practice. Of particular interest in this example was the fact that leg-shaving would typically be viewed as Girly and therefore antithetical to 'real' lesbianism, but the idea of sexual attractiveness carried more weight. This suggests that, despite the lack of sex talk occurring in the group, the women *did* recognise that sexual desire defined, to some extent, their joint engagement as a CoP. Nonetheless, the data here also reveals that the most interesting thing about language use in a queer group will not always be the communication of erotic desire.

Rather than revealing that the study of desire is fruitless, or that the study of sexual identity should be prioritised over research into the erotic, then, the research presented in this book implies instead that desire may be a complementary notion to sexual identity if taken in a more generalised sense. More than this, the objections made and concerns raised about the feasibility of research into speakers who define themselves in accordance with a particular sexual label have been shown, as a result of this research, to be unfounded. In this sense, research into sexual desire should be encouraged and explored, but not at the expense of continuing research into language and sexual identity. When sexual identity is viewed from a bottom-up, sociocultural linguistics perspective, the broader ideologies surrounding ideas of 'gay communities' and 'authentic lesbian identities' may be better understood as structures and systems which play a crucial role in the construction of locally prevalent personae which, in turn, allow speakers to make sense of who they are. Though these ideologies may at times be harmful, reflecting broader patriarchal, hegemonic ideals which disadvantage those of a minority sexual orientation, their very existence means that they can be challenged and that there may be some definable notion which brings otherwise disparate groups of people together. The following, penultimate, section considers this in more detail, focusing explicitly on – and considering the ramifications of – broader ideological structures on lesbian identity construction.

10.3   The study of language and lesbian identity

It has been argued already in this book (see Section 3.3, for example) that there is relatively little sociocultural linguistics research which is focused on lesbian culture and identity, particularly when compared to research concerning heterosexual women or homosexual men. An aim of this book, therefore, has been to begin to redress this balance by drawing on research within both language and gender (which most often focuses on straight women) as well as language and sexuality (which frequently focuses on gay men). A further aim, however, has been to move away from the concept of a homogeneous lesbian identity or discourse style; a lack of understanding about lesbian culture within mainstream society – due the prevalence of male identities within queer culture – must not lead to broad assumptions which merely reflect the stereotypes. In this sense, it is arguably a risky strategy to produce a body of work which, to some extent, reveals a CoP of women reproducing ideologies of butch/femme. Yet, as argued in Section 10.2, the use of broad stereotypes and ideologies about queer culture and identity does not render such research awkward or unworkable; it demonstrates the importance of understanding that broader ideologies may be reworked by social actors in order to make sense of themselves. The challenge, then, is to ensure that research which appears to rework prevalent stereotypes does not play a role in the reproduction of those stereotypes but, instead, furthers our understanding of the structures and symbols which enable minority groups to develop a coherent, fulfilled and definitive sense of who they are within the wider world.

One important aspect of this understanding is the recognition that the women who engaged in the Stomper group did not necessarily identify as Dykes in other contexts. In different environments, such as in the workplace or with their families, their sexuality may have had little or no bearing on the personality they projected in those moments. The women's continuous negotiation of what a lesbian was, and what that meant to them, simply reveals that the identities that they embraced within various Stomper contexts were moments of social positioning – they were not necessarily an articulation of an inner self or an inherent identity. Using the concept of persona within the sociocultural framework allows for the emphasis on performance and the projection of social positions to be clear. It is significant, nonetheless, that the Stomper women were reliant on the specific binary stereotype of butch and femme.

The Stomper women's reliance on broader notions of dichotomous gender, with heteronormative femininity necessarily positioned as antithetical to the 'authentic' butch Dyke, illustrates the prevalence of binary ideologies within lesbian culture more broadly. Given the women's limited levels of intimacy or knowledge of one another on a personal level, it is somewhat unsurprising that they invoked (perhaps unrealistic) ideologies related to the one element of each other's identity of which they felt certain: lesbianism. The women utilised the shared ideals surrounding their sexuality which were most accessible to them. In this way, the authenticity that they constructed may be seen as constrained by the wider hegemonic ideologies surrounding their sexuality. That the Stompers' local authenticity emerged from such stereotypes, then, demonstrates that the women achieved their joint sense of self via *widely available* cultural ideologies. This reflects many of the findings regarding language and lesbian identity already undertaken and discussed in Section 3.3, including Queen's (2005) observation that the lesbians in her study told jokes which revolved around lesbian stereotypes. Her (1997) investigation similarly demonstrated that lesbian norms were used to represent lesbian characters in cartoon strips, whilst Morrish and Sauntson's (2007) analysis of lesbian conversation also found that lesbian discourses often invoked stereotypes such as lesbian couples tending to own cats (2007: 53). Importantly, these ideologies have been shown to be flexible, with the Stomper women choosing to align themselves with them to differing degrees according to whether or not they themselves shaved their legs or used an iron, for instance (see Interaction 7.1). In this way, the Stomper women clearly had agency over their identity construction, despite their apparent reliance on stereotypes in order to achieve it.

Morrish and Sauntson (2007) argue that the apparent adherence to such stereotypes – as typically seems to occur within lesbian interactions – is unsurprising. Using the concept of interpellation (see Althusser 1971), they suggest that any individual who defines themselves in line with a particular identity category will, to some extent, embrace it and acknowledge its relevance to them. In this sense, that individual is bound to acknowledge certain stereotypical elements of the category, even if they do so reluctantly or by rejecting them (Morrish and Sauntson 2007: 15). This important point reflects the finding that the Stomper women positioned themselves in different ways – in line with different stances and personae, for example – throughout their various interactions. Because they were simply using the characteristics and traits associated with the category of 'lesbian' to their advantage, they were able to project a fluid and changeable identity. In other words, they were not reduced to an essentialised type of lesbian, but instead were dynamic and active in their reworking of ideals to best suit their needs in a given moment.

Evidence for the fact that the Stomper women did not simply reproduce the categories of butch and femme is illustrated in Chapters 4 and 5 by the women's evident reworking of them. In Chapter 4, the women were shown to actively construct the personae Dyke and Girl, and in Chapter 5 they were shown to negotiate what was 'authentic' for the Dyke persona. Though the term 'Dyke' does not appear in every extract presented in this book, its use nonetheless provides a tangible way of defining the group's contextually specific orientation to butch practices and styles within lesbian culture. By doing so, it is highlighted that the Stompers' construction of authentic lesbian identity reflects not merely that of 'a butch', a woman who may 'identify primarily as masculine or prefer masculine signals, personal appearance and styles' (Rubin 1992: 467), but instead as a non-heteronormative woman who eschews traditional femininity. In this sense, though the women invoked lesbian stereotypes, the meaning of these stereotypes was particular to the group.

Although the Stomper women's unique take on the broader stereotypes of butch and femme may have been specific to them, those stereotypes are nonetheless salient in broader lesbian culture; as indicated above, the butch/femme dichotomy is found in most studies of lesbian identity. It was also reworked in a way which was specific to the Stomper women's needs and desires, however. For example, it is clear that, for the Stompers, the rejection of heteronormative femininity was intrinsically related to their experiences as middle-aged lesbian women. Chapters 7 and 8 revealed how the women presumed one another's political orientation, and it is clear why when one considers the social change (in terms of the growth of women's and gay rights campaigns and activism) throughout their adult lives. These chapters also reveal why the women might have rejected hegemonic forms of femininity; as the dominant and naturalised gender style for women in the mainstream, it represents 'typical' women and their subordination.

Despite the apparent influence of feminism in the women's identity construction, their embrace of a non-feminised identity may also be perceived as positioning masculinity as superior to femininity, however. The fact that the Stomper women deconstructed the category of 'woman' and rejected what would be ideologically imposed as their 'natural' gender, though, can also be seen to subvert the notion of inherent femininity (see Section 3.3 for more on this concept). In this sense, the behaviour of these Stompers echoes that of feminists during the women's liberation movement (a time that many of these women experienced) which rejected those feminine styles perceived as functioning as patriarchal tools of objectification and oppression (Craig 2003: 20). As outlined in Chapter 8, of course, there were exceptions to this, namely Claire, but overall the women did seem to construct a particularly feminist-oriented identity for the group. Their use of butch/ femme as a salient tool in the construction of a 'queer woman' identity, therefore, can be partly explained in this way.

What is unavoidable in the analysis of the data obtained during this study, however, is some recognition of the fact that the Stomper women, despite their apparently feminist aims, did ultimately reproduce an ideological dichotomy through their rejection of traditional femininity and their embrace of non-normative female styles. In claiming that a Girl was not a lesbian, as in Section 5.2.2 for example, the women did make a clear distinction between what was authentic and what was illegitimate in terms of lesbian style. Certainly, one could argue that this divided and essentialised way of viewing sexuality is somewhat anti-feminist in nature. However, as has been argued above, constructing an identity within a given context will always rely on some kind of relational structure; one is either real or fake, an insider or an outsider, authentic or inauthentic. By constructing a clear dichotomy between a 'real lesbian' (or Dyke) and an inauthentic one (a Girl) as a result, the women can be seen to be engaged in typical identity work. Their use of the persona Girl to symbolise heteronormative style, and Dyke as symbolic of recognisable lesbianism, therefore, shows that they simply created something which was meaningful to them, using available cultural resources to do so.

It is also unsurprising that the women produced a positive/negative dichotomy, given that wider society is structured in such a way (with male/female and straight/gay arguably examples of this). Furthermore, the 'wave' of feminism that most of the group members identified with was focused more on the equality of women and men than on gender politics in a broader sense – this came somewhat later in the development of feminist thought (see Section 2.3 for more on this). Importantly, the use of such a recognisable structure for the Stomper women's identity construction enabled newcomers to learn the norms of the group quickly, to contribute to the construction of meaning in the CoP, and for all of the women engaged in the Sapphic Stomper group to rework heteronormative assumptions and construct a normative identity for themselves. The typically playful nature of their identity construction and the fact that the women typically only knew one another through this group also suggests, of course, that they did not consciously aim to make political statements through their identity construction. It may be argued, instead, that they took on those stereotypes and ideals which were most accessible in order to construct a meaningful, shared identity in the most straightforward and direct way.

As indicated above, similarities have been found between the Stompers and lesbians studied in other research projects, in terms of the role that gender ideologies and those of butch and femme play within lesbian culture. This ought not to be considered as evidence for some universal lesbian identity, however. Rather, this may be explained by the fact that, typically, such studies have involved white, middle-class, middle-aged, educated women. Though members of a minority sexual group, speakers such as the Stompers nonetheless reflect the hegemonic norm and the research trends typical in language and gender research, whereby the demographic group most accessible to the typically white, middle-class academics carrying out the studies has been disproportionately represented (an issue highlighted by Hall 2003: 354). A research field which predominantly considers the white and mainly middle class arguably merely creates, and maintains, an ideology of what is 'normal' (Morgan 2004: 252); as Mills (2007: 11) argues, this must be challenged. Those who research non-normative sexual identity construction should therefore extend their investigations to account for all minority groups. In doing so, we might begin to ensure that no single experience is ever taken as broadly representative or normative. For this reason, research now needs to be carried out into a broad range of CoPs defined by sexuality, but also by age, class and ethnicity. Such research will enable a greater understanding of the role that broader sociocultural experiences play in sexual identity construction and its connection with gender.

In particular, CoPs of lesbian women who do not match the generational, class-based or ethnic demographic of the Stompers may well reinterpret butch/femme categories in an entirely different way, to the extent that they may not be relevant at all. Whilst butch and femme identities currently remain prevalent in lesbian culture (as evident from the presence of 'Shane' in *The L Word*, for example), the meaning of these is likely to change depending on the individuals who comprise a CoP. For example, it seems likely that a CoP of much younger women who identify as lesbian (and engage together as such) might rework butch or femme styles in different ways and for different reasons from the Stompers. A shift in the cultural value of feminism for young adults in the twenty-first century, for example, may have reduced the desire to subvert a patriarchal concept of femininity. As Zucker (2004) argues, it is not uncommon in the twenty-first century to hear the phrase 'I'm not a feminist, but ...' followed by the declaration of a value reminiscent of the movement. This suggests that the concept of feminism has changed and that the label itself may be being abandoned; this factor alone is likely to lead to a shift in how younger generations of lesbians engage with what the older Stompers clearly perceived as a central part of their identity. As Roof (1998: 35) also suggests, the objectives of young lesbians in the 1990s differed from those of the 1970s, as they were concerned less with correcting structures of oppression and more with extending their 'political freedoms in relation to personal choices'. Similarly, it may be that research into younger lesbian groups *now* will reveal that these women feel less – or at least *differently* – constrained by the ideologies linking gender to sexual orientation. For this reason, an outcome of the research presented in this book will hopefully be that more work in this area – with a broader range of social groups – will develop to challenge the findings presented here.

10.4   Concluding points

Through the research outlined in these chapters, I have argued that both the CoP approach and a sociocultural framework are relevant and useful tools in any study of language and sexual identity. The analyses have unpicked the indexical relationships which exist between local practices and prevalent, global ideologies of both sexuality and gender in the Stomper group, focusing on the construction of authenticity as it emerges within given interactions. Importantly, this has revealed that CoPs should not, in themselves, be viewed as homogeneous units, but that homogeneity may be both constructed and disrupted during members' engagement together, depending on the identity goals of a given moment. The analyses provided have aimed to demonstrate how, through the use of discourse analysis and local-level, ethnographic research methods, it is possible to understand the process of social positioning as it is achieved via stance-taking towards CoP-specific personae. The personal account of the methodological approach taken for this particular study also offers, I hope, the useful benefit of hindsight gained from my own experiences conducting ethnographic research, particularly that which takes place outside of a typical CoP context.

The focus on the Stomper CoP in this study has provided an insight into the prevalence of stereotypical notions such as butch and femme within lesbian culture, yet has also argued that the orientation to those stereotypes depends on a complex array of factors. Though the women in this study have been shown to use broadly available cultural resources in order to position themselves in relation to the wider world, their changing identity construction in a range of contexts has demonstrated that these resources are used varyingly, flexibly and in an agentive way. Indeed, it has been argued that the Stompers constructed not only a specifically *lesbian* identity, but a specifically *female* one; their assumed experiences as middle-class, middle-aged women dictated what this meant to them. In this sense, whilst the focus on identity construction here was on how the women oriented to their sexuality, it was perhaps inevitable that their gender would play an equally relevant role in their performance of authentic identities.

Whilst this research has been led by the desire to explore new ways of approaching language and sexuality, it has also been influenced by the lack of current research into queer women's discourse. By examining language in interaction, it has been shown that, though these findings are specific to just one group of women, the sociocultural influences on lesbian identity construction may emerge largely from broader, heteronormative culture. Tellingly, the data collected for this book has illustrated that the broader sociocultural ideologies associated with gender and sexuality – those which may be defined as heteronormative in nature – are all pervasive in the construction of identity in a fundamentally queer group. For the women to make sense of themselves as a coherent unit, they have been shown to draw on available resources with connotations in the broader, mainstream culture, and to rework them for mutual gain. Whilst they did so in a unique, agentive way, it has nonetheless been evident throughout the analyses that the women's identity construction was ultimately shaped by these heteronormative discourses. A positive note on this seems to be, however, that the women were able to disrupt what is perceived as 'normal' and to subvert expectations of gender conformity.

As argued in Section 3.3.1.1, the society in which the Stomper women were based is one which tends to position lesbians as incomplete women, as threatening to the heteronormative order of things, or as objects of sexual titillation, or simply in ways which marginalise them or render them invisible. Certainly, the cultural context is beginning to change, and younger queer women may identify with their sexuality differently from the Stompers as a result, but the impact of patriarchy on broader culture has inevitably led to a degree of invisibility for lesbian women. In order to address this, and to challenge misogynistic ideas about what it means to be a gay woman, it is important to promote an understanding of *why* ideological categories such as butch and femme may be drawn upon in order to deconstruct and rework lesbianism for particular identity goals. The construction of identities, including personae such as Dyke and Girl, is far more complex than the simple reproduction of masculine and feminine practices and styles, and it is a responsibility of those with the tools to do so to help to explain this. By engaging in research into queer women's lives, scholars have the ability to raise awareness – both within and outside of academia – of why non-normative gender styles and practices by lesbians may well be viewed as subversive acts, but should also be viewed as agentive responses to dominant discourses. These discourses position queer women in a negative way due to their failure to adhere to what is perceived as being normal and valued, and society as a whole must begin to question why this is. By engaging in research which uncovers these ideologies, showing them to be ingrained within popular culture, we may begin to reveal – and challenge – the potentially harmful structures which constrain social interaction and the construction of local identities.

Notes

1 Introduction

1. This name, as with all names and geographical places mentioned in this book, is a pseudonym. It reflects the originality and use of poetic techniques in the original label the group chose for themselves. The term 'Sapphic' is often used as a synonym for 'lesbian', from the Ancient Greek poet Sappho (of Lesbos) who wrote of love and sex between women, hence my use of it here. In reflecting my familiarity with the group and the abbreviation of their actual name that the more regular members routinely used, I typically refer to them as just the 'Stompers'.
2. Gay Pride is a movement which promotes unity and self-respect amongst members of gay communities worldwide. During the summer months (in Europe and North America in particular), marches, demonstrations, political rallies and festivals take place in order to raise public awareness, acceptance and tolerance of gay people.

2 Sociocultural Approaches to Linguistics

1. For an excellent review of indexicality, see Moore and Podesva (2007).

3 Approaches to Language and Sexuality

1. Heterosexism is a term associated with heteronormativity; it describes the ideology that heterosexuality is normative, and that non-heterosexual behaviours or relationships are stigmatised (Herek 1990: 319). The term is more common in the field of psychology, and is distinct from heteronormativity in its explicit correlation with sexism (i.e. inequality and derision).
2. It is important to be clear, here, that research detailed in this book relates almost exclusively to Western women; as Koller (2008: 6) points out, 'lesbian' is itself a Western term and a Western identity category, and I use the term to imply a social identity which is salient in this culture.

5 *Dyke* and *Girl*

1. This chapter extends upon the analysis provided in Jones (2011).
2. The rainbow is a symbol used throughout Europe and North America to represent lesbian, gay and bisexual pride and identity. The colours represent diversity within the gay community, and were established in 1970s San Francisco.
3. This styling undoubtedly takes place on a wider level beyond the Stompers, given existing attempts within the social sciences to pin down non-verbal

communicative cues that signal a 'gaydar' in gay men and lesbians (such as Nicholas 2004).
4. 'Bi-curious', a term which emerged in the 1990s, typically refers to heterosexuals who may be interested in homosexual activity as a titillating experience.
5. The initial capitalisation of Dyke and Girl represents the personae specific to the Sapphic Stomper group; if presented without capitalisation from this point onwards, the term is being used in a non-identity-specific way.
6. Research has found that drink choices are culturally recognised as being gendered. For instance, Aitkin et al. (1988: 495) found that children as young as 12 viewed a pint of beer as a 'man's drink', and associated women with drinks such as Martini cocktails.

6   Negotiating Authentic Style and Practice

1. In colloquial British English, 'sad' is often synonymous with 'pathetic'.

7   Indexing Authenticity via Cultural Knowledge

1. Civil partnerships in Britain were brought into law in 2004 to provide same-sex couples with a union which affords them the same legal rights and responsibilities as marriage does for heterosexual couples. Though widely heralded as a considerable step towards equality for gay and lesbian people, civil partnerships are, at the time of print, available only for gay couples and only straight couples may be 'married'. Whilst it is clear that those with cultural authority have begun to recognise and legitimise queer relationships, therefore, it may also be argued that, by refraining from making civil partnerships entirely equal to heterosexual marriage, heterosexuality has been upheld as comparatively 'normal' behaviour.
2. In universal politeness theory, positive face is considered to be the image that a person holds of themselves and their desire to be respected in accordance with it, whereas negative face is the desire to be free, independent and unimpeded upon. Comments or demands from interlocutors which challenge either the positive or negative face of a person are therefore known as face-threatening acts (Brown and Levinson 1978: 61).

8   Political Difference and Maintenance of Shared Identity

1. 'The love that dare not speak its name' is a phrase found in a poem by Lord Alfred Douglas from the nineteenth century. It was used in 1895 during Oscar Wilde's gross indecency trial for homosexuality, is most commonly associated with Wilde, and may still be used as a euphemism for gay relationships.
2. It is important to evaluate the extent to which Claire's awareness of being recorded might have impacted on her decision to present herself as non-feminist in this moment. Her apparent desire to state her identity 'for the tape' (line 4) illustrates her consciousness that an audio recorder is present. In this sense, it could be argued that her interaction (and that of the other women) is not entirely spontaneous or 'natural'. However, if we are to view

language use as meaningful within a CoP, and meaning as shifting depending on the interactive moment, it is clear that there can be no such thing as 'natural' data, rather simply language which is used within the context in which it is produced. A sociocultural approach acknowledges that interaction is specific to the context in which it occurs at that moment, but my decision to record Stomper interactions after at least a year of engagement with them was designed to reduce the impact of my presence and the subsequent observer's paradox. Whilst stating that her identity claim is 'for the tape', therefore, Claire's turn here is likely to be consistent with her self-interpretation as a Stomper at that moment.

3. I am grateful to the audience members who, at the presentation of this data extract at Sociolinguistics Symposium 18 (Southampton, UK, 2010), directed me towards this particular insight.

4. My thanks to Justine Coupland for drawing the significance of 'like' to my attention with regard to this analysis.

References

Aitken, P.P. et al., 1988. Television advertisements for alcoholic drinks do reinforce under-age drinking. *British Journal of Addiction*, 83(12), 1399–419.

Alim, H.S., 2004. Hip hop nation language. In E. Finegan and J. Rickford, eds *Language in the USA: Themes for the twenty-first century*. Cambridge: Cambridge University Press, pp. 387–409.

Allan, K. and Burridge, K., 2006. *Forbidden words: Taboo and the censoring of language*. Cambridge: Cambridge University Press.

Althusser, L., 1971. *Lenin and philosophy*. New York: Monthly Review.

Anderson, B., 1983. *Imagined Communities: Reflections on the origin and spread of nationalism*. London: Verso Books.

Austin, J.L., 1976. *How to do things with words: the William James lectures delivered in Harvard University in 1955*. Oxford: Oxford Paperbacks.

Baker, P., 2008. *Sexed texts: Language, gender and sexuality*. London: Equinox.

Bakhtin, M., 1981. Discourse in the novel. In M. Holquist, ed. *The dialogic imagination: Four essays by M. M. Bakhtin*. Austin: University of Texas Press, pp. 259–422.

Bani-Shoraka, H., 2008. Challenging social hierarchy: Playing with oppositional identities in family talk. *Multilingua – Journal of Cross-Cultural and Interlanguage Communication*, 27(1–2), 13–35.

Barrett, R., 1995. Supermodels of the world, unite!: Political economy and the language of performance among African American drag queens. In W. Leap, ed. *Beyond the lavender lexicon: Authenticity, imagination and appropriation in lesbian and gay languages*. New York: Gordon and Breach Press, pp. 207–26.

Barrett, R., 1997. The 'homo-genius' speech community. In A. Livia and K. Hall, eds. *Queerly phrased: Language, gender, and sexuality*. New York: Oxford University Press, pp. 181–201.

Barrett, R., 1998. Markedness and styleswitching in performances by African American drag queens. In C. Myers-Scotton, ed. *Codes and consequences: Choosing linguistic varieties*. New York: Oxford University Press, pp. 139–61.

Behan, D., 1995. What's an orgasm? The language of sex reassignment surgery and transgender identities on the internet. Paper presented at the Third Annual Lavender Languages and Linguistics Conference, American University.

Bem, S., 1993. *Lenses of gender: Transforming the debate on sexual inequality*. New Haven: Yale University Press.

Bergvall, V., 1996. Constructing and enacting gender through discourse: Negotiating multiple roles as female engineering students. In V. Bergvall, J. Bing and A. Freed, eds *Rethinking language and gender research: Theory and practice*. Oxford: Blackwell, pp. 173–201.

Bolton, R., 1995. Tricks, friends and lovers: Erotic encounters in the field. In D. Kulick and M. Wilson, eds *Taboo: Sex, identity and erotic subjectivity in anthropological fieldwork*. London: Routledge, pp. 140–67.

Brown, G., 1977. *Listening to spoken English*. London: Longman.

Brown, P. and Levinson, S.C., 1987. *Politeness: Some universals in language usage.* Cambridge: Cambridge University Press.

Bucholtz, M., 1999. 'Why be normal?': Language and identity practices in a community of nerd girls. *Language in Society*, 28(02), 203–23.

Bucholtz, M., 2003. Theories of discourse as theories of gender: Discourse analysis in language and gender studies. In J. Holmes and M. Meyerhoff, eds *The handbook of language and gender.* Oxford: Blackwell, pp. 43–68.

Bucholtz, M., 2004. Changing places: Language and woman's place in context. In M. Bucholtz, ed. *Language and woman's place: text and commentaries.* New York: Oxford University Press, pp. 121–8.

Bucholtz, M. and Hall, K., 2004. Theorizing identity in language and sexuality research. *Language in Society*, 33(04), 469–515.

Bucholtz, M. and Hall, K., 2005. Identity and interaction: a sociocultural linguistic approach. *Discourse Studies*, 7(4–5), 585–614.

Bucholtz, M. and Hall, K., 2008. All of the above: New coalitions in sociocultural linguistics. *Journal of Sociolinguistics*, 12(4), 401–31.

Butler, J., 1990. *Gender trouble: Feminism and the subversion of identity.* London: Routledge.

Butler, J., 1993. *Bodies that matter: On the discursive limits of sex.* London: Routledge.

Cameron, D., 1990. Demythologizing sociolinguistics: Why language does not reflect society. In J. Joseph and J.T. Taylor, eds *Ideologies of Languge.* London: Routledge, pp. 79–75.

Cameron, D., 1998. Performing gender identity: Young men's talk and the construction of heterosexual masculinity. In J. Coates, ed. *Language and gender: a reader.* Oxford: Blackwell, pp. 270–84.

Cameron, D. and Kulick, D., 2003. *Language and sexuality.* Cambridge: Cambridge University Press.

Cameron, D. and Kulick, D., 2005. Identity crisis? *Language and Communication*, 25(2), 107–25.

Case, S.E., 1993. Toward a butch–femme aesthetic. In H. Abelove, M. Barale and D. Halperin, eds *The lesbian and gay studies reader.* New York: Routledge, pp. 294–306.

Chen, K.H.Y., 2008. Positioning and repositioning: Linguistic practices and identity negotiation of overseas returning bilinguals in Hong Kong. *Multilingua – Journal of Cross-Cultural and Interlanguage Communication*, 27(1–2), 57–75.

Chirrey, D.A., 2011. Formulating dispositions in coming out advice. *Discourse Studies*, 13, 283–98.

Clark, B., 2010. Constructing flight attendant identity in safety reports to a government agency. Paper presented at the Sociolinguistics Summer School. Edinburgh University, Edinburgh.

Clark, J., forthcoming. *Language, sex and social structure.* Palgrave Macmillan.

Coates, J., 1996. *Women talk: Conversation between women friends.* Oxford: Wiley-Blackwell.

Coates, J. and Jordan, M.E., 1997. Que(e)rying friendship: Discourses of resistance and the construction of gendered subjectivity. In A. Livia and K. Hall, eds. *Queerly phrased.* New York: Oxford University Press, pp. 214–32.

Connell, R.W., 2005. *Masculinities.* Cambridge: Polity Press.

Coupland, J. and Coupland, N., 2009. Attributing stance in discourses of body shape and weight loss. In A. Jaffe, ed. *Stance: Sociolinguistic perspectives.* New York: Oxford University Press, pp. 227–50.

Coupland, N., 2007. *Style: Language variation and identity.* Cambridge: Cambridge University Press.

Craig, S., 2003. Madison Avenue versus the feminine mystique: the advertising industry's response to the women's movement. In S. A. Inness, ed. *Disco divas: Women and popular culture in the 1970s.* Philadelphia: University of Pennsylvania Press, pp. 13–23.

Dailey-O'Cain, J., 2000. The sociolinguistic distribution of and attitudes toward focuser 'like' and quotative 'like'. *Journal of Sociolinguistics,* 4(1), 60–80.

Davies, B., 2005. Communities of practice: Legitimacy not choice. *Journal of Sociolinguistics,* 9(4), 557–81.

De Andrade, L.L., 2000. Negotiating from the inside. *Journal of Contemporary Ethnography,* 29(3), 268–90.

Denfield, R., 1995. *The new Victorians: Why young people are abandoning the women's movement.* London: Simon & Schuster.

Doan, L., 2001. *Fashioning sapphism: the origins of a modern English lesbian culture.* New York: Columbia University Press.

Dougherty, K. and Strassel, S., 1998. A new look at variation in and perception of American English quotatives. Paper presented at New Ways of Analyzing Variation in English 27. University of Georgia.

Du Bois, J.W., 2007. The stance triangle. In R. Englebretson, ed. *Stancetaking in discourse: Subjectivity, evaluation, interaction.* Amsterdam: Benjamins, pp. 139–82.

Eckert, P., 1989. *Jocks and burnouts: Social categories and identity in the high school.* New York: Teachers' College Press.

Eckert, P., 2000. *Linguistic variation as social practice: the linguistic construction of identity in Belten High.* Oxford: Wiley-Blackwell.

Eckert, P., 2005. Variation, convention, and social meaning. Paper presented at the Annual Meeting of the Linguistic Society of America. Oakland, California.

Eckert, P. and McConnell-Ginet, S., 1992. Think practically and look locally: Language and gender as community-based practice. *Annual Review of Anthropology,* 21(1), 461–88.

Eckert, P. and McConnell-Ginet, S., 1995. Constructing meaning, constructing selves: Snapshots of language, gender and class from Belten High. In M. Bucholtz and K. Hall, eds *Gender articulated: Language and the socially constructed self.* New York: Routledge, pp. 469–507.

Eckert, P. and McConnell-Ginet, S., 2003. *Language and gender.* Cambridge University Press.

Eckert, P. and McConnell-Ginet, S., 2007. Putting communities of practice in their place. *Gender and Language,* 1(1), 27–37.

Eckert, P. and Wenger, E., 2005. What is the role of power in sociolinguistic variation? *Journal of Sociolinguistics,* 9(4), 582–89.

Edelman, E., 2008. Cirque noir: Trans bodies and the cultivation of a homoerotic haven. Paper presented at the Fifteenth Annual Lavender Languages and Linguistics Conference. American University.

Eggins, S. and Slade, D., 2004. *Analysing casual conversation.* London: Equinox.

Foucault, M., 1972. *The archaeology of knowledge.* New York: Pantheon Books.

Foucault, M., 1978. *The history of sexuality*. Volume 1: *An introduction*. New York: Pantheon.

Freedman, J. 2001. *Feminism*. Buckingham: Open University Press.

Gaudio, R.P., 1994. Sounding gay: Pitch properties in the speech of gay and straight men. *American Speech*, 69, 30–57.

Gaudio, R.P., 2001. White men do it too: Racialized (homo) sexualities in postcolonial Hausaland. *Journal of Linguistic Anthropology*, 11(1), 36–51.

Gee, J.P., 2005. Meaning making, communities of practice, and analytical toolkits. *Journal of Sociolinguistics*, 9(4), 590–4.

Gee, J.P. and Green, J.L., 1998. Discourse analysis, learning and social practice: a methodological study. *Review of Research in Education*, 23, 119–69.

Geertz, C., 1973. *Thick description: Toward an interpretive theory of culture*. New York: Basic Books.

Goodwin, D., Pope, C., Mort, M. and Smith, A., 2003. Ethics and ethnography: an experiential account. *Qualitative Health Research*, 13(4), 567–77.

Grogan, S., 2008. *Body image: Understanding body dissatisfaction in men, women, and children*. New York: Routledge.

Gumperz, J.J., 1982. *Discourse strategies*. Cambridge: Cambridge University Press.

Gumperz, J.J. and Hymes, D. eds, 1964. *The ethnography of communication*. Washington, DC: American Anthropological Association.

Halberstam, J., 1998. *Female masculinity*. London: Duke University Press.

Hall, K., 1995. Lip service on the fantasy lines. In M. Bucholtz and K. Hall, eds *Gender articulated: Language and the socially constructed self*. New York: Routledge, pp. 183–216.

Hall, K., 2003. Exceptional speakers: Contested and problematized gender identities. In J. Holmes and M. Meyerhoff, eds *The handbook of language and gender*. Oxford: Blackwell, pp. 353–80.

Hammersley, M. and Atkinson, P., 1995. *Ethnography: Principles in practice*. London: Routledge.

Haraway, D., 1991. A cyborg manifesto: Science, technology, and socialist-feminism in the late twentieth century. In D. Haraway, ed. *Simians, cyborgs and women: the reinvention of Nature*. New York: Routledge, pp. 149–81.

Harvey, K. and Shalom, C., 1997. *Language and desire: Encoding sex, romance, and intimacy*. London: Routledge.

Heller, D., 2006. How does a lesbian look? Stendhal's syndrome and The L Word. In K. Akass and J. McCabe, eds *Reading The L Word: Outing contemporary television*. New York: I.B.Tauris, pp. 55–68.

Hemmings, C., 2002. *Bisexual spaces: a geography of sexuality and gender*. London: Routledge.

Henry, G.W., 1948. *Sex variants: a study of homosexual patterns*. New York: Hoeber.

Herek, G.M., 1990. The context of antigay violence: Notes on cultural and psychological heterosexism. *Journal of Interpersonal Violence*, (5), 316–33.

Holmes, J. and Meyerhoff, M., 1999. The community of practice: Theories and methodologies in language and gender research. *Language in Society*, 28(02), 173–83.

Hudson, R.A., 1975. The meaning of questions. *Language*, 51(1), 1–31.

Hughes, J., 2012. 'Gold–star lesbians': How do lesbians in Portland, Oregon use virginity, performance, and bar culture to build community? Paper presented at the Nineteenth Annual Lavender Languages and Linguistics Conference. American University.

Hymes, D., 1962. The ethnography of speaking. In T. Gladwin and W. C. Sturtevant, eds *Anthropology and human behavior*. Washington, DC: Anthropological Society of Washington, pp. 15–53.

Inness, S.A., 1997. *The lesbian menace: Ideology, identity, and the representation of lesbian life*. Amherst, Mass.: University of Massachusetts Press.

Irvine, J., 2001. Style as distinctiveness: the culture and ideology of linguistic differentiation. In P. Eckert and J. R. Rickford, eds *Style and sociolinguistic variation*. Cambridge: Cambridge University Press, pp. 21–43.

Irvine, J. and Gal, S., 2000. Language ideology and linguistic differentiation. In P. Kroskrity, ed. *Regimes of language: Ideologies, polities, and identities*. Santa Fe: New Mexico: SAR Press, pp. 35–83.

Jacobs, G., 2002. Discourse analysis of gay male chatroom chatter. Paper presented at the Ninth Annual Lavender Languages and Linguistics Conference. American University.

Jaffe, A., 2009. *Stance: Sociolinguistic perspectives*. Oxford: Oxford University Press.

Jaworski, A., 1993. *The power of silence: Social and pragmatic perspectives*. Newbury Park: Sage Publications, Inc.

Johnston, J., 1974. *Lesbian nation: the feminist solution*. New York: Simon and Schuster.

Jones, L., 2011. 'The only dykey one': Constructions of (in)authenticity in a lesbian community of practice. *Journal of Homosexuality*, 58, 719–41.

Kaminski, M., 2004. *Games prisoners play: the tragicomic worlds of Polish prison*. Princeton: Princeton University Press.

Kiesling, S.F., 2001. 'Now I gotta watch what I say': Shifting constructions of masculinity in discourse. *Journal of Linguistic Anthropology*, 11(2), 250–73.

Kiesling, S.F., 2004. Dude. *American Speech*, 79(3), 281–305.

Kinsey, A.C., Pomeroy, W.R. and Martin, C.E., 1948. *Sexual behavior in the human male*. Philadelphia: WB Saunders.

Koller, V., 2008. *Lesbian discourses: Images of a community*. London: Routledge.

Kulick, D., 2000. Gay and lesbian language. *Annual Review of Anthropology*, 29(1), 243–85.

Labov, W., 1972. *Sociolinguistic patterns*. Philadelphia: University of Pennsylvania Press.

Lakoff, R.T., 1975. *Language and woman's place*. New York: Harper and Row.

Lave, J. and Wenger, E., 1991. *Situated learning: Legitimate peripheral participation*. Cambridge: Cambridge University Press.

Lawson, R., 2006. 'I'd be worried if I was called a Ned': Sociolinguistic constructions of identity in a Glasgow high school. Paper presented at Sociolinguistics Symposium 16. University of Limerick.

Leap, W., 1996. *Word's out: Gay men's English*. Newark: University of Minnesota Press.

Leap, W., 2008. The 'hermaphrodite', the rattlesnake, and the chubby: How gay sexual cinema regulates meanings of transgender embodiment. Paper presented at the Fifteenth Annual Lavender Languages and Linguistics Conference. American University.

Legman, G., 1941. The language of homosexuality: an American glossary. In Henry, G.W., ed. *Sex variants: a study of homosexual patterns*, Vol. 2. New York: Hoeber, pp. 1149–79.

Livia, A., 1995. I ought to throw a Buick at you: Fictional representations of butch/femme speech. In K. Hall and M. Bucholtz, eds *Gender articulated: Language and the socially constructed self*. London: Routledge, pp. 245–78.

Livia, A. and Hall, K. eds., 1997. *Queerly phrased: Language, gender, and sexuality*. Oxford: Oxford University Press.

Madison, N., 2012. The articulation of bisexual identities in new mediascapes: Negotiating (in)visibility online. Paper presented at the Nineteenth Annual Lavender Languages and Linguistics Conference. American University.

Maher, M. and Pusch, W., 1995. Speaking 'out': the implications of negotiating lesbian identity. In W. Leap, ed. *Beyond the lavender lexicon: Authenticity, imagination, and appropriation in lesbian and gay languages*. Amsterdam: Gordon and Breach, pp. 19–44.

Malinowski, B., 1935. *Coral gardens and their magic: a study of the methods of tilling the soil and of agricultural rites in the Trobriand Islands*. New York: American Book Company.

Maltz, D. and Borker, R., 1982. A cultural approach to male–female miscommunication. In J. J. Gumperz, ed. *Language and social identity*. Cambridge: Cambridge University Press, pp. 196–216.

Martin, D. and Lyon, P., 1972. *Lesbian/woman*. New York: Bantam.

Mendoza-Denton, N., 2008. *Homegirls: Language and cultural practice among Latina youth gangs*. Malden: Blackwell.

Mills, S., 2007. Communities of practice and politeness. Paper presented at the School of English Departmental Research Seminar Series. University of Sheffield.

Milroy, L., 1980. *Language and social networks*. Oxford: Blackwell.

Moore, C. and Schilt, K., 2006. Is she man enough? Female masculinities on The L Word. In K. Akass and J. McCabe, eds *Reading The L Word: Outing contemporary television*. London: I.B.Tauris, pp. 159–72.

Moore, E., 2003. Learning style and identity: a sociolinguistic analysis of a Bolton high school. Unpublished PhD thesis, University of Manchester.

Moore, E. and Podesva, R., 2007. Style, indexicality, and the social meaning of tag questions. *Language in Society*, 38, 447–85.

Morgan, M., 2004. 'I'm every woman': Black women's (dis)placement in women's language study. In R. T. Lakoff and M. Bucholtz, eds *Language and woman's place: Text and commentaries*. Oxford: Oxford University Press, pp. 252–9.

Morgan, R. and Wood, K., 1995. Lesbians in the living room: Collusion, co-construction, and co-narration in conversation. In W. Leap, ed. *Beyond the lavender lexicon: Authenticity, imagination and appropriation in gay and lesbian languages*. New York: Gordon and Breach, pp. 235–48.

Morrish, L. and Leap, W., 2007. Sex talk: Language, desire, identity and beyond. In H. Sauntson and S. Kyratzis, eds *Language, sexualities and desires: Cross-cultural perspectives*. Basingstoke: Palgrave Macmillan, pp. 17–40.

Morrish, E. and Sauntson, H., 2007. *New perspectives on language and sexual identity*. Basingstoke: Palgrave Macmillan.

Namaste, V., 2000. *Invisible lives: the erasure of transsexual and transgendered people*. Chicago: University of Chicago Press.

Nestle, J., 1992. The femme question. In J. Nestle, ed. *The persistent desire: a femme-butch reader*. Boston: Alyson, pp. 138–46.

Newton, E., 1984. The mythic mannish lesbian: Radclyffe Hall and the new woman. *Signs*, 9(4), 557–75.

Nicholas, C., 2004. Gaydar: eye-gaze as identity recognition among gay men and lesbians. *Sexuality and Culture*, 8(1), 60–86.

Nichols, M., 2006. Psychotherapeutic issues with 'kinky' clients. *Journal of Homosexuality*, 50(2), 281–300.

O'Barr, W. and Atkins, B., 1980. 'Women's language' or 'powerless language'? In S. McConnell-Ginet, R. Borker and N. Furman, eds *Women and language in literature and society*. New York: Praeger, pp. 93–110.

Ochs, E., 1990. Indexicality and socialization. In J. Stigler, R. Shweder and G. Herdt, eds *Cultural psychology: the Chicago Symposia*. Cambridge: Cambridge University Press, pp. 287–308.

Ochs, E., 1991. Indexing gender. In A. Duranti and Goodwin, eds *Rethinking context: Language as an interactive phenomenon*. Cambridge: Cambridge University Press, pp. 335–58.

Pascoe, C.J., 2007. *Dude, you're a fag: Masculinity and sexuality in high school*. Los Angeles: University of California Press.

Pichler, P., 2007. Gender, ethnicity and religion in spontaneous talk and ethnographic-style interviews: Balancing perspectives of researcher and researched. In K. Harrington, L. Litosseliti, H. Sauntson and J. Sunderland, eds *Language and gender research methodologies*. Basingstoke: Palgrave Macmillan, pp. 56–70.

Pichler, P., 2009. *Talking young femininities*. Basingstoke: Palgrave Macmillan.

Podesva, R.J., 2007. Phonation type as a stylistic variable: the use of falsetto in constructing a persona. *Journal of Sociolinguistics*, 11(4), 478–504.

Queen, R., 1997. I don't speak Spritch: Locating lesbian language. In A. Livia and K. Hall, eds *Queerly phrased: Language, gender, and sexuality*. Oxford: Oxford University Press, pp. 233–56.

Queen, R., 1998. 'Stay queer!'Never fear!': Building queer social networks. *World Englishes*, 17(2), 203–14.

Queen, R., 2005. How many lesbians does it take …: Jokes, teasing, and the negotiation of stereotypes about lesbians. *Journal of Linguistic Anthropology*, 15(2), 239–57.

Rampton, B., 1992. Scope for empowerment in sociolinguistics. In D. Cameron, E. Frazer, P. Harvey, B. Rampton and K. Richardson, eds *Researching language: Issues of power and method*. London: Routledge, pp. 29–64.

Rich, A., 1980. Compulsory heterosexuality and lesbian existence. *Signs*, 5(4), 631–60.

Richardson, D., 1996. Constructing lesbian sexualities. In S. Jackson and S. Scott, eds *Feminism and sexuality: a reader*. Edinburgh: Edinburgh University Press, pp. 276–86.

Rodgers, B., 1972. *The queens' vernacular: a gay lexicon*. San Francisco: Straight Arrow Books.

Romaine, S. and Lange, D., 1991. The use of like as a marker of reported speech and thought: a case of grammaticalization in progress. *American Speech*, 66(3), 227–79.

Roof, J., 1998. 1970s lesbian feminism meets 1990s butch-femme. In S.R. Munt, ed. *Butch/femme: Inside lesbian gender*. London: Cassell, pp. 27–35.

Rose, M., 2006. Language, place and identity in later life. Unpublished PhD thesis, Stanford University.

Rose, M. and Sharma, D., 2002. Introduction: Ideology and identity in practice. In S. Benor et al., eds *Gendered practices in language*. Stanford: CSLI Publications, pp. 1–20.

Rubin, G., 1992. Of catamites and kings: Reflections on butch, gender, and boundaries. In J. Nestle, ed. *The persistent desire: a femme-butch reader*. Boston: Alyson, pp. 466–82.

Rust, P., 1996. Sexual identity and bisexual identities: the struggle for self-description in a changing sexual landscape. In B. Beemyn and M. Eliason, eds *Queer studies: a lesbian, gay, bisexual, and transgender anthology*. New York: New York University Press, pp. 64–86.

Salih, S. ed., 2004. *The Judith Butler reader*. Oxford: Wiley-Blackwell.

Sanjek, R., 1990. A vocabulary for fieldnotes. In R. Sanjek, ed. *Fieldnotes: the makings of anthropology*. Ithaca: Cornell University Press, pp. 92–121.

Sauntson, H., 2008. The contributions of queer theory to gender and language research. In K. Harrington, L. Litosseliti and H. Sauntson, eds *Gender and language research methodologies*. Basingstoke: Palgrave Macmillan, pp. 271–82.

Sauntson, H. and Kyratzis, S. eds, 2007. *Language, sexualities and desires: Cross-cultural perspectives*. Basingstoke: Palgrave Macmillan.

Schilling-Estes, N., 2004. Constructing ethnicity in interaction. *Journal of Sociolinguistics*, 8(2), 163–95.

Silverstein, M., 2003. Indexical order and the dialectics of sociolinguistic life. *Language and Communication*, 23(3–4), 193–229.

Spender, D., 1980. *Man made language*. London: Routledge.

Spiro, M.E., 1996. Postmodernist anthropology, subjectivity, and science: a modernist critique. *Comparative Studies in Society and History*, 38(04), 759–80.

Tagliamonte, S. and Hudson, R., 1999. *Be like* et al. beyond America: the quotative system in British and Canadian youth. *Journal of Sociolinguistics*. 3(2), 147–72.

Talbot, M., 1995. A synthetic sisterhood: False friends in a teenage magazine. In M. Bucholtz and K. Hall, eds *Gender articulated: Language and the socially constructed self*. London: Routledge, pp. 143–65.

Tannen, D., 2007. *Talking voices: Repetition, dialogue, and imagery in conversational discourse*. Cambridge: Cambridge University Press.

Thorne, A. and Coupland, J., 1998. Articulations of same-sex desire: Lesbian and gay male dating advertisements. *Journal of Sociolinguistics*, 2(2), 233–57.

Thorne, L., 2012. 'But I'm attracted to women': Identity claims and normative ideologies in bisexual women's accounts of experience. Paper presented at the Nineteenth Annual Lavender Languages and Linguistics Conference. American University.

Trudgill, P. and Giles, H., 1978. Sociolinguistics and linguistic value judgement: Correctness, adequacy and aesthetics. In F. Coppieters and D. L. Goyvaerts, eds *Functional studies in language and literature*. Ghent: Story-Scientia, pp. 167–90.

Turner, G., 2008. 'The road to the lesbian nation is not an easy one': 'Us' and 'them' in Diva magazine. *Social Semiotics*, 18(3), 377–88.

Tusting, K. and Maybin, J., 2007. Linguistic ethnography and interdisciplinarity: Opening the discussion. *Journal of Sociolinguistics*, 11(5), 575–83.

Valentine, D., 2003. 'I went to bed with my own kind once': the erasure of desire in the name of identity. *Language and Communication*, 23, 123–38.

Vicinus, M., 1992. 'They wonder to which sex I belong': the historical roots of the modern lesbian identity. *Feminist Studies*, 18(3), 467–97.

Wagner, S., 2010. Bringing sexuality to the table: Language, gender and power in seven lesbian families. *Gender and Language*, 4(1), 33–72.

Wales, K., 1999. North and South: a linguistic divide? Available at: http://www.leeds.ac.uk/reporter/439/kwales.htm [Accessed 16 July 2008].

Wareing, S., 1996. What do we know about language and gender? Paper presented at the Eleventh Sociolinguistic Symposium. Cardiff University.

Warner, M., 1991. Introduction: Fear of a queer planet. *Social Text*, 9(4), 3–17.

Weeks, J., 1987. Questions of identity. In P. Caplan, ed. *The cultural construction of sexuality*. London: Routledge, pp. 31–51.

Wenger, E., 1998. *Communities of practice: Learning, meanings, and identity.* Cambridge: Cambridge University Press.

West, C. and Zimmerman, D., 1987. Doing gender. *Gender and Society*, 1(2), 125–51.

Whittle, S., 1996. Gender fucking or fucking gender? Current cultural contributions to theories of gender blending. In R. Ekins and D. King, eds *Blending genders: Social aspects of cross-dressing and sex-changing*. London: Routledge, pp. 196–214.

Williams, T.J., Pepitone, M., Christensen, C., Cooke, B., Huberman, A., Breedlove, N., Breedlove, T., Jordan, C. and Breedlove, S., 2000. Finger-length ratios and sexual orientation. *Nature*, 404(6777), 455–6.

Wilson, E. and Weir, A., 1986. *Hidden agendas: Theory, politics, and experience in the women's movement*, London: Tavistock.

Wolfson, N., 1976. Speech events and natural speech: Some implications for sociolinguistic methodology. *Language in Society*, 5(02), 189–209.

Wood, K., 1999. Coherent identities amid heterosexist ideologies: Deaf and hearing lesbian coming-out stories. In M. Bucholtz, A. C. Liang and L. A. Sutton, eds *Reinventing identities: the gendered self in discourse*. New York: Oxford University Press, pp. 46–63.

Woolard, K.A., 1985. Language variation and cultural hegemony: Toward an integration of sociolinguistic and social theory. *American Ethnologist*, 12(4), 738–48.

Young, R., 2008. English and identity in Asia. *Asiatic*, 2(2), 2–13.

Zucker, A.N., 2004. Disavowing social identities: What it means when women say, 'I'm not a feminist, but ...'. *Psychology of Women Quarterly*, 28(4), 423–35.

Zwicky, 1997. Two lavender issues for linguists. In A. Livia and K. Hall, eds *Queerly phrased: language, gender, and sexuality*. New York: Oxford University Press, pp. 21–34.

Index